EARLY PUBLIC LIBRARIES

EARLY PUBLIC LIBRARIES

A History of Public Libraries in Great Britain before 1850

By
THOMAS KELLY
M.A., PH.D., F.R.HIST.S.
Director of Extra-Mural Studies in the
University of Liverpool

THE LIBRARY ASSOCIATION
1966

"Everything is older than we think"
—W. G. HOSKINS

First published 1966
Reprinted 1969
by The Library Association
7 Ridgmount Street, Store Street, London, W.C.1

© Thomas Kelly, 1966

SBN : 85365 381 X

Printed in 11 on 12-pt. Bell

Made and printed in England by
STAPLES PRINTERS LIMITED
at their Rochester, Kent, establishment

PREFACE

WHEN I accepted the invitation of the Library Association to write a new *History of Public Libraries in Great Britain* I asked if I might be permitted to deal not only with the rate-aided public libraries which have their beginnings in the mid-nineteenth century but also with their precursors in earlier times. I had in mind the old town and parish libraries, the subscription libraries, and the libraries of bodies such as the mechanics' institutes. I suspected there was a field here which needed exploration, but I must confess I had no idea how plentiful and how rich in interest the material would prove to be. The result is that what was originally intended to provide a preliminary chapter or two has grown into a book, which is here offered as a forerunner to the main volume on the history of the rate-aided libraries.

Even so I cannot regard the present work as more than a preliminary survey. I have tried to provide an outline of the story, and to reveal the main pattern of development. I have also suggested, in an appendix, what seems to me the most appropriate system of nomenclature. Clearly, however, there is still much scope for further research, especially on a local basis. Only when this has been done, and the details of the picture have been filled in, will a definitive history of this aspect of our cultural development be possible.

I have done my best to present the story in a way which will be of interest to the general reader as well as to the scholar. In such a case footnotes are always a difficulty: in this instance I have compromised by providing a bibliography at the end of each chapter, reserving footnotes for out-of-the-way references and the identification of quotations.

I should like to say how much I appreciate the generous assistance that has been given to me by librarians and archivists, and their staffs, all over the country. Among chief librarians of public libraries I must mention especially Mr. M. K. Milne of Aberdeen, Mr. J. W. Forsyth of Ayr, Mr. W. S. Haugh of Bristol, Mrs. M. D. McLean of Dumfries, Mr. W. S. Taylor of Dundee, Mr. J. S. English of Gainsborough, Mr. C. W.

Black of Glasgow, Mr. P. Hepworth of Norwich, Mr. E. MacGillivray of Orkney, Miss J. A. Downton of Preston, Miss O. S. Newman of Shropshire, and Mr. S. Robinson of Sowerby Bridge; and among archivists Miss Elizabeth Ralph of the Bristol Archives Office, Miss M. C. Hill of the County Record Office at Shrewsbury, Mr. E. H. Sargeant of the County Record Office at Worcester, Mr. A. E. Barker of the Society for Promoting Christian Knowledge, and Mrs. Belle Pridmore of the United Society for the Propagation of the Gospel. The Rev. Canon R. T. Holtby, Librarian of Carlisle Cathedral, Mr. A. R. B. Fuller, Librarian of St. Paul's Cathedral, the Rev. Canon J. P. Boden, Librarian of Winchester Cathedral, Mr. C. B. L. Barr, Sub-Librarian of York Cathedral, Dr. Claire Cross of the Reading University, Mr. A. Anderson, Sub-Librarian, Southampton University, Mr. R. C. Rider, Sub-Librarian, St. David's College, Lampeter, Mr. J. E. Vaughan, Librarian, Liverpool University Institute of Education, Mr. F. Beckwith, Librarian of the Leeds Library, Rev. J. Ramsay, of Easton-in-Gordano, Somerset, Mr. T. Evans, of Llansaint, Carmarthenshire, and Sir William Arbuckle, of Edinburgh, have also given particularly valuable help. To all these, and to the scores of other people who have so patiently answered my inquiries, and often taken a great deal of trouble on my behalf, I offer my very sincere thanks.

Mr. N. R. Ker of Magdalen College, Oxford, has assisted me at many points from his unrivalled knowledge of mediaeval and parochial libraries; Dr. Paul Kaufman of the University of Washington Library has been prodigal of help in the field of eighteenth-century library history which he has made so specially his own; Rev. J. A. Fitch, of Reydon, Suffolk, has provided information on the parochial libraries of that county, and kindly allowed me to read in MS. his recently published paper on this subject; and Mr. F. J. Hill of the British Museum Library has been kind enough to read the first draft of Chapter VII. Professor Raymond Irwin of University College, London, has undertaken the heroic labour of reading the entire work in typescript, and has favoured me, from his wide knowledge of this field, with comments and suggestions on a number of points. I am deeply grateful to them all. Finally I must express my thanks to the Librarian of the Library Association, Mr. L. J.

Preface   7

Taylor; to its Publications Officer, Mr. F. J. Cornell; to Miss
Helen Williams of the Liverpool University Extra-Mural
Department; and not least to the Librarian and staff of the
Liverpool University Library, without whose assistance the
whole thing would have been impossible.

July 1965   T. K.

CONTENTS

9

LIST OF ILLUSTRATIONS

11

ACKNOWLEDGMENTS

GRATEFUL acknowledgment is made to Messrs. Macmillan and Co.; the Bodleian Library; Messrs. Photo Precision Ltd.; the York Minster Library; *Country Life*; Mr. Robert Lee; Chetham's Library, Manchester; the Norfolk and Norwich Records Committee; the United Society for the Propagation of the Gospel; the Trustees of the Innerpeffray Library; the British Museum; the Bristol City Libraries; the Liverpool City Libraries; the Wisbech and Fenland Museum; and the Leathersellers' Co., London; for permission to reproduce illustrative material as indicated in the text; and to Messrs. Robert Hale Ltd., and J. Allan Cash for permission to use the illustration on the jacket.

CHAPTER I

Mediaeval Origins

To most people today, the term "public library" stands for the rate-aided library round the corner, which is public in the dual sense that it is supported from public funds and freely available for public use. To a minority, mostly professional scholars, the term may also be held to include the great national libraries such as the British Museum, which are also maintained from public funds though public access is not quite unrestricted. These publicly-financed libraries are, however, a comparatively recent phenomenon: there were very few rate-aided libraries before the Public Libraries act of 1850; and the British Museum Library, the oldest of the national libraries, dates only from 1753. If we think of public libraries simply as libraries for the use of the public (irrespective of finance), their history is a much longer one. The idea was not born suddenly, but emerged slowly and gradually in response to a developing public need. It is the purpose of this volume to trace the evolution of this idea, and the many and varied institutions in which it is embodied, prior to the year 1850. To find our point of departure we have to go back a very long way, for the public libraries, like so many of our great educational institutions, find their remote origins in the mediaeval church. We have to begin, therefore, by considering the situation as it was in the closing centuries of the Middle Ages.

We must note, first, that before the fifteenth century, or at any rate the late fourteenth century, there was no "general public" for books in the sense in which we use the phrase today. Books were for the most part in Latin: they were, therefore, for the learned, and learning was virtually a monopoly of the clergy "The laity", declared a fourteenth-century author bluntly, "who look at a book turned upside down just as if it were open in the right way, are utterly unworthy of any communion with books."[1]

---

[1] Richard de Bury, *Philobiblon*, ed. E. C. Thomas (1902), p. 108. On the authorship of this work see below, p. 26.

It should be noted, however, that the ranks of the clergy included not only the members of the religious orders, and the hierarchy of the secular church, but also many who would nowadays be laymen – clerks, secretaries, stewards, lawyers, teachers, physicians and civil servants. It was this body which constituted the "public" for books, and its needs, though varied, were strictly professional.

MONASTIC, CATHEDRAL AND UNIVERSITY LIBRARIES

In judging the extent of the provision which existed to meet these professional needs we must bear in mind one basic fact, namely that books were, by our standards, fantastically expensive. The labour of copying was, of course, tremendous – a single volume could easily take six months to transcribe – and parchment and binding were also very costly. Any attempt to measure mediaeval book-prices in terms of modern money is bound to be hazardous and misleading, but some idea of comparative values may be gained if we note that a fairly common price for a bound volume in the later Middle Ages was 20s., and that for this sum a man might buy, about 1450, two cows, a dozen sheep, or a tolerable horse, or, if he were convivially inclined, about 20 gallons of wine or 10 barrels of beer. Alternatively, the same sum would purchase the services of an agricultural labourer for a period of ten weeks. Probably, therefore, we should think of such a volume as worth, in modern times, the equivalent of not less than £100.

Many books, of course, were cheaper. On the other hand a large book such as a Bible, or a book elaborately bound or illuminated, would be correspondingly dearer: it is on record, for example, that the London Franciscans, about 1421, paid the stupendous sum of 100 marks (£66 13s. 4d.) for a copy in two volumes of the *Commentaries* of Nicholas de Lyra – a well-known and much-prized work by a French Franciscan.

In these circumstances, though some of the clergy, as we shall see, managed to assemble small libraries of their own, most of them necessarily relied on institutional libraries. These were much more numerous and varied than is commonly supposed. The existence of libraries in the monasteries and other religious houses, and in the universities, is well known; but it is not as generally known that libraries, or at least collections of books, were to be found also in the secular cathedrals,[1] in collegiate churches, in parish churches, and even, towards the close of the Middle Ages, in a few schools.

But if there were many libraries there were very few books, for all were by modern standards very small. The largest libraries known to us were those of three great Benedictine houses – Bury St. Edmunds; St. Augustine's Abbey, Canterbury; and the Cathedral Priory of Christ Church, Canterbury. Each of these numbered by the close of the fifteenth century about 2,000 volumes.[2] The Cathedral Priory of St. Cuthbert, Durham, probably had upwards of 1,000 volumes at this period, and its collection may perhaps have been matched by that of another great Benedictine house, St. Albans, which is known to have had an outstanding library. Of the non-Benedictine houses, the Austin Canons at Leicester and the Bridgettines at Syon in Middlesex had collections approaching the thousand mark. No other religious house of any order is known to have possessed more than a few hundred volumes. This applies even to the houses of the friars, who had something of a reputation as book-collectors.

As to the secular cathedrals, it is doubtful if any of them at any time possessed as many as 500 volumes; and the largest collegiate church library of which we have precise knowledge is that of Bishop Auckland, which amounted in 1499 to fewer than fifty volumes. The ordinary parish church rarely had more than a handful of books, though a few London churches had more substantial collections: St. Peter's upon Cornhill had sufficient, in the fifteenth century, to warrant a separate library building.

The universities, though latecomers on the scene, benefited more than other institutions by the munificence of pious donors, but even here the largest collections recorded – at Magdalen and Merton Colleges, Oxford – probably did not exceed 1,000 volumes. The Oxford and Cambridge University libraries (as

---

[1] The secular cathedrals were those which were served, not by monastic communities, but by chapters of secular canons. They were in England, Chichester, Exeter, Hereford, Lichfield, Lincoln, London (St. Paul's), Salisbury, Wells, and York; in Wales, Bangor, Llandaff, St. Asaph, and St. David's; and in Scotland, Aberdeen, Brechin, Elgin (Moray), and Glasgow.

[2] These and other figures in this chapter exclude service-books.

distinct from the college libraries) were substantially smaller
than this, and none of the Scottish university libraries attained
any considerable size during the mediaeval period. Among
schools we need take account only of three important foundations – Winchester, Eton, and Rotherham. All these were in
form chantries with schools attached, and they had small
libraries for the use of the clergy and fellows. Rotherham, the
last to be founded (1483), acquired its library only in 1500,
when it inherited over a hundred volumes from its patron
Thomas Rotherham, Archbishop of York.

All in all, it is doubtful if all the libraries in Britain put
together could muster as many as 100,000 volumes. It should
be borne in mind, however, that in the Middle Ages a *volume* is
not to be equated, as it usually can be today, with a *book*, since
it was the common practice to bind smaller manuscript works
together into large volumes (often without much regard for
the contents). Thus at Christ Church, Canterbury, the
fourteenth-century catalogue lists 1,831 volumes, but these
contain 4,157 separate titles. A more striking example still
comes from Glasgow, where in 1475 Bishop John Laing presented to the University library thirty-two works of philosophy
and theology bound in two volumes – one of parchment, containing twenty-four works, and the other of paper, containing
the remaining eight.[1] In order, therefore, to form a just idea of
the number of books in mediaeval libraries we should probably
multiply the number of volumes by a factor of three or four.
Even so the total book resources in the manuscript age
were pitiably small, especially if we bear in mind the recent
recommendation of a Government committee that a basic public
library service should allow for an annual addition of 7,200
titles.[2]

All these mediaeval libraries, were, of course, basically
theological. If we look at the catalogue of the Benedictine
priory of St. Martin at Dover, compiled in 1389, we find that
the books were divided into nine classes or Distinctions. The
first Distinction was devoted to Bibles and books of the Bible;
four were devoted to theology; two to civil and canon law;

---

[1] *Munimenta Alme Universitatis Glasguensis* (1854), Vol. III, pp. 403–4.
[2] Ministry of Education, *Standards of Public Library Service in England
and Wales* (1962), p. 18.

one to logic, philosophy, rhetoric, medicine, chronicles and romances; and one to poetry, grammar and dictionaries. Here we have the basic elements which are to be found in nearly all mediaeval libraries, but of course the emphasis on the different subjects varied according to the use the library was intended to serve.

The monastic libraries were intended for devotional purposes, and were rich in Biblical texts and the writings of the early Fathers. The libraries of the friars, on the other hand, reflected the preaching duties of these orders: they were strong in commentaries and sermons, and paid less attention to the Fathers and more to the scholastic theologians of their own time. The libraries of the cathedrals served the needs of the cathedral clergy (a vast horde in the Middle Ages), and also, we must suppose, of the clergy of the diocese in so far as they were within reach, and their distinguishing feature was the relatively large place accorded to works on canon and civil law. Books on law usually found a place, too, in the small collections recorded in the non-cathedral churches. These also were intended for the use of the clergy, since even churches which were not collegiate often had numerous chantry priests in addition to the parish clergy. The university libraries, naturally, concentrated on the theological and philosophical texts required by the regent masters for their lectures and by the graduate fellows for their higher studies (the average undergraduate had to be content to hear books rather than read them).

Individual libraries had, of course, their special features. Durham Priory, for example, was unusually rich in the classics; St. Albans was strong on the historical side; St. Augustine's, Canterbury, and the Austin Friars at York were remarkable for scientific works, and Leicester Abbey and Titchfield Abbey for medical books; the Oxford Franciscans and the Benedictines of Ramsey Abbey had small but notable collections of Hebrew works; and the Oxford Franciscans also had some Greek texts. The University library at Oxford was distinguished for the splendid collection of close on 300 manuscripts presented, mostly between 1439 and 1444, by the great humanist and book-lover Humphrey, Duke of Gloucester – a collection which included not only theology but astronomy, medicine, a remarkable selection of the classics, and works of Dante, Petrarch and

Boccaccio. Special collections such as these, small though they were, were very precious amid the prevailing scarcity.

It is interesting to observe these mediaeval libraries, small as they were, beginning to grapple with those problems of library organization which later had to be solved by the public library system.

A word may be said, to begin with, as to how books were acquired. In the early Middle Ages, when almost the only libraries were those of the monasteries, the books were for the most part copied by the monks themselves, and in some Scottish houses this practice was continued, at least to some extent, into the sixteenth century. In general, however, as the Middle Ages wore on, the output of the monastic *scriptoria* declined. The friars, with the exception of the Franciscans, seldom produced their own books, preferring to employ lay scribes, who were often attached to the convents for this purpose. In the fourteenth and fifteenth centuries a very large proportion of books came by way of gift or bequest.

The university and college libraries in particular benefited in this way. The college libraries were often endowed by their founders: William of Wykeham, for example, gave 240 volumes to New College in 1379, and William of Waynflete, a century later, presented 800 volumes to Magdalen College. Gifts of this kind represented the donor's private collections, and they were the product, in the first instance, either of hired scribes or of the commercial booksellers. These were numerous in London and the university towns, and were to be found also in other towns. Well-to-do nobles and ecclesiastics, travelling abroad in the service of King or Church, also had the opportunity to purchase books in Paris, Rome, and other continental centres.

The commercial booksellers, or "stationers", revolutionized the production of books. In the university centres they concentrated on producing plain texts of the books most in demand. The format was reduced, the handwriting condensed, the binding simplified, and all unnecessary ornamentation eliminated. Teams of scribes were frequently employed, each responsible for a single section of the manuscript, which when complete

was either bound and sold or hired out in unbound sections
(*peciae*) for copying or study. The texts thus produced were
very different from the large, beautifully written and handsomely illuminated manuscripts which we particularly associate
with the Middle Ages, but the reduction in cost was very
considerable.

When books were few, in the early Middle Ages, the problem
of storage presented little difficulty: they were kept in chests or
cupboards, usually in or near the cloister, otherwise in the
church. The precentor, who acted as librarian in monastic
libraries, was known also as *armarius*, "the keeper of the cupboards". The Cistercian houses, and occasionally others, had a
special store-room adjoining the cloister. In non-monastic
establishments books were often chained in the church.[1] The
royal collegiate chapel at St. George's, Windsor, for example,
possessed at the beginning of the fifteenth century thirty-four
volumes, of which twenty-two were law-books kept in a cupboard, and the remainder were chained in the church. These
latter included, oddly enough, a copy of the *Roman de la Rose*
and another volume of French romance.

The practice of chaining books in the church continued to the
close of the Middle Ages, even where other provision had been
made. At Exeter, as late as 1506, though the majority of the
cathedral's 363 volumes were in the library, eight were chained
near the west door, seven (a Bible, a Concordance, and de Lyra's
Commentaries), behind the treasurer's stall, and fourteen law-
books behind the precentor's stall. Examples of the same
practice are to be found at Canterbury, York and Glasgow.[2]

By the mid-fifteenth century, however, it was becoming
increasingly common to have a special library room, often built
over a cloister or over an aisle of the church, and fitted with
lecterns to hold the books and provide accommodation for
reading. Usually, it seems, the books were chained to the
lecterns. Libraries of this kind became the general rule at the
universities and in the secular cathedrals, and were to be found
also in many of the larger monasteries and friaries. In the
secular cathedrals, where many of the canons and other cathedral
clergy were non-resident, it was particularly useful to have a

---

[1] At Exeter, in early times, some books seem to have been kept in boxes
secured to the pillars.   [2] For York see below, p. 25.

central place where books could be readily consulted and at the same time adequately safeguarded.

The drawback of the lectern system was that the lecterns could hold very few books, so that in the case of the larger collections only a portion of the books could be housed in the library. Leicester Abbey, for example, had at the close of the fifteenth century a collection of nearly 1,000 volumes, but the library accommodated less than a quarter of them. M. R. James believed that these books were chained, and that they constituted "a sort of reference library, available to members of the house, and very likely to members of the public also, or at least to properly accredited persons".[1] The rest remained in cupboards and were available for lending.

Thus the distinction between the reference library and the lending library was early established. The libraries of the secular cathedrals, which were relatively small, were apparently for reference only, and so were the two university libraries at Oxford and Cambridge, except that at Oxford there was a separate set of books, kept in a chest called "the chest of three philosophies and the seven liberal sciences", which were available for lending to masters teaching in arts. The college libraries, however, had loan collections as well as chained reference collections. The books for lending (*libri distribuendi*) were periodically distributed, usually once a year, to the fellows of the college. Each fellow could thus have at his disposal a small collection of books, which he would no doubt exchange from time to time with those borrowed by others, but for which he was responsible until the time of the next allocation.

The growth in the size of libraries made it necessary to provide some kind of catalogue. The earliest records of this kind are mere booklists, inventories of valuables rather than library catalogues. Later, however, it was found convenient to arrange the books in some kind of subject order. Since so many volumes contained more than one work, however, even a subject catalogue was apt to be difficult, and from the Benedictine Abbey of Peterborough we have what seems to have been a special list, compiled in the late fourteenth century, of the contents, other than the first item, of composite volumes.

[1] M. R. James (ed.), "Catalogue of the Library of Leicester Abbey", in *Trans. Leics. Archaeol. Soc.*, Vol. XIX (1935–37), pp. 120, 127.

By this date the best catalogues had already attained a surprising degree of elaboration. A remarkable example is the catalogue to which reference has already been made above, compiled in 1389 by John Whytefeld, librarian of the Benedictine priory of St. Martin at Dover (a daughter house of Christ Church, Canterbury).[1] This was a triple catalogue, comprising a shelf list, a list showing the individual works of each volume, and an alphabetical list, by titles, of all the works in the library. As we have noted above, the books were divided into nine classes or Distinctions, and it appears that these corresponded to nine presses in the priory bookroom (there was no library room at this stage). Each press had seven shelves, numbered from the bottom to facilitate the addition of extra shelves at the top, if required; and the shelf-list indicated for each volume its Distinction, its shelf, and its location on the shelf. The shelf-list also recorded the number of separate titles in the volume and the total number of folios, i.e. leaves; and following the common mediaeval practice it identified each volume individually by citing the opening words from the second or some subsequent folio of the first title. (This was a simple but effective method of identification, since in manuscript books the pagination inevitably varied from copy to copy.) Each volume bore a press-mark corresponding to the shelf-list.

If we take a single example from the shelf-list, we find that St. Augustine's *De Civitate Dei* was the first title in the sixth volume on the sixth shelf from the foot of Distinction C, which was one of the Distinctions devoted to theology. The volume contained two other works, with 178 folios in all, and the opening words of the fifth folio of the *De Civitate Dei* were *-tinere compertum*.[2]

The first attempt at an inter-library catalogue, or union catalogue as we should call it today, was a list known as the *Registrum librorum Angliae*, which seems to date from the second half of the thirteenth century. It was compiled by the Franciscans, no doubt for the use of travelling Franciscan preachers, and listed the works of over eighty authors with the monastic

---

[1] See above, pp. 16–17.
[2] M. R. James, *The Ancient Libraries of Canterbury and Dover* (Cambridge 1903), p. 418.

libraries in which they might be found. It covered no fewer than 183 libraries, including seven in Scotland.

Early in the fifteenth century a monk of Bury St. Edmunds, using the *Registrum* and other lists, and drawing also on personal knowledge of certain libraries, set out to produce a more comprehensive catalogue – "a list in alphabetical order of all the authors, pagan and secular, of whom any knowledge was to be had, with their dates, the titles of the works, and for each work the number of books contained in it, its first and last words, and references as far as possible to libraries in Great Britain in which it might be consulted."[1] He added four monasteries and four priories to the Franciscan list of libraries, and extended the scope of the work to cover 673 authors; but this great *Catalogus scriptorum ecclesiae* was never completed.[2]

HOW FAR WERE THESE LIBRARIES PUBLIC?

J. W. Clark's claim that the monastic libraries were "the public libraries of the Middle Ages"[3] is a picturesque exaggeration, but it is true that although the monastic libraries and the other libraries we have described were provided primarily for the use of the members of the institutions concerned, some of them did fulfil, in some measure, the functions we now associate with public libraries.

The monastic libraries, it appears, were reasonably accessible for purposes of reference to all who required to use them, which meant, in practice, to clergy and students. The inter-library catalogue compiled by the Franciscans, for example, presupposes that travelling friars would be admitted to monastic libraries. There is no reason to suppose that similar privileges would be refused to laymen able and willing to take advantage of them, but these must have been few, and until the fifteenth century drawn exclusively from the well-to-do and the well

[1] R. A. B. Mynors, "Latin Classics Known to Boston of Bury", in *Fritz Saxl: Memorial Essays* (1957), p. 159.
[2] This catalogue, long attributed to John Boston, was printed in part by D. Wilkins in his edition of T. Tanner, *Bibliotheca Britannico-Hibernica* (1748), pp. xviii–xliii. The question of the authorship is at present being re-examined by Mr. R. H. Rouse, of Harvard University, who is preparing a new edition.
[3] J. W. Clark, *The Care of Books* (Cambridge, 1901, 2nd edn. 1902), pp. 55, 64.

connected. William Worcester, secretary to Sir John Fastolf and one of our earliest English antiquaries, was apparently able to draw freely for information on the libraries of religious houses in his journeyings through England in the 1460s and 1470s.

It is also true that both monasteries and friaries sometimes lent books to outsiders. The extent to which this happened may have been exaggerated, for some of the evidence commonly quoted relates to France and is not necessarily applicable to this country. It is, however, sufficiently astonishing that books should be lent at all, in view of their value. Naturally, such loans were made only under the most stringent precautions. A striking but not unique example comes from Winchester, where in 1299 Bishop John of Pontoise borrowed from his own cathedral monastery "a Bible in two volumes well glossed", which had been bequeathed by a former bishop. In doing so he undertook in the most solemn terms to restore the book, and in the event of its not being restored at the time of his death the monastery was empowered to distrain upon all his goods, temporal and ecclesiastical, until it should have been recovered.[1]

As a rule every loan was the subject of a formal legal agreement, and very often a deposit of equal value was also called for, either in money or in some other form, e.g. another book. The Prior and Chapter at Durham, for example, decided in 1235 that "no book should be lent to anyone by the librarian, or by any other person, except on receipt of a pledge of equal value; unless it should be at the request of the Lord Bishop".[2] The Durham records afford several instances of such transactions, and also two examples, from the fourteenth century, of lawbooks lent to outsiders without pledge. Probably such exceptions were fairly freely made for local people well known to the monastery concerned: thus at Ely, in 1320, the Prior and Chapter recovered from the executors of Roger de Huntingfeld, Rector of Balsham, ten volumes of theology which he formerly borrowed, upon indenture but apparently without pledge. In 1431 the Abbot of Easby in Yorkshire (a Premonstratensian

---

[1] C. Deedes (ed.), *Registrum Johannis de Pontissara*, Vol. II (Cant. and York Soc., Vol. XXX, 1924), pp. 712–13.

[2] J. Raine (ed.), *Catalogi veteres librorum ecclesiae cathedralis Dunelmensis* (Surtees Soc., Vol. VII, Durham 1838), p. 21.

house) went to law to recover from John Eseby, parson of Fulbeck in Lincolnshire, sixteen books valued at 100 marks.[1]

At Christ Church, Canterbury, where loans both within and without the monastery were recorded on boards or tablets (*tabulae*), a list of books missing in 1337 includes seventeen volumes "in the hands of seculars" (*in manibus secularium*). Most of the books borrowed were law-books, and most of the borrowers were secular clergy, but the list does include one layman – no other than the late King Edward II, who had borrowed the Miracles of St. Thomas, and lives of St. Thomas and St. Anselm.[2]

It should be remembered, in this connection, that the cathedral monasteries, and also some friaries, were at times centres for theological teaching. At Christ Church, Canterbury, in 1324, auditors were flocking to the theology lectures in great numbers (*copiosius affluant*), and at Norwich the Franciscan school was famous enough to attract students from abroad.[3] Such students would naturally be glad to make use of the library.

The secular cathedrals were particularly active in the provision of instruction in theology, and some, e.g. Glasgow, provided lectures in law also. At Salisbury the building of the library was specifically associated with educational work of this kind: in 1445 the Chapter decided that as it was desirable,

"for divers reasons, to have certain schools suitable for lectures, together with a library for the safe keeping of books and the convenience of those who wish to study therein – which library up to the present they have been without – such schools and library shall be built as soon as possible over one side of the cloister of the church."[4]

It is in these secular cathedral libraries, rather than in the monastic libraries, that we find ourselves closest to the modern concept of a public library. The monastic libraries, however

[1] For other examples of loans to secular clergy see the entries listed under *accomodare* in the glossary appended to the List of Donors, etc., in N. R. Ker, *Mediaeval Libraries* (1941, 2nd edn., 1964), p. 326.
[2] Another royal borrower was Edward's daughter Joanna, Queen of Scotland, who in 1362 (the year of her death) borrowed from the Benedictines of Abingdon a glossed copy of the Apocalypse – Ker, *op. cit.*, p. 226.
[3] W. A. Pantin, *The English Church in the Fourteenth Century* (Cambridge 1955), pp. 117–19.
[4] *Chapter Act Book*, quoted by J. W. Clark, *The Care of Books* (Cambridge 1901, 2nd edn., 1902), p. 115.

accessible, remained essentially private. In many cases their books were still stored in cupboards or bookrooms. The cathedral libraries, on the other hand, were almost invariably chained reference libraries. They seldom lent books – Aberdeen was exceptional in this respect – but they were open for consultation by the cathedral clergy (both resident and non-resident), visiting scholars and students, and no doubt to such of the parish clergy from round about as were learned enough to make use of them. The same was true, though in a very minor degree, of the small collections of books held by non-cathedral churches.

In the case of books given or bequeathed for chaining in churches, it was frequently made clear that they were intended for general use. In 1378, for example, Thomas of Farnylaw, Chancellor of York, bequeathed a Bible and Concordances to the church of St. Nicholas, Newcastle, to be chained in the north porch "for the common use". And at York Minster itself, about a century earlier, Canon John le Cras presented a copy of a well-known Latin dictionary, the *Summa Hugucionis*,[1] with an inscription by the scribe which begins:

"Here ends the *Summa* of Master Hugutio concerning the derivations, composition, meanings and interpretations of words, which Master John le Cras, canon of the church of the Blessed Peter at York, caused to be written at his own expense, for the convenience and use of the priests and clerks frequenting the choir of the aforesaid church, and likewise of other clerks, as well scholars as those at leisure, or travelling, to be placed in a common, safe and honourable place, so that should anyone seek information concerning some point of doubt, scholarship, or disputation, it may easily be found according to the letters of the alphabet. And whosoever shall alienate it from the precincts of the Blessed Peter of the church of York, or falsify it, or misappropriate it, or in any way remove it from the aforesaid community, by the authority of Blessed Peter, Prince of the Apostles, may he be anathema. Amen."[2]

The concluding denunciation of whoever shall remove the book is typical of many mediaeval manuscript inscriptions.

[1] By Hugutio of Pisa, written *c.* 1200.
[2] I am indebted for this inscription to Professor C. R. Cheney, of Cambridge, and Mr. Bernard Barr of the York Minster Library. Copies of the same work are recorded as chained in the lady chapel at St. Edmund's, Salisbury (1472), and All Saints, Derby (*c.* 1525) – J. C. Cox, *Churchwarden's Accounts* (1913), pp. 107, 120.

The most exclusive of the mediaeval libraries were those of Oxford and Cambridge. The two university libraries were, as has been noted above, mainly reference libraries, and their use was restricted to graduates and others of similar standing.[1] In the colleges the use of the reference collections was restricted to the fellows, and to others of similar standing with the permission of the fellows. Loans to outsiders from college libraries were in many cases specifically forbidden, and where they were permitted, as at University College and All Souls College, Oxford, it was only upon indenture and upon the deposit of a pledge of greater value than the book.

It has been supposed that the regulations drafted by that great fourteenth-century bibliophile, Richard of Bury, for the library he planned to bestow on Durham Hall, Oxford, envisaged the establishment of a public lending library. He did indeed propose that duplicate books should be available for loan to "any scholar, secular or religious", but the word secular refers here to the secular clergy, and the text makes it clear that the plan was intended for the benefit of "the scholars and masters, as well regulars as seculars, of the university".[2] In the end, unfortunately, it was never carried out.

PRIVATE LIBRARIES AND THE GROWTH OF
THE READING PUBLIC

The fifteenth century saw not only the continued growth of institutional libraries of all kinds, and a rapid improvement in library facilities, but also a great increase in the number of books in private circulation. Until the late fourteenth century private libraries were predominantly clerical, and usually quite small. Richard of Bury's library, just mentioned, seems to have been an outstanding exception. Bishop of Durham from 1333 until his death in 1345, holder of many royal offices, and reputed author of the *Philobiblon*,[3] Bury was a bibliomaniac rather than

---

[1] See above, p. 20. The St. Andrew's University library, founded in 1456, was unchained, but books were not lightly lent – J. B. Salmond and G. H. Bushnell, *Henderson's Benefaction* (St. Andrews 1942), p. 30.

[2] See Richard de Bury, *Philobiblon*, ed. E. C. Thomas (1902), pp. 114–17.

[3] Though the *Philobiblon* is autobiographical in form, it has sometimes been attributed to Bury's friend Robert Holcot, an eminent Dominican scholar.

a scholar. He scoured Europe for manuscripts, and used his money and his position without scruple to further his passion. He is said to have possessed no fewer than 1,500 volumes – the largest private library in mediaeval England – but this estimate is almost certainly much exaggerated.[1] In the fifteenth century private libraries multiplied. Humphrey, Duke of Gloucester, who has already been referred to in connection with his benefactions to the University of Oxford, and whose library must have amounted to at least five or six hundred volumes, was but one of a number of notable collectors, both lay and ecclesiastical. Many of them were deeply influenced by the Italian Renaissance, and the libraries they assembled included rare or hitherto unknown Latin works, Latin translations from the Greek (often specially commissioned), and even, in some cases, manuscripts in the original Greek. In this respect the private collectors were far in advance of the institutional libraries of their time, and many of their treasures have survived to enrich our national libraries today.

Even more interesting from our present point of view, as illustrating the spread of the reading habit, are the humbler libraries of lesser men – the dozen or so volumes of poetry, romance, heraldry and the classics in the possession of Sir John Paston, and the miscellaneous volumes, mostly devotional in character, bequeathed by city merchants. About 20 per cent of London wills of personal property in the fifteenth century mention books. This change from earlier epochs reflects at once the fall in the relative price of books, the growing wealth of the community, and above all the spread of literacy, which in turn was due to the increase in the number of grammar schools, and especially the multiplication of more elementary schools teaching reading and writing.

Most of these schools were attached to cathedrals, collegiate churches, or chantries, and it is paradoxical that the result of

---

[1] It derives from J. de Ghellinck, "Un bibliophile au XIVe siècle: Richard de Bury", in *Revue d'histoire ecclésiastique*, Vol. XIX (1923), p. 175, and is based on a statement by the chronicler Adam Murimuth that "five great carts (*carectae*) were insufficient for the carriage of his books". But obviously everything turns on the accuracy of the chronicler and the size of the carts. Cf. *Adae Murimuth Continuatio Chronicarum*, ed. E. M. Thompson (Rolls Ser. 1889), p. 171. There is an interesting essay on Bury in R. Irwin, *The Heritage of the English Library* (1964), Ch. x.

the Church's teaching should have been to break down the long clerical monopoly of learning. So, however, it was. Geoffrey Chaucer, who died in 1400, was a portent of the new age – one of the first great lay scholars, and incidentally, as is evident from his works, the possessor of a considerable library. The revival of English as a literary language, with which he was pre-eminently associated, did much to foster the habit of reading among the middle classes by making available a much wider range of reading material: chronicles, ballads and romances, sermons and manuals of devotion, books on heraldry, etiquette and medicine, and translations of the classics.

To generalize about the extent of literacy is difficult, but it is perhaps fair to say that by the mid-fifteenth century literacy, in the sense of an ability to read and write in English, was almost universal among the gentry and the merchant class of London and south-east England, and was becoming increasingly common among the ranks of craftsmen and shopkeepers. Many of these people, too, had some competence in Latin. The same statement might hold good of important urban centres outside London, such as Norwich and Bristol, but in Wales and in the rural areas of northern England and Scotland illiteracy must still have been the general rule.[1] Everywhere the standard of literacy amongst men was higher than amongst women.

We must, of course, keep in mind that the number of manuscripts of English works in circulation was exceedingly limited. Pious people sometimes had religious works copied "for a comyn profite", that is to say, on the understanding that the holder, when not using the book himself, should lend it to someone else, and that he should ultimately bequeath it for circulation in the same way, "so it be delivered and committed from persoone to persoone, man or womman, as longe as the book endureth".[2]

Books were also circulated sometimes by commercial copyists. One of these, John Shirley, who died in 1456, was in business in London on a large scale, and made a speciality of

[1] John Durkan's chapter on "Education" in D. McRoberts (ed.), *Essays on the Scottish Reformation* (Glasgow 1962), pp. 145 seq., is a warning against underestimating the extent of literacy in Scotland.
[2] H. S. Bennett, "The Production and Dissemination of Vernacular Manuscripts in the Fifteenth Century", in *The Library*, 5th Ser., Vol. I (1947), pp. 170–1.

anthologies containing a number of pieces, sacred and profane, to suit a variety of tastes. Many of his books were inscribed with a rhyme which ends:

> "Whanne ye this booke haue ouer-redde and seyne,
> To Johan Shirley restore yee hit ageyne."[1]

THE FIRST PUBLIC LIBRARIES

It is against this background of increasing literacy that the first public libraries make their appearance. Three such libraries are known to have existed in the fifteenth century, the first, the Guildhall Library of London, being associated with the name of that famous citizen, Richard Whittington.

Whether Whittington himself had any hand in the foundation is uncertain. He did not mention it in his will, made in 1421,[2] but we know he was interested in libraries – the magnificent library of the London Greyfriars was built and furnished largely at his expense – and he assisted also in the building of the Guildhall. What is certain is that soon after his death in 1423 his executors, together with those of another wealthy mercer, William Bury, completed and handed over to the Mayor, Aldermen and Commonalty of the City of London a new building adjoining the Guildhall for the purposes of a library. In September, 1425, the custody of this building was handed back to the executors with authority to make all necessary arrangements concerning the provision of books. Later the library came to be regarded as attached particularly to the Guildhall College (a chantry foundation), and it seems to have been the regular practice for one of the College chaplains to act as librarian.

It seems probable that some at least of the credit for this new foundation should go to Whittington's chief executor, John Carpenter, a wealthy and influential man who served as Common Clerk, or as we should say Town Clerk, from 1417 to 1438, twice represented the City in Parliament, and compiled the now invaluable *Liber Albus* describing its laws and customs. A bequest which he made for the maintenance of poor scholars led

---

[1] H. S. Bennett, *Chaucer and the Fifteenth Century* (Oxford 1947), pp. 116-18.

[2] Printed in E. F. Jacob (ed.), *The Register of Henry Chichele*, Vol. II (Cant. and York Soc. 1937), pp. 240-3.

in the fulness of time to the foundation of the City of London
School. Carpenter was himself a booklover: his will, proved in
1442, specified twenty-five books by name (amongst them
Richard of Bury's *Philobiblon*), and directed that

"if any good or rare books shall be found among the said residue of
my goods, which . . . may seem necessary to the common library of
the Guildhall, for the profit of the students there, and those dis-
coursing to the common people, then I will and bequeath that those
books should be placed by my executors and chained in that library,
under such form that the visitors and students thereof may be the
sooner admonished to pray for my soul."[1]

This passage suggests that, as we should expect, the Guildhall library was a chained library of reference. It also suggests
that it was predominantly theological in character. This is
confirmed, a century later, by a description of the library (in a
schedule of the possessions of the Guildhall College, July 1549)
as "a house appointed by the saied Maior and cominalitie for . . .
resorte of all students for their education in Divine Scriptures".[2]

The library would, however, almost certainly include provision for the study of canon law, and it would be surprising, in
view of Carpenter's own interests, if it did not also include, at
least at the outset, a substantial section on civil law. Such a
library would be a boon to clergy of all kinds – parish priests,
preaching friars, diocesan officials, clerks in the royal service,
chantry priests in charge of schools, and so forth – and it would
be used also by university students on vacation and by the
students of the inns of court, whose curriculum included divinity
as well as law. The earliest reference to a library at one of these
institutions is at Lincoln's Inn in 1475.

That the library was well used, at least in its earlier years, is
suggested by the petition of Master John Clipstone, librarian,
in 1444, to be confirmed in his office, and in the occupation of
the house and garden which went with it, in consideration of
"the great attendaunce and charge which he hath with it, and

---

[1] For the will, and an account of Carpenter's books, see T. Brewer,
Memoir of the Life and Times of John Carpenter (1836, 2nd edn. 1856),
pp. 121–44.
[2] J. E. Price, *A Descriptive Account of the Guildhall of the City of London*
(1886), p. 139.

in waytenge thereupon".[1] The library was still in existence, as
we have seen, in July, but the last reference we have to the
books occurs on 31st January of that year, when the Court of
Common Council agreed that "Mr. Cycyll" should be permitted
to borrow

"all suche boks of St. Augustyns works and other as he nowe desyreth
that Remayne in the guylde hall chappell with this gentle Requeste
to be made to hym upon the delyuerye of the same that this howse
trusteth that he havynge perused theym wyll Restore theym to the
seid lyberarye there to Remayne to such vse as they were provyded
for."[2]

This was an ominous request, and the fear implied in the
concluding words was only too well founded, for William Cecil
(the same who was afterwards Lord Burghley) was at this time
secretary to Protector Somerset. The sequel came later in the
year, and is described by John Stow, writing in 1598:

"Adioyning to this chappell on the south side was sometime a
fayre and large library, furnished with books, pertayning to the
Guildhall and colledge: The books as it is said were in the raign of
Edward the 6. sent for by *Edward* Duke of Somerset, Lorde Protector,
with promise to be restored shortly: men laded from thence three
carries with them but they were never returned."[3]

A "carry" was a small two-wheeled cart, and "three carries"
does not suggest a very large library. Probably by this time the
library was out of date and not extensively used. At any rate
the City fathers seem to have made little effort to resuscitate it:
in 1550 they sold the lecterns to the highest bidder and let the
building as a market-house for the sale of clothes.[4]

The other two fifteenth-century public libraries were established later in the century, one at Worcester and one at Bristol.
Their founder was another John Carpenter, who was Bishop of
Worcester from 1444 to 1476. The coincidence of names is more
than accidental, for there is evidence that the two Carpenters

[1] R. R. Sharpe (ed.), *Calendar of Letter-books of the City of London*, Vol. K
(1911), p. 295.
[2] *City of London Letter-book Q*, f. 275a, quoted by C. Welsh, "The
Guildhall Library and its Work", in *The Library*, Vol. I (1889), p. 322.
[3] *Survey of London*, ed. C. L. Kingsford (Oxford 1908), Vol. I, p. 235.
Somerset fell from power in October, 1549.
[4] The present Guildhall Library is a nineteenth-century foundation.

were intimate friends, and we may surmise that they were in some way kinsmen. The libraries founded by Carpenter of Worcester were similar in scope and purpose to the Guildhall library, and it is difficult to believe that they were not influenced by the earlier enterprise.

Carpenter of Worcester was a powerful, wealthy and industrious prelate, who before becoming a bishop had been Fellow, Dean, and Provost of Oriel, Master of St. Anthony's Hospital, London, and for a year (1438–39), Chancellor of Oxford University. His cathedral at Worcester was a monastic one, and had of course its own monastic library, but Carpenter, concerned about the education of the parish clergy, evidently felt that this was insufficient. He therefore built at his own expense a new library – a chained reference library – which was to be open to all.

This new library was attached to the chantry chapel which had long been associated with the cathedral charnel-house. The chapel was under the charge of the sacristan, who was bound to maintain a chantry chaplain there. Carpenter decreed that this chaplain should henceforth be qualified in theology, and have the custody of the library; and a house was erected at the end of the library for his use. In 1458 Carpenter endowed the priory with additional revenues in order to ensure that these provisions should be properly carried out.[1]

In 1464 Carpenter founded a similar library in the great mercantile centre of Bristol, the largest city in his diocese. We may perhaps compare the Worcester library with the chained reference libraries of the non-monastic cathedrals, but in establishing such a library in a non-cathedral city Carpenter was breaking new ground. The Bristol foundation was attached to an ancient and rather curious body known as the Gild of Kalendars or Kalendaries. This was a religious gild associated with the church of All Saints. It was open to both men and women, and made provision for the usual functions of such gilds – monthly meetings of members, prayers for the souls of members and departed members, the care of the poor and the sick, and so

[1] J. W. Clark, *The Care of Books* (Cambridge 1901, 2nd edn. 1902), pp. 121–3, was the first to print an account of this library, but wrongly supposed that it was founded in 1464. Other writers have given 1459 or 1461. See below, p. 34n. 1.

1. FINAL PAGE OF THE "REGISTRUM LIBRORUM ANGLIE"
(MS. Tanner 165, fol. 120 v.)

This page shows the location of works by Richard of St. Victor. Each number in the column on the right represents a monastic library.

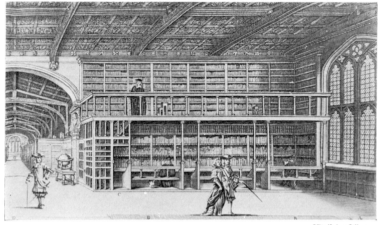

2. WALL BOOKCASES AT THE BODLEIAN (ARTS END)

The first example of this type of shelving known in this country, built in 1610–12. The books on the upper shelves were unchained.

3. THE CHAINED LIBRARY AT HEREFORD CATHEDRAL

The stalls (a development of the mediaeval lectern, for which see p. 78) date from 1611 and were copied from those in Duke Humphrey's Library at the Bodleian. The volumes are shelved, as usual, with the fore-edge outwards, the chain being attached to the fore-edge of the cover.

on. It had a meeting-place and chapel on the north side of the church, and its affairs were conducted under the direction of a prior, who was assisted in the celebration of masses by a number of chaplains or chantry priests.

Carpenter constructed his library in a room recently built for the house of Kalendars over the Lady Chapel, and placed the prior of the Gild in charge, with the provision that he should be duly qualified in theology. Since there was some uncertainty as to the manner of his election, Carpenter decreed that he should be chosen by the Mayor of Bristol, in consultation with the town council and the chaplains of the Gild. These arrangements were set forth in an indenture of 5th April, 1464, which was subscribed by the Prior and the Mayor on 17th April, and which included detailed regulations for the conduct of the library. On 5th May, 1464, regulations in almost identical terms were made for the library already established at Worcester.

The regulations decreed that the keeper of the library should be a bachelor of divinity, or at least a graduate, sufficiently instructed in Holy Scripture, and a ready preacher, and provided that

"on every weekday, for two hours before None and two hours after None, all who wish to enter that library for the purpose of study shall be free to come and go; and the aforesaid Master and Keeper shall, when duly required, expound doubtful and obscure passages of Holy Scripture to the ignorant, to the best of his knowledge."[1]

Careful arrangements were made for the chaining and cataloguing of the books, and any book lost through the negligence of the keeper was to be replaced by him on pain of a fine of 40s. The keeper was also to deliver a public lecture in the library once a week, and at Worcester he was to preach a sermon in the cathedral or at the cross in the cemetery on Holy Thursday. For these services he was to receive the handsome annual allowance of £10, at Bristol from the sacristan. At

---

[1] *quolibet die feriato per duas horas ante nonam et duas post nonam quibuscunque illam librariam eruditionis causa intrare volentibus libere pateant accessus et excessus; dictusque Magister et Custos cum debite requisitus fuerit, dubia et obscura sacre scripture ignorantibus iuxta facultatis sue scientiam declarabit . . .* (Register of Bishop Silvestro de' Gigli, f. 134, Worcestershire County Record Office). The office of None varied from 2 to 4 p.m. according to the season of the year.

Worcester he was also to receive four yards of woollen cloth to make him a gown and hood.[1]

Unfortunately we know little or nothing of the subsequent history of these two interesting libraries. At Bristol there is a reference in the parish records to the library building in 1486–87, and it is recorded that the possessions of the Gild in 1548 still included a chamber called the library. We do not know, however, whether this chamber continued to serve its original purpose.[2] At Worcester, in January, 1475, towards the close of Carpenter's episcopate, we have a record of the institution as librarian of his suffragan Richard Wolsey, formerly Bishop of Down and Connor.[3] Since it is unlikely that a suffragan bishop would perform the duties of such a humble office, the presumption is either that the library was neglected or that someone else was hired to do the work. In 1513 the Bishop's

[1] The Register of John Carpenter (Worcestershire County Record Office), contains the charters of 1458 relating to the Worcester library (Vol. I, f. 175) and the regulations for the Bristol library (ff. 197–8). The regulations for the Worcester library were recited in the record of an inquiry of 1513 (see below) which is in Silvestro de' Gigli's Register, ff. 132–6. There is a transcript of these pages from Gigli's Register in Prattinton MSS., Misc. Vol. VII, pp. 377–83, in the library of the Society of Antiquaries.

[2] There are still preserved at All Saints' Church three fifteenth-century MSS. and five fifteenth- and early sixteenth-century printed books (all theological works) which have been thought by some to be remnants of the Gild Library. If this could be established it would mean that the library was still functioning in the early sixteenth century. Unfortunately, none of the books bears any evidence of having belonged to the Gild; rather they are the sort of books that might have been bequeathed by some early sixteenth-century parson. See for a description T. W. Williams, "Gloucestershire Mediaeval Libraries", in *Transactions of the Bristol and Gloucestershire Archaeological Society*, Vol. XXXI (1908); and cf. N. R. Ker, *Mediaeval Libraries of Great Britain* (1941, 2nd edn. 1964), p. 13, and Central Council for the Care of Churches, *The Parochial Libraries of the Church of England* (1959), p. 71. Mr. Ker has pointed out to me that one of the books listed by Williams as a MS. (No. 4) is in fact a printed book.

The early history of the Gild Library has been confused by misreading of the records and by the forgeries of Thomas Chatterton, and it may therefore be as well to make clear, first, that there is no record of any library at the Gild before 1464, and second, that there is no evidence for the destruction of the Gild Library by fire in 1466. I am indebted to Miss Elizabeth Ralph, of the Bristol Archives Office, for generous assistance in unravelling these obscurities.

[3] Register of John Carpenter, Vol. II, f. 59. Wolsey was appointed to the see of Down and Connor by papal provision in 1451, but it is doubtful

official, Thomas Hannibal, conducted an inquiry into the disappearance of the copy of the foundation deed of the library which was supposed to be held by the sacristan. Prior John, formerly sacristan, testified that his predecessor as prior, Thomas Mildenham, had sent for the deed, and, as he believed and had heard from many, had burned it. Others testified to the same effect, but Prior John and another witness were so familiar with the deed that they were able to verify the accuracy of another copy which was produced at the inquiry, and which was thereupon duly authenticated. This rather puzzling incident at least suggests that the library was still in existence, but whether it was still in active use is another matter.

There is just one other place in fifteenth-century England where one might expect to find some kind of public library, and that is Norwich. It is, therefore, of interest to find in the will of John Leystofte, Vicar of St. Stephen's in that city, in the year 1461, the following bequest:

"Item, I will that, if a library be begun in Norwich, within two years after my decease, I bequeath to the same, my book called *Repyngton.*"[1]

This suggests that the idea of a library was at least under discussion, but there is no evidence to suggest that it ever came into existence.

whether he ever visited his bishopric. From 1452 until his death he was in England, acting successively as suffragan to the Bishops of Lichfield, Worcester (1475–79) and Hereford, besides holding other benefices. Another bishop was provided to Down and Connor in 1453, but Wolsey still clung to the title, and is described as Bishop in the record of institution.

[1] J. Kirkpatrick, *History of the Religious Orders . . . of Norwich* (Norwich 1845), p. 80. Cardinal Philip Repingdon was Bishop of Lincoln 1404–20; five MSS. of his Sermons on the Gospels survive in the Bodleian and other Oxford libraries.

Bibliographical Note

The best survey of the mediaeval libraries of this country for the general reader is still E. A. Savage, *Old English Libraries* (1911). J. W. Thompson (ed.), *The Medieval Library* (Chicago 1939, 2nd edn. New York 1957), which covers the whole of Europe, is systematic and comprehensive but sometimes inaccurate on detail. F. Wormald and C. E. Wright (eds.), *The English Library before 1700* (1958), is the most up-to-date and scholarly account for those aspects of the subject with which it deals. R. Irwin, *The Origins of the English Library* (1958), and *The Heritage of the English Library* (1964), has some interesting and far-ranging chapters on the subject: Part II of the former has a chapter on private libraries, for which see also R. Weiss, *Humanism in England during the Fifteenth Century* (Oxford 1941, 2nd edn. 1957). On library organization J. W. Clark, *The Care of Books* (Cambridge 1901, 2nd edn. 1902), is invaluable, and B. H. Streeter, *The Chained Library* (1931), is definitive within its special field. M. R. James, "The List of Libraries prefixed to the Catalogue of John Boston and the Kindred Documents", in *Collectanea Franciscana*, Vol. II (Manchester 1922), is best on inter-library catalogues. For book-prices see H. E. Bell, "The Price of Books in Mediaeval England", in *The Librarian*, 4th Ser., Vol. XVII (1936–37).

For the English monastic libraries D. Knowles, *The Religious Orders in England*, Vol. II (Cambridge 1955), Ch. xxvi, provides a useful brief survey; and the opening essay in F. A. Gasquet, *The Old English Bible* (1897, 2nd edn. 1908), is still worth reading. For the Scottish houses E. A. Savage, "Notes on the Early Monastic Libraries of Scotland", in *Papers of the Edinburgh Bibliographical Society*, Vol. XIV (1926–30), provides a starting-point for further research. A. Gwynn, *The English Austin Friars* (1940), deals with the libraries of that order, and H. M. Colvin, *The White Canons in England* (Oxford 1931), with those of the Premonstratensian order. For the Franciscan order there are a number of detailed studies, e.g. A. G. Little, *The Grey Friars in Oxford* (Oxford Historical Society 1891), C. L. Kingsford, *The Grey Friars of London* (Aberdeen 1915), W. M. Bryce, *The Scottish Grey Friars* (2v. Edinburgh [1909]), and J. H. R. Moorman, *The Grey Friars in Cambridge* (Cambridge 1952); but the most comprehensive survey is K. W. Humphreys, *The Book Provisions of the Mediaeval Friars, 1215–1400* (Amsterdam 1964).

Regional studies are few, but there are two by T. W. Williams, viz., *Somerset Mediaeval Libraries* (Somerset Archaeological and Natural History Society, Bristol 1897), and "Gloucester Mediaeval Libraries", in *Transactions of the Bristol and Gloucestershire Archaeological Society*, Vol. XXXI (1908). For London, R. A. Rye, *Students' Guide to the Libraries of London* (1908, 3rd edn. 1927) has useful historical material.

For much significant detail it is necessary to turn to the histories of individual libraries and institutions. These are too numerous to list, but bibliographical references to printed library catalogues, many of which contain valuable introductions, are to be found in N. R. Ker, *Medieval Libraries of Great Britain: a List of Surviving Books* (Royal Historical Society 1941, 2nd edn. 1964). Two studies of outstanding interest are J. Raine (ed.), *Catalogi veteres ecclesiae cathedralis Dunel-*

mensis (Surtees Society, Vol. VII, Durham 1838), and M. R. James, *The Ancient Libraries of Canterbury and Dover* (Cambridge 1903). For the former institution H. D. Hughes, *A History of Durham Cathedral Library* (Durham 1925), provides a more popular account; and James's work is supplemented, as far as Christ Church is concerned, by M. Beazeley, "The History of the Chapter Library of Canterbury Cathedral", in *Transactions of the Bibliographical Society*, Vol. VIII (1904–06).

On the growth of literacy see M. Deanesly, *The Lollard Bible* (Cambridge 1920), Ch. viii; C. L. Kingsford, *Prejudice and Promise in XVth Century England* (Oxford 1920), Ch. ii; J. W. Adamson, *"The Illiterate Anglo-Saxon"* (Cambridge 1946), Ch. iii; S. L. Thrupp, *The Merchant Class of Medieval London* (Michigan 1948, repr. 1962), Ch. iv; and for a convenient summary Ch. xi of R. Irwin's *Heritage of the English Library* (1964).

E. M. Borrajo, "The Guildhall Library", in *Library Association Record*, Vol. X (1908), is a brief general account. The early years are dealt with in detail in R. Smith, "The Library at Guildhall in the 15th and 16th Centuries", Parts I and II, in *Guildhall Miscellany*, Vol. I, Nos. 1 and 6 (1952–56). The original records of the public libraries at Worcester and Bristol are in the episcopal registers as noted above, but see for Worcester J. W. Clark, *The Care of Books* (*ut sup.*), pp. 121–3, and for Bristol W. Barrett, *The History and Antiquities of Bristol* (1789), pp. 448–58, and the Introduction to R. Ricard, *The Maire of Bristowe is Kalendar*, ed. L. T. Smith (Camden Society 1872). The two works last named, however, should be used with caution, and should be read in the light of E. G. C. F. Atchley, "On the Parish Records of the Church of All Saints, Bristol", in *Transactions of the Bristol and Gloucestershire Archaeological Society*, Vol. XXVII (1904). Many of the records relating to the Gild of Kalendars are printed in Vol. II of F. B. Bickley (ed.), *The Little Red Book of Bristol* (2v., Bristol 1900). The origin of these two libraries is also briefly touched on in a MS. thesis on John Carpenter by M. J. Morgan (M.A. Birmingham 1960), pp. 47–9.

CHAPTER II

Destruction and New Beginnings

FROM the point of view of library history, the sixteenth century is marked by two conflicting developments. On the one hand the introduction of printing made possible the multiplication of books on a scale hitherto undreamt of, and thereby laid the foundation upon which alone an extended public library service could be built. On the other hand, in mid-century, the virtual destruction of most of the old mediaeval libraries brought to an end such public facilities as these institutions had been able to offer. The pioneer public libraries founded in the previous century disappeared at the same time, if not earlier. It was not until the closing decades of Elizabeth's reign that the work of reconstruction was seriously taken in hand, and provision again began to be made, on a small scale, for public reading.

THE ADVENT OF PRINTING

The art of printing from movable type, perfected by Johann Gutenberg of Mainz about 1450, spread rapidly to other continental centres, especially in Germany, France, Italy and the Low Countries. It reached England in 1476, when William Caxton established his press at Westminster. For a long time operations were, by modern standards, on a very small scale. By 1500 (nine years after Caxton's death) there were about six printers in England; by 1550 there were still only about twenty, producing rather more than 200 books during the year, usually in small editions of not more than 600 or 700 copies. Though books were occasionally printed at provincial centres – St. Albans, Oxford and Cambridge, Canterbury and York, Ipswich and Worcester – London remained the great publishing centre, and St. Paul's Churchyard the great resort of booksellers. Wynkyn de Worde (Caxton's successor) and Richard Pynson, another London printer, were alone responsible for about two-thirds of all books printed in England between 1500 and 1530.

In Scotland, though Walter Chepman and Andrew Myllar, of Edinburgh, were granted a royal licence to print books in 1507, and a few other printers are known to have been at work either in Edinburgh or at St. Andrews before 1560, printing was in the main a post-Reformation development.[1] Both in England and in Scotland printed books were subject to a measure of political and religious censorship. In England this came to be exercised through the medium of the Stationers' Company – the special organ of the printing trade, formally incorporated in 1557.

In spite of the relatively small scale of production, the total achievement of these early years is impressive. Though many of the older generation of book collectors scorned printed books as inferior to the product of the scrivener's craft, the printing press quickly established itself as the normal method of book production. Its products ranged the whole gamut from children's ABCs to learned works of law and theology, and they were of course much cheaper than manuscript books. Apart from the saving in the cost of production, the use of paper instead of parchment or vellum, and of paper boards instead of wooden boards for binding, did much to bring prices down. By the middle of the sixteenth century a Bible might be had for 10s., a New Testament for 2s., ballads and broadsheets for 1d. apiece – and this in spite of the substantial rise in prices during the Tudor period. John Dorne, an Oxford bookseller, sold in 1520, in less than a year, 1,850 books, enough to stock a sizable mediaeval library.

A very significant feature of this period is the number of books printed in English. If we include works printed abroad, more than 5,000 editions of English works are recorded up to 1557. This fact lends colour to the oft-quoted but rather puzzling comment made by Sir Thomas More, in 1533, on the subject of popular literacy. Speaking of the argument that the English people should have the Bible available in their own tongue, he remarks that "farre more than four partes of the whole dyvyded into tenne, could never read englishe yet",[2] which would seem to imply that more than half the population *could* read. This

---

[1] There is no certain evidence of printing in Wales until 1718, when Isaac Carter began printing at Trefhedyn in Cardiganshire, but Welsh works were printed in England from 1546 onwards. See I. Jones, *A History of Printing and Printers in Wales* (Cardiff 1925).

[2] Sir T. More, *Apologye* (E.E.T.S. 1930), p. 13.

cannot possibly have been true of the country as a whole, but it may have been true of the more literate south-east.

The first complete English translation of the Bible was actually printed two years later, in 1535. This was Miles Coverdale's version, which incorporated some of William Tyndale's work, and provided the foundation for later translations, including the Authorized Version of 1611. John Strype tells us with what joy the English Bible was received by the people:

> "Everybody who could bought the book, or busily read it, or got others to read it to them, if they could not themselves; and divers more elderly persons learned to read on purpose."[1]

No fewer than thirty editions of the complete Bible, and fifty of the New Testament alone, appeared by 1557. Thomas Cromwell, as Vicar-General to Henry VIII, encouraged people to read the Bible, and in 1536 enjoined that it should be available in every parish church. This policy, however, was soon found to have its dangers, and an Act of Parliament of 1543 forbade the reading of the English Bible by artificers, apprentices, journeymen, serving-men of the rank of yeomen and under, husbandmen and labourers, and women other than noblewomen and gentlewomen. Here again we have evidence of the spread of literacy among ordinary people, and of the part played by the printing press in encouraging it.[2]

The advent of printing was reflected, as we should expect, in the growth of private libraries. John Fisher, Bishop of Rochester, who was beheaded in 1539 for his opposition to Henry VIII, is said to have had the "notablest Library of Books in all England, two long galleries full, the Books were sorted in stalls and a Register of the names of every Book at the end of every stall".[3] The library of Thomas Cranmer, Archbishop of Canterbury, is described by Strype as "the storehouse of ecclesiastical writers of all ages: and which was open for the use of learned men". Hugh Latimer, Bishop of Worcester, the famous preacher, was one of those who made use of its treasures.[4] There were other

---

[1] J. Strype, *Memorials of Thomas Cranmer* (1694, new edn. 1812), Vol. I, p. 91.
[2] The ban was lifted under Edward VI.
[3] Quoted in W. Y. Fletcher, *English Book Collectors* (1902), p. 17.
[4] Strype, *op. cit.*, Vol. I, p. 631.

substantial collections in the pre-Reformation period, both in England and in Scotland.

Even more striking, however, as indicating the extent of the change that was taking place, is the inventory drawn up in 1556 of the books of Sir William More, a well-to-do country gentleman of Surrey. Sir John Paston, a century earlier, had been happy in the possession of a dozen volumes or so: of More's library we read:

"Around the room is a collection of about 120 volumes of books, among them are some of the best chronicles of the time; as Fabyan, Langton, Harding, Carion, &c.; translations from the classics, as well as some in their original language; for magisterial business there are the statutes of Henry VIII, Edward VI and Mary, and all the statutes before, as well as the New Book of Justices, and other legal works; for medical use we find a Book of Physic, the Glass of Health, and a book against the Sweat, as well as a Book of Medicines for Horses; while for lighter reading there are such books as Chaucer, Lydgate, Skelton, and others, not only in English but also in French and Italian and for religious study, besides a Bible and Testaments in various languages, the Scala Perfectionis, Flores Bibliae, &c."[1]

Our knowledge of institutional libraries during the first half of the sixteenth century is still rather patchy, but it is clear that they were much slower than private collectors in responding to the new opportunities opened up by the age of printing. We do indeed catch glimpses, here and there, of vigorous life. The Bridgettines of Syon Monastery, for example, evidently did their best to keep pace with the new learning: their catalogue for 1526 lists some 400 printed books, including many humanist works. William More, Prior of Worcester, was a purchaser of books, both for himself and for his monastery, on visits to London between 1518 and 1533. In 1530 Thomas Chrystall, the reforming abbot of the Cistercian monastery of Kinloss, in Perthshire, refounded the library there, and this house became "a radiating centre for learning in the whole of the north of Scotland".[2] At Oxford, Corpus Christi College, founded in 1517, was endowed with a collection of manuscript and printed

[1] J. Evans, "Extracts from the Private Account Book of Sir William More", in *Archaeologia*, Vol. XXXVI (1855), p. 285.
[2] J. Durkan, "The Beginnings of Humanism in Scotland", in *Innes Review* (1953), p. 15.

works which Erasmus declared would attract more scholars to Oxford than had formerly been attracted to Rome. Later, between 1535 and 1550, several of the Colleges were renewing their stocks by extensive purchases of printed books: some colleges even sold plate for this purpose.

In general, however, one has the impression that the old mediaeval libraries, if not actually sinking into decay, as was the case with Duke Humphrey's library at Oxford, were growing only very slowly. How far they continued to serve a wider public is not clear, but it may perhaps be significant that when, shortly before the Dissolution, John Leland visited the library of Glastonbury Abbey, and stood amazed at the wonderful treasures assembled there, he found the library was "not accessible to all" (*non omnibus perviam*).[1] The same was probably true of some of the Scottish monasteries: the German Marcus Wagner, who visited St. Andrews and a number of neighbouring houses in 1553, found many rare and beautiful books, but all too often they were thick with dust or damaged by mice or other vermin.[2] As to the three public libraries mentioned in the last chapter, the only one which we can feel reasonably certain was still in active existence at the time of the Dissolution was the Guildhall Library in London.

THE DISPERSION

Both in England and in Scotland the Reformation led to the wholesale destruction or dispersion of the great mediaeval libraries. The dissolution of the English and Welsh monasteries took place under the acts of 1536 and 1539, and the seventeenth-century historian Thomas Fuller has described very accurately what happened to their libraries at this time:

"As brokers in England, when they buy an old suit, buy the linings together with the outside; so it was conceived meet, that such as purchased the buildings of monasteries should, in the same grant, have the libraries (the stuffing thereof) conveyed unto them. And now these ignorant owners, so long as they might keep a ledger-book or terrier, by direction thereof to find such straggling acres as be-

[1] J. Leland, *Commentarii de Scriptoribus Britannicis*, ed. A. Hall (1709), Vol. I, p. 41.

[2] J. H. Baxter (ed.), *Copiale Prioratus Sanctiandree* (1930), pp. xx–xxxi.

longed to them, they cared not to preserve any other monuments. The covers of books, with curious brass bosses and clasps, intended to protect, proved to betray them, being the baits of covetousness. And so, many excellent authors, stripped out of their cases, were left naked, to be burned or thrown away."[1]

For a vivid contemporary description we can turn to the words of the Protestant John Bale, afterwards Bishop of Ossory, Bale was a renegade friar and a bitter enemy of monasticism, but he was also an antiquarian and a booklover. In 1549 he wrote:

"Neuer had we bene offended for the losse of our lybraryes, beynge so many in nombre and in so desolate places for the more parte, yf the chiefe monumentes and most notable workes of our excellent wryters, had bene reserued. If there had bene in euery shyre of Englande, but one solempne lybrary, to the preseruacyon of these noble workes and preferrement of good lernynges in oure posteryte, it had been yet sumwhat. But to destroye all without consyderacyon, is and wyll be vnto Englande for euer, a most horryble infamy amonge the graue senyours of other nacyons. A great nombre of them whych purchased those superstycyous mansyons, reserued of these lybrarye bokes, some to serue theyr iakes, some to scoure theyr candelstyckes, and some to rubbe their bootes. Some they solde to the grossers and sopesellers, and some they sent ouersee to the bokebynders, not in small nombre, but at tymes whole shyppes full, to the wonderynge of the foren nacyons. . . . I know a merchant man which shall at thys tyme be namelesse, that boughte the contentes of two noble lybraryes for xl shyllynges pryce, a shame it is to be spoken. Thys stuffe hath he occupyed in the stede of graye paper by the space of more than these x years, and yet he hath store ynough for many yeares to come."[2]

John Aubrey, the antiquary, tells us that when he went to school in Wiltshire, nearly a hundred years after the Dissolution, the leaves of illuminated manuscripts were still used for covering schoolbooks, and the local rector vowed there was nothing like a sheet of parchment for stopping a barrel of ale. "In my grandfather's dayes", adds Aubrey, "the manuscripts flew about like butterflies."[3]

[1] T. Fuller, *The Church History of Britain* (1655, new edn. 1837), Vol. II, p. 246.
[2] J. Bale, *The Laboryouse Journey and Serche of Johan Leylande for Englandes Antiquitees* (1549), Preface to Leland's New Year's Gift.
[3] J. Aubrey, *The Natural History of Wiltshire*, ed. J. Britton (1847), pp. 78–9.

The monastic collections did not, of course, entirely perish. Some volumes survived by chance, others were saved by their former owners, or by antiquaries such as Leland and Bale. Over a hundred volumes from the Augustinian house of Lanthony, in Gloucestershire, for example, were carried off by the former prior, and ultimately found their way to the Lambeth Palace Library. At Monk Bretton in Yorkshire the books were divided among the dispossessed prior and monks, and were still intact nearly twenty years after the Dissolution, but in this case the final outcome was less happy, for only two Monk Bretton books – a Bible and a breviary – now survive.

Leland, who as Keeper of the King's libraries was commissioned by Henry VIII in 1533/4 "to peruse and diligently to serche all the libraries of monasteries and colleges of this yowre noble reaulme, to the intente that the monumentes of auncient writers as welle of other nations, as of this yowr owne province mighte be brought owte of deadeley darkenes to lyvely lighte",[1] was particularly active in arranging the transfer of books from the monastic libraries to his master's collection. He also, he tells us, retained some books in his own possession, while others which he had discovered were sent abroad to be printed in Germany or Switzerland.

In spite of these attempts at salvage, however, there were many fine monastic libraries from which only a handful of books can now be traced.

The dissolution of the chantries, collegiate churches and religious guilds, planned in Henry VIII's reign but mainly carried out in Edward VI's reign under an act of 1547, was of lesser significance in library history, but it must have been at this stage that the public libraries of Worcester and Bristol, if they still existed, disappeared.

The cathedral and university libraries, though they suffered less than the monastic libraries, did not escape. Of the monastic cathedrals only Durham and Worcester, and of the secular cathedrals only Exeter, Hereford, Lincoln, Salisbury, and St. Paul's are known to have retained any substantial number of their mediaeval texts. Many books were discarded as out of date; others were purged as heretical or superstitious. At Oxford and Cambridge useful reforms in teaching were accom-

[1] J. Leland, *Itinerary*, ed. L. T. Smith, Vol. I (1907), pp. xxvii–xxviii.

panied by much senseless destruction, and although some of the college libraries got off fairly lightly the two university libraries suffered severely.

The first casualty here was scholastic theology, which at Oxford was quite literally scattered to the winds. One of the commissioners sent to the University by Thomas Cromwell in 1535 reported with satisfaction that on the occasion of their second visit to New College they found "all the gret quadrant court full of the leiffcs of Dunce [i.e. Duns Scotus], the wynde blowyng them into evere corner".[1] A Mr. Greenfield, a gentleman of Buckinghamshire, was gathering up some of the leaves to make scarecrows to keep his deer within bounds.

In 1550, following the Act of that year against Superstitious Books and Images, came a new attack. A later but well informed Oxford historian, Anthony Wood, laments that many manuscripts were destroyed for no other reason than that they had red letters on their covers or titles, or that they contained mathematical diagrams.[2]

By 1556 the Oxford University library, which had once housed the splendid gifts of Duke Humphrey, stood empty, and orders were given that the useless lecterns should be sold. The Cambridge University library was in little better shape. In 1543 the main library had been converted into a theological school, "since it is now of no use to anybody". In 1556 a smaller room still contained 172 books, mostly manuscripts, "but very sore cut and mangled for the lymned lettres and pictures".[3]

Our information concerning the fate of the mediaeval libraries of Scotland is less complete than for England, but we have many accounts of the plundering and destruction of monasteries, cathedrals and churches in the reforming fury of the years 1559–61. John Spottiswoode, who became Archbishop of St. Andrews in the reign of James I, writes of "Bibliothecks destroied, the volumes of the Fathers, Councells, and other books of humane learning, with the Registers of the Church, cast into the streets, afterwards gathered in heapes, and con-

[1] T. Wright (ed.), *Three Chapters of Letters relating to the Suppression of Monasteries* (Camden Soc. Vol. XXVI, 1843), p. 71.

[2] *The History and Antiquities of the University of Oxford*, ed. J. Gutch, Vol. II, i (1796), pp. 106–7.

[3] C. Sayle, "Annals of Cambridge University Library", in *The Library* 3rd Ser., Vol. VI (1915), pp. 151–3.

sumed with fire";[1] and this is confirmed by the fact that from all the institutional libraries of mediaeval Scotland (including those of the universities) the careful researches of Mr. Ker have identified only 92 manuscripts.[2]

THE BEGINNINGS OF RECOVERY

In all English history from the central period of the Middle Ages onward there is no period so barren of facilities for public reading as the fifty years following the suppression of the monasteries. From the point of view of library provision this was indeed the "bleak age". At the outset of the period the monastic libraries had vanished beyond recall; most of the cathedral libraries had been plundered or dispersed; and the smaller collections of the collegiate and parish churches had been purged out of existence. Only the depleted university libraries (inaccessible to the public) and the shattered remnants of half a dozen cathedral libraries, remained to bear witness to former glories. It is indeed surprising that at this time, when the minds of so many men were occupied with the search for new knowledge, when grammar and elementary schools, after the temporary setback caused by the Reformation, were rapidly increasing in number, when literacy was spreading, and the products of the printing press were multiplying year by year, there was hardly a place in all Britain (except perchance at the house of a friend) where a man could turn to borrow a book, and precious few where he could even consult a work of reference.

Yet it is in this same period that we can trace the first beginnings of recovery. By about 1560 in England, a little later in Scotland, the worst of the destruction was over, and scholars were beginning to reassemble the scattered remains of the mediaeval libraries. Among those most active in this work, in Elizabethan England, were Matthew Parker, Archbishop of Canterbury, Henry Fitzalan (Earl of Arundel), his son-in-law

[1] Quoted by R. Keith, *History of the Affairs of Church and State in Scotland*, Vol. III (1735, Spottiswoode Soc. Edinburgh 1850), p. 37. Cf. Spottiswoode's *History of the Church of Scotland*, Vol. I (1665, Spottiswoode Soc. 1847), p. 372.

[2] N. R. Ker, *Mediaeval Libraries* (1941, 2nd edn. 1964), p. xi. Printed works, from the period 1470 to 1560, are more numerous, and are listed by J. Durkan and A. Ross, *Early Scottish Libraries* (Glasgow 1961).

Lord Lumley, Sir William Cecil (Lord Burghley), Dr. John Dee, Sir Thomas Bodley, and Sir Robert Cotton. (The last three all survived into the seventeenth century, the youngest, Sir Robert Cotton, dying in 1631.) The same sort of thing was going on, though inevitably on a much smaller scale, in Scotland, where William Gatherer, a burgess of Elgin, rescued many of the books formerly owned by Kinloss Abbey. It would be inappropriate here to deal in detail with these private collections, but a word must be spared for that interesting character Dr. John Dee, parson, mathematician, astrologer, and reputed sorcerer, who claimed to have assembled in his house at Mortlake, Surrey, a library of nearly 3,000 printed books and nearly 1,000 manuscripts. The claim was probably exaggerated, but his was undoubtedly one of the largest libraries in Elizabethan England.[1] Some of his books were destroyed in 1583 by a mob which suspected him of witchcraft; and others were sold to buy bread in his poverty-stricken old age.

Several people in England had the idea of collecting the scattered manuscripts into a single repository – the first germ of the idea of a national library. John Leland, as early as 1536, had sought the help of Thomas Cromwell in securing the transfer of monastic books to the royal library, but in the end only about 250 books were saved in this way. Bale, as we have seen,[2] favoured a central library in each county. Dee reverted to the idea of the royal library, and proposed to Queen Mary in 1557 that commissioners should be appointed with power to demand that possessors of manuscripts should send them to be copied for the Queen's library. Something of this kind was actually attempted in 1568, when Archbishop Parker was appointed by Queen Elizabeth to have a special care for the monastic records, and private persons possessing such records were commanded to hand them to the Archbishop's deputies for inspection, so that their contents might be known. Parker, with doubtful legality, used this order to make inquiries among the cathedral

---

[1] J. Dee, *A Compendious Rehearsal*, 1592, printed in T. Hearne (ed.), *Johannis Glastoniensis Chronica*, Vol. II (Oxford 1726), App., p. 529. The catalogue of his MSS. drawn up in 1583 lists only some 200 volumes, including some 720 separate titles – see M. R. James, "Lists of Manuscripts formerly owned by Dr. John Dee", in *The Library*, 4th Ser., Suppl. I (1921).

[2] Above, p. 43.

libraries, and to take into his possession a number of valuable manuscripts, especially Anglo-Saxon manuscripts. The idea of a national repository is found again in a petition presented to the Queen, about 1602, by Sir Robert Cotton and two other members of the Society of Antiquaries which had been formed about 1586. The petition proposed the establishment of an Academy for the Study of Antiquity and History, with a library in which "divers old books concerning Matter of History of this Realme, original Charters and Monuments"[1] should be preserved.

The Queen's death, in 1603, put an end to this project, but in fact by this date most of what could be saved had already been secured by private collectors. Fortunately most of the great collections passed ultimately into public hands: Parker's to Corpus Christi College, Cambridge; Bodley's to the Bodleian Library at Oxford; Arundel's, Lumley's and Cotton's to the British Museum. Cotton's library, even in his own lifetime, was regularly consulted by historians, antiquaries, and politicians in search of precedents, and indeed the records he succeeded in amassing (some of them by rather dubious means) played no insignificant part in the constitutional issues of James's reign.

So far we have spoken merely of the recovery of the old. Even more important, from our present point of view, is the birth of the new. For the starting-point of the new development we may turn back to Thomas Cromwell's injunction of 1536, already referred to, concerning the provision of the Bible in churches. He enjoined

"that every parson, or proprietary of any parish church within the realm, shall on this side the feast of *S. Peter ad Vincula* next coming, provide a book of the whole Bible both in Latin, and also in English, and lay the same in the choir, for every man that will to look and read thereon, and shall discourage no man from the reading of any part of the Bible, in Latin or in English, but rather comfort, exhort, and admonish every man to read the same as the very word of God, and the spiritual food of man's soul. . . . "[2]

This passage clearly illustrates a feature of Protestantism

---

[1] Quoted in J. Evans, *A History of the Society of Antiquaries*, (1956), p. 8.
[2] W. H. Frere and W. M. Kennedy, *Visitation Articles and Injunctions of the Period of the Reformation* (1910), Vol. II, p. 9.

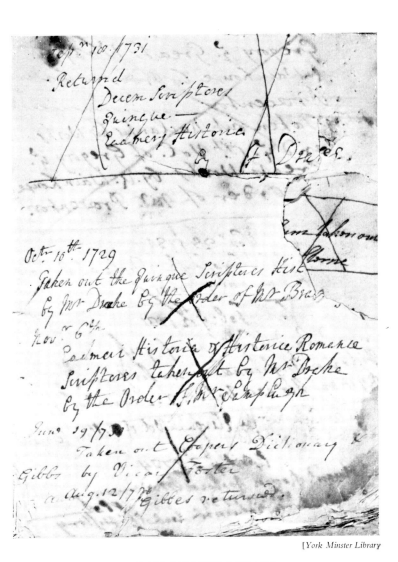

5. YORK MINSTER LIBRARY

Extract from an eighteenth-century borrowers' book.

6. LANGLEY MARISH LIBRARY

Notice the elaborately painted cupboard doors. The portrait inside the door on the
left is that of the founder, Sir John Kederminster.

7. GORTON PARISH LIBRARY

The cupboard bears the inscription: "The Gift of Humphrey Chetham, Esquire,
1655".

that has often been remarked, namely that it is "a book religion",[1] in which the accessibility of the sacred scriptures to the laity is a fundamental principle. It is true that, as we have noticed, Henry VIII became alarmed at the consequences of this policy, and sought to restrict Bible-reading to the upper classes, but this was a temporary measure. Under Edward VI, and again under Elizabeth, free access to the Bible by all classes was restored. The later injunctions stipulated only the provision of an English Bible, the reference to a Latin version being dropped.

From the provision of an English Bible for the use of parish-ioners it was a short step to the provision of other works of piety, and so there came into existence, in parish churches throughout the country, those collections of chained volumes, occasionally growing into small libraries, of which the remnants can still frequently be seen.

Alongside the education of the laity went, inevitably, the education of the clergy, which was desperately needed because of the deterioration in standards resulting from the confusion and upheavals of the Reformation era. Matthew Parker, Arch-bishop of Canterbury, confessed in 1560 that to meet the shortage "sundry artificers and others", and "some that were of base occupations", had been pressed into service.[2] Even at the close of the century more than half the English clergy were neither graduates nor licensed preachers.[3]

One obvious measure, in England, was the revival of the cathedral libraries, and the first step towards this was taken in 1547, when injunctions in the name of Edward VI prescribed that the authorities of each cathedral and collegiate church should within the space of one year provide a library in some convenient place in their church, and lay therein the works of the Fathers, Erasmus, and other good writers. These injunctions were repeated by Elizabeth in 1559, and reinforced by the exhortations of bishops and archbishops. Many chapters, prob-ably for financial reasons, were slow to act in the matter, but about half the English cathedrals had libraries of some sort,

[1] E. Halévy, *A History of the English People in 1815*, trans. E. I. Watkin and D. A. Barker (1924), p. 457.
[2] A. T. Hart, *The Country Clergy in Elizabethan and Stuart Times* (1958), p. 24.
[3] R. G. Usher, *The Reconstruction of the English Church*, Vol. I (New York 1910), Ch. x.

either newly founded or surviving from the Middle Ages, by the end of the century.

Unfortunately the cathedral libraries were not of much value to the ordinary parish clergy, who for the most part had neither the time nor the money to travel to a distant cathedral city. Here the initiative came not from the ecclesiastical authorities, but from the clergy themselves, from the gentry, and in some cases from municipal corporations. There are traces of the formation of parochial libraries, apparently for the use of the clergy, as early as the mid-sixteenth century – at Ecclesfield in Yorkshire (by 1549), at Ludlow in Shropshire (1557), and at Steeple Ashton in Wiltshire (1569). The main movement, however, came rather later – in the 'eighties and 'nineties and the opening years of the seventeenth century, and was associated, as we shall see, with the rise of Puritanism.

Such, then, were the beginnings of the religious libraries of the post-Reformation period. In the next three chapters their history will be considered in more detail.

Bibliographical Note

The most useful survey of early printing is H. S. Bennett, *English Books and Readers, 1475–1557* (Cambridge 1952). This may be supplemented from older works such as G. H. Putman, *Books and their Makers during the Middle Ages* (2v. New York 1898), E. G. Duff, *A Century of the English Book Trade, 1457–1557* (1905), and for Scotland R. Dickson and J. P. Edmond, *Annals of Scottish Printing* (Cambridge 1890). The early chapters of S. H. Steinberg, *Five Hundred Years of Printing* (1955), provide a brief survey.

Many of the general works on mediaeval libraries cited at the end of Chapter I carry the story up to the Reformation, e.g. E. A. Savage, *Old English Libraries* (1911); J. W. Thompson, *The Medieval Library* (Chicago 1939, 2nd edn. New York 1957). The same is true of many of the histories of individual libraries there cited. For the dispersal and what followed the fullest account is in F. Wormald and C. E. Wright (eds.), *The English Library before 1700* (1958), but see also the Introduction to N. R. Ker, *Medieval Libraries of Great Britain: a List of Surviving Books* (Royal Historical Society 1941, 2nd edn. 1964). For Leland and his work see the Introduction to L. T. Smith's edition of his *Itinerary*, Vol. I (1907). R. Irwin, *The Origins of the English Library* (1958), has chapters on the dispersal and on private libraries. On the latter subject W. Y. Fletcher, *English Book Collectors* (1902), assembles much useful information. For the situation in Scotland see J. Durkan and A. Ross, *Early Scottish Libraries* (Glasgow 1961), and chapters by the same authors, and by the editor, in D. McRoberts (ed.), *Essays on the Scottish Reformation* (Glasgow 1962).

For the cathedral and church libraries of the later sixteenth century see the Bibliographical Notes to the next three chapters.

CHAPTER III

University and Cathedral Libraries
After the Reformation

THE INFLUENCE OF OXFORD AND CAMBRIDGE

THE university libraries have never been public libraries, in the modern period any more than in the Middle Ages.[1] It is not possible, however, to write the story of library development in the seventeenth and eighteenth centuries without some reference to the role of Oxford and Cambridge. The Scottish university libraries we can ignore, for they remained very small until in the eighteenth century they began to profit by the Copyright Act of 1709. The Oxford and Cambridge libraries, however, after the disappearance of the monastic libraries, became and long remained the most important institutional collections in the country, and the methods of library organization which they developed were widely imitated.

At Oxford the lead was taken by the University library. Duke Humphrey's old library stood empty after the Reformation until, between 1598 and 1602, it was re-equipped and refurnished with books by the munificence of Sir Thomas Bodley. Thereafter, however, progress was rapid, and by 1620 the Bodleian, with some 16,000 volumes, was one of the largest libraries in Europe. Obviously such a collection could not be accommodated on lecterns of the old mediaeval type, and Bodley, foreseeing this, had re-fitted the library with lecterns of a new kind, with three shelves above the reading desk. These are known to library historians as "stalls". The books were still chained, but they now stood upright upon the shelves instead of lying flat as was the mediaeval practice. In order to keep the length and weight of chain to a minimum, it was found

[1] The general university libraries were often termed *bibliothecae publicae*, but this was merely to distinguish them from the college libraries, and did not imply any use by the general public.

convenient to shelve the books with the edges of the leaves facing outwards.

Even before Bodley's death in 1613, additional accommodation was urgently needed, and an extra wing, now known as Arts End, was furnished in a quite new way with bookcases all round the walls from floor to ceiling. The larger books, which were still chained, were stored on the lower shelves, but the upper shelves, reached by galleries, were used for the smaller volumes which were unsuitable for chaining.

These developments set the pattern for the Oxford college libraries. Stall fittings were popular in the seventeenth century, and wall shelving came into widespread use in the eighteenth century. A particularly sophisticated example of wall shelving is to be found in the Radcliffe Camera, a massive circular building which was opened as a Physic Library in 1749 and is now part of the Bodleian.

At Cambridge, where the chaining of books began to be abandoned as early as 1627, the stall system was never widely used, since it was no longer necessary to have a reading-desk attached to each bookcase. The library of St. John's College, completed in 1628, was thus able to have free-standing bookcases in the modern style, with shelves almost to floor-level, and this example was followed both in the University library and at other colleges. At Trinity College, in 1676, Wren combined wall cases with free-standing cases to provide the book-lined "cells" or alcoves familiar in so many later libraries.

In spite of all these developments the practice of chaining books continued in many places, especially at Oxford, until well into the eighteenth century. Even at the Bodleian the chains were not removed until 1757 onwards, and at Magdalen College they lasted until 1799.

The new methods of book-shelving inevitably influenced other large libraries outside the universities, especially the cathedral libraries, and non-university libraries of all kinds profited also by the advances made at the Bodleian in the arrangement and cataloguing of books. In the later mediaeval libraries, as we have seen, it was a common practice to arrange the books on the shelves or lecterns, and to catalogue them in the same order. Where the books were shelved, a press-mark might be used to indicate precisely by letters or numbers the bookcase or press, the shelf, and the position of the book on the shelf.

Such a method was suited only to a small and more or less static library. The multiplication of printed books from the sixteenth century onwards created a whole new range of problems for librarians, who now had to cope with libraries which were not only much larger than anything known in the Middle Ages, but also constantly expanding. These problems confronted Bodley's first librarian, Dr. Thomas James, the man whom a contemporary refers to as "the incomparably industrious and learned Bibliothecary of Oxford".[1]

The Bodleian Library was arranged, at the insistence of its founder, into four faculties – Theology, Medicine, Law and Arts. Within each faculty the books fell into three groups. The folio volumes, and a few large quartos, were chained to the stall bookcases, the remaining quartos and the octavos, too small for chaining, were in locked cupboards or on shelves. In each faculty, and in each size, the books were arranged in alphabetical order of authors. At the end of each stall was a list showing the contents of the stall shelf by shelf, and James's first printed catalogue, published in 1605, was actually based on these lists. A page of the catalogue was allotted to each shelf. At the head of the page stood the folios, and in the space that was left, or if necessary on additional pages, the quartos and octavos were added, as far as possible in their due alphabetical order.

The system of press-marking was interesting. The folios and large quartos bore a letter and two numbers, e.g. A.3.10, where A denoted the press, 3 the shelf, and 10 the order of the book on the shelf. At first sight this seems exactly like the mediaeval system which has been mentioned in connection with the library of St. Martin's, Dover,[2] but at the Bodleian the letter A represented not, as at Dover, an actual press but a block of shelves carrying books of which the author's names began with that letter. The arrangement was the same for all the other letters of the alphabet. For the press with a limited number of shelves James had thus substituted a notional press which could include any number of shelves required. This was a great advance in flexibility, but there was still the difficulty that the number of

[1] *The Bodleian Library in the Seventeenth Century* (Oxford 1951), p. 14.
[2] See above, p. 21.

each book on the shelf was fixed, and had to be changed if additions made it necessary to move books along.

The small quartos and octavos, which James rather despised, were shelved on a different plan. Each of these, also, bore a press-letter corresponding to the author's initial, but there were no shelf or place numbers: in each faculty, instead, the quarto volumes under each letter were numbered consecutively beginning with no. 1, and the octavo volumes the same, so that the press-marks were in the form 4° A30, or 8° R17. The difference may seem trivial, but it was important, because with a system of consecutive numbering it was possible to add any number of books without changing the press-marks. A difficulty that might occur to the modern reader, namely that the added books would be out of strict alphabetical order, did not apply, since James's alphabetical order extended only to the first letter.

Here, then, was a method of press-marking independent of the actual position of the books on the shelves. In technical terms, it was, as Dr. G. W. Wheeler has pointed out, a system of "relative location" as opposed to the "fixed location" adopted for the larger books.[1] It is this system of relative location that forms the basis of all modern library shelving arrangements – it is indeed the only possible system for a constantly expanding collection. It was to be some time yet before librarians perceived the possibility of a complete alphabetical arrangement according to the successive letters of the author's name, and still longer before such an arrangement became common practice, but once this was realized it became obvious also that the numbering of books could be dispensed with, and relative location could be determined by alphabetical arrangement alone. Thus under the Dewey system, which is the one most commonly used in modern English public libraries, the books are grouped into subject divisions and sub-divisions, each of which has its number, and within each sub-division the books are shelved in alphabetical order of authors.

James found the arrangement of books under subjects very troublesome. At this time the mediaeval practice of binding several works together still persisted, and in consequence, even though he had to contend only with a broad division into the four faculties, there were many volumes which were impossible

[1] *The Earliest Catalogues of the Bodleian Library* (Oxford 1928), pp. 28–9.

in Bibliotheca Bodleiana. 263

HYG

Ecclesiarum Lutheran, *Witeb.*1608.8º. H.66.

Sadeel ellenchomenos, *Witeb.*1602.8º. H.92.

Hygenus

De limitibus agrorum constituendis. 4º.A.11.*Art.*

C. Iulius *Hyginus*

Fabulæ.*Baf.*1570.P.6.8.

Poëtica, Astronomica,&c. Ib.

De Sphæra Cœlesti *MS.*V.1.8.*Iur.*

Mauricius *Hilaretus*

In Evang.Dominicalia.*Par.*1604.8º.H. 53.54.

Hymnarium

Et Collectarium.*MS.*4º.H.13.

Hymni expositio,vnâ cum Textu.1488. W.4.3.4º.H.5.

Hymni sacri antiquorum Patrum.

Expositio Hymnorum.*Eborac.*1507.V. 6.7.

The Hymnes throughout the whole yeare.8º.P.62.

Andr. *Hyperius*

In Ep.ad Hebræos.*Tig.*1584.H.5.9.

In Ethica Aristotelis.*Lichæ* 1598.M.6.1

In Epist.Pauli & Iudæ.*Tig.*1584.H.6.3.

Opuscula var.a.*Baf.*1580.8º. H.28.

Topica Theologica. *Baf.*1573.lb.

In Isaiam 8º.H.29.*Baf.*1574.

De ratione studij Theolog. *Baf.*8º.H. 4º.

De S. Scripturæ lectione quotidiana. *Baf.*8º.H.45.

Dialectica & Rhetorica. *Baf.*1585.8º. H.20.

Compendium Physices Aristotelis. Ib.

Theses de Trinitate.T.7.6.

Hypsicles

In Euclidem. 1516.

Leon. *Iacchinus*

IN nonum Rasis,cum alijs opusc. *Baf.* 1579.8º.I.1.

Abraham *Iackson*

Sorrowes leuitis. Lond.1614.8º.N.

IAC

15.*Th.*

Will. *Iackson*

The Celestiall husbandry.Lond.1616 I.6.10.

Io. *Iackson*

A discourse defending the immortality of the soule.Lond.1611.8º.E.82.

Tho. *Jackson*

Peters Teares.Lond.1612. S.125.

The eternall truth of Scriptures, and Christian beliefe. Lond.1613. 1.part. I.4 13.

The third booke.1614.4º.I.6.

R. *Iacob* Salomonis filius.

Collectanea.*Par.*1572.8º.C.8.*Th.*

Dom. Card. *Iacobatius*

De Conc.*Romæ* 1538.L.1.2.T.3.8.

Io. *Iacobinus*

Sygismundi Principis Transfylvaniæ res gestæ.H.3.1.T.2.3.

Iacobinus de S. Georgio

De Feudis, homagijs, & Roydis. *Ben.* 1575.I.1.8.

De Homagijs.*Fr.*1606.8º.I.4.

Sup.1m et 2m.Dig.vet.*Ben.*1575.L.1.8.

Super 1. & 2.Cod.lb.I.1.8.

De feudis.T.3.4.

Cynosura iuris feudalis. *Fr.*1606 8º. I.4.

Iacobus S. Georgij

De Iubileo Anno, cum scholijs Iulij Rosei.B.5.11.

Henr. *Iacob*

A defence of the Churches and ministery of England,against Fr.Ihonson. *Middleb.*1599.4º.I.12.

Jacobus R.

Dæmonologia Anglicè. Lond.1603.4º. I.7.

A fruitfull Meditation vpon the 7.8. 9.and 10. Uerses of the 20. Chapter of the Revelation.Lond.1603.8º.I.19. & Lat.lb.8º.I.20.

The Lawes of free Monarchie. Lond. 1603.8º.I.37. & Edinburgi 1598.8º.

βασιλικον Δωρον Anglicè.*Edinburgi* 1603.

R 4 &

4. A PAGE FROM THE BODLEIAN CATALOGUE OF 1620

Note the arrangement under alphabetical order of authors, and the press-marks.

to classify satisfactorily. In the preface to his second printed catalogue, of 1620, he therefore advised librarians to arrange their books according to size – folio, quarto, and octavo – and then to number them consecutively as they stood on the shelves.

The proper place for subject divisions, James thought, was not in the library but in the catalogue. Given a good subject catalogue, and an index of authors, the arrangement on the shelves should be as simple as possible. The 1620 catalogue was, in fact, an alphabetical author index of all the books in the library, irrespective of size or faculty. This was the first large-scale catalogue of this kind. It was very carefully compiled, giving for each entry the author, brief title, place and date of publication, and except in the case of folio works, the size. There was some attempt at alphabetical arrangement beyond the first letter of the author's name. A weakness was that as a rule there was no indication (other than the subject) of the faculty to which the book belonged, so that there were often four works bearing the same press-mark. The production of this catalogue brought James up against some of the many problems involved in alphabetical cataloguing, not least that of where to put anonymous works. This is a problem which is still debated to this day: James's solution was to put them under a general heading *Anonymi* or under some key word of the title, e.g. *A Warning for Tobacconists* (1602), figured under "Warning", *The Mirror of Martyrs* (1612) under "Mirrors", and *The Lamentable Burning of Teverton* (1612) under "Teverton".

This alphabetical index was complemented by four elaborate subject catalogues, one for each faculty, which were completed by James between 1607 and 1625. They were never printed, and only three – theology, law and arts – now remain. The theology catalogue extended to 784 folio pages and included some 10,000 entries. The numerous headings (all in Latin of course) are arranged in alphabetical order, and usually divided under sub-headings, each with a list of works referring to the topic in question. Often the references are to a specific section or even page. Thus under the heading *Mundus*, "the World", there were sub-headings *De mundi creatione, De fine mundi, De contempta mundi, De vanitate mundi*, and so on. In the subject catalogue for arts, in the section on Grammatical Works, we

find as the thirteenth sub-heading English Language, which
reads as follows:

13.   *De Lingua Anglica*

De recta Linguae Anglicanae scriptione. Lut. 1568. 4°P.8. per Tho.
  Smithaeum.
Geo Lilij Grammatica Anglo-Lat. Lond. 1617.
Jo. Minshewes, Guide into Tongues. Lond. 1617. S.5.14 Art.
Riders Dictionary enlarged. Lond. 1633. S.9.13 Art.
Th. Thomasii Diction. Lond. 1615.[1]

It is not difficult to pick holes in James's methods – he did
not, for example, always clearly distinguish between a subject
catalogue and a title catalogue, with the result that the same
subject is likely to appear in several places because of differences
in the titles. Nothing, however, can detract from the merit of
this great pioneering achievement. James's author and subject
catalogues laid the foundation of modern library cataloguing.

His methods were further refined in the revised catalogue
published in 1674. This covered the printed books only, the
manuscripts being embraced within a larger work, the *Catalogi
librorum manuscriptorum Angliae et Hiberniae* (1697), which
covered most of the manuscript collections of England and
Ireland. Thomas Hyde, the librarian who compiled the 1674
catalogue, complains in the preface of the weariness and dis-
comfort of his labours in the unheated library. He took nine
years over the task, but the resulting catalogue quickly
established itself as a standard work of reference and a model of
cataloguing practice. Many other libraries, both inside and outside the universities, long made use of an interleaved copy of
this work as a substitute for a catalogue of their own.

THE CATHEDRAL LIBRARIES OF ENGLAND AND WALES

Until the close of the seventeenth century virtually the only
libraries which were in any degree accessible to the public were
religious libraries. Most of them were to be found in cathedrals
and churches; a few were under the control of municipal corporations, but their character was the same. The cathedral libraries
were not sufficiently numerous to make any significant contribu-

---

[1] I take these examples from Wheeler, *op. cit.*, Ch. vii. The entry for
  Rider's *Dictionary* is a later addition to the MS.

tion to public provision, but their story, which has been strangely neglected, is not without interest.

We have noted in the previous chapter that the restoration of these libraries was a matter of concern as early as 1547, and that by the end of the sixteenth century about half the English cathedrals had a library of some kind. At others, however, progress was slow, and it was not until the latter part of the seventeenth century that effective working libraries were generally established. In the meantime, all too often, such books as survived from the Middle Ages were neglected and many of them were lost. Some collections were rifled by antiquaries, some were damaged by damp, fire, or vermin, others were plundered or destroyed during the Civil War or its aftermath.

A few examples will illustrate what happened. At Canterbury, the old monastic library was partly destroyed by fire in 1538, and for ninety years it remained derelict, a prey to the antiquarian proclivities of Archbishops Parker and Whitgift and Dean Thomas Neville, whose acquisitions went ultimately to enrich the libraries of Corpus Christi College and Trinity College, Cambridge. A few books accumulated in the early seventeenth century were sold during the Commonwealth period, and it was only after the Restoration that the task of restocking and reorganization was vigorously taken in hand. By the rules drawn up in 1672, books might be borrowed only by the Dean and prebends, but "any of the six Preachers or of the Petty Canons or any other Gentleman or any Minister may be allowed if brought in by any of the Chapter or by the Library Keeper to studdy there".[1]

Exeter Cathedral, in 1506, possessed a chained library of 387 volumes, of which more than a hundred remained after the Reformation; but one of the most precious manuscripts – a copy of the Anglo-Saxon Gospels – was presented to Parker in 1556, and most of the rest, including other rare Anglo-Saxon books, were given to the Bodleian in 1602. During the Civil War, tradition has it that volumes from the library were offered for sale in the Cathedral Close, but an Exeter physician, Dr. John

---

[1] M. Beazeley, "History of the Chapter Library of Canterbury Cathedral" in *Bibliographical Society Transactions*, Vol. VIII (1904–06), p. 160, quoting *Acta Capituli, 1670–1710*.

Vilvaine, rescued at least some and afterwards built a new library in the Lady Chapel. It was not, however, until 1676 that a bequest of 1,200 volumes from the Cathedral Treasurer, Dr. Edward Cotton, laid the foundations of the modern cathedral library. Of some 5,000 volumes catalogued in 1752, only twenty had been listed in 1506.

The modern history of the famous chained library at Hereford Cathedral dates from the new statutes drawn up in 1583, following a visit by the Queen's Commissioners in the previous year. At that time the old library over the west cloister still possessed over a hundred of the original mediaeval manuscripts, together with a number of manuscripts from other religious houses, and a few printed books, but it was "covered with dirt and mould, and almost falling down with age".[1]

Under the new regulations the books were to be chained and placed in the custody of one of the canons residentiary, who was to collect from each canon, at his inauguration, the sum of 40s. towards the cost of books. Two catalogues were to be prepared, in addition to a shelf-list at the end of each lectern, and there was to be a stocktaking four times a year.

In 1595 the books were removed to the Lady Chapel, and in 1611 the lecterns were replaced by stall bookcases on the model of those at the Bodleian. In the course of various removals in the nineteenth century the bookcases and benches were substantially altered, and many of the chains taken off, but in 1929-31, after much patient investigation by Canon B. H. Streeter, the library was restored as far as possible to its original form, partly in the old treasury chamber and partly in a room over the west cloister. There are now about 1,500 chained books.

Lichfield Cathedral library was one of the casualties of the Civil War. Many of its mediaeval manuscripts were abstracted by an antiquarian Dean, Laurence Nowell, who died in 1576, and these afterwards found their way into the Cotton collection; nearly all the rest perished during the later years of the Civil War. The starting-point of the present library was a gift by the Duchess of Somerset, in 1673, of the library of her late husband, William, the second Duke.

Most of the mediaeval manuscripts of St. Paul's Cathedral seem to have remained almost undisturbed on their shelves

[1] B. H. Streeter, *The Chained Library* (1931), App. IV.

until 1647, when by a decree of the Lord Mayor of London the entire library, consisting at that time of 152 manuscripts and 67 printed books, was moved to Sion College, in order that it should be available to a wider public. When the Great Fire came in 1666 these books, and those of the College's own library, were piled on carts for conveyance to the Charterhouse outside the city walls, but the flames advanced so rapidly that most of them were consumed. Of the St. Paul's books only three manuscripts and twenty-three printed books were saved. When Wren rebuilt the Cathedral, a new library room was provided, fitted with wall-shelving from floor to ceiling, but this did not come into use till 1709. The purchase of the library of Mr. Gery, Vicar of Islington, for £500 in 1708 helped to provide the initial stock.

Westminster Abbey was converted at the Dissolution into a collegiate church, but its mediaeval library was for the most part dispersed, and the Abbey possessed few books until the seventeenth century. Between 1620 and 1626 Dean John Williams, Bishop of Lincoln and afterwards Archbishop of Canterbury, reconstructed the library, equipped it with stall bookcases, and furnished it with 2,000 books. On his death in 1650 he also left to the library a collection of 230 manuscripts, which unfortunately was destroyed by fire in 1694.

An account written about 1700 says Williams founded the library "for public use, every day in term time from 9 to 12, and from 2 to 4";[1] and the register of benefactors, begun in 1623, describes it as "the Publicque Librarie att Westminster".[2] This might mean only that it was open to all the clergy, but the account given by Williams's chaplain and biographer, John Hacket, afterwards Bishop of Lichfield, suggests a wider use:

"he converted a wast Room, situate in the East side of the Cloysters into *Plato's* Portico, into a goodly Library, model'd it into decent Shape, furnished it with Desks and Chairs, accoutred it with all Vtensils, and stored it with a vast Number of Learned Volumes: to which use he lighted most fortunately upon the Study of that Learned Gentleman Mr. *Baker* of *Highgate*, who in a long and industrious Life had Collected into his own possession the best Authors in all Sciences,

[1] *Report from the Select Committee on Public Libraries* (1849), p. 229.
[2] J. A. Robinson and M. R. James, *The Manuscripts of Westminster Abbey* (Cambridge 1909), pp. 39, 42.

in their best Editions, which being bought at 500l. (a cheap Peny worth for such precious War) were removed into this Store-House. When he received Thanks from all the professors of Learning in and about *London* far beyond his expectation, because they had free admittance to such Hony from the Flowers of such a Garden, as they had wanted before, it compell'd him to unlock his Cabinet of Jewels, and bring forth his choicest Manuscripts."[1]

At Winchester, in spite of repeated injunctions from 1547 onwards, there was still no library in 1571, but a library of some kind had come into existence before the Civil War. Following the abolition of the Dean and Chapter, John Woodman, solicitor for sequestrations for the city, sold the books to Thomas Matthews, a London grocer, and Augustus Garland, M.P., and they were carried off to London. By order of the Government, however, they were recovered and despatched to Winchester College, "there to remain for public use".[2] Most of them were returned after the Restoration and these books, together with a substantial bequest from Bishop George Morley on his death in 1604, were the nucleus of the modern library.

The Welsh cathedral libraries, as might be expected, were small. At St. David's the mediaeval library was destroyed at the Reformation, and though another library was accumulated over the years, it still amounted to fewer than 500 volumes in 1795. It was reorganized with the help of the Associates of Dr. Bray in 1807. The libraries of Bangor and Llandaff were preserved at the Reformation, but the former perished during the Civil War, and the latter, which had been removed for safety to Cardiff Castle, was burnt by the Puritans on the capture of the Castle in 1655. "The Cavaliers of the Country, and the Wives of several sequester'd Clergymen", we are told, "were invited to the Castle, in a cold Winter's Day, to warm themselves by the Fire, which was then made of the Books that were there burnt."[3] The Llandaff library was refounded in 1670, but Bangor had to wait until 1710, when the S.P.C.K. presented books to the value of about £60 to form a diocesan lending

[1] J. Hacket, *Scrinia Reserata* (1693), Vol. I, pp. 46 *seq.*, quoted Robinson and James, *op. cit.*, p. 18.
[2] W. R. W. Stephens and F. T. Madge (eds.), *Documents relating to the History of the Cathedral Church of Winchester in the Seventeenth Century* (Hamps. Rec. Soc. 1897), p. 73.
[3] Browne Willis, *Survey of Llandaff Cathedral* (1719), p. 32.

library. A year later the same body came to the rescue, in the same way, at St. Asaph, where apparently there had been no library to speak of since the mediaeval library was destroyed by fire in 1402.[1]

On the whole the cathedral and collegiate church libraries were not extensively used by non-clerical readers. Many of the reasons for this can best be understood from the reports of a Royal Commission on the Cathedral and Collegiate Churches which was appointed in 1852. These reports show, first, that most of the libraries were very small. The largest were at Durham and Westminster (about 11,000 volumes each). York and St. Paul's had about 8,000 volumes each. At the other end of the scale were Bristol, Ripon, Rochester, Southwell, and the four Welsh cathedrals, all with fewer than 2,000 volumes each. All the remaining libraries ranged between 2,000 and 5,000 volumes.[2]

Moreover, although many of these libraries contained manuscripts and early printed works which are now regarded as great treasures, they were in general heavily loaded with theological texts, many of them in Latin or Greek. A comment made on the library at Carlisle in 1849 is typical: "The principal feature of this Library is theological, ponderous folios of obsolete divinity in dark, unlettered calf, and smaller controversial treatises, now deservedly forgotten, occupying a large space upon these dusty shelves."[3] At Rochester also the same observer found "a considerable quantity of obsolete divinity", upon which "the worms seem tacitly permitted to feed".[4]

The conditions under which the books were kept were also discouraging. Few of these libraries had any regular source of income: Durham had £200 a year, Canterbury about £550, the rest depended almost entirely on the installation fees of the canons and other casual income, or on *ad hoc* grants from

[1] For the work of the S.P.C.K. and the Bray trustees, see below, pp. 110–12.
[2] All these figures exclude MSS. Bristol had at one time 6,000 volumes, but most of these perished in the flames of the Bishop's palace during the Reform riots of 1831.
[3] B. Botfield, *Notes on the Cathedral Libraries of England* (1849), p. 50.
[4] *Op. cit.*, p. 391.

chapter funds. The librarian, if there was one, was usually part-time, and access even by the clergy was as a general rule exceedingly restricted. Even as late as 1878 there were only five cathedrals – Chester, Chichester, St. Paul's, Winchester and Worcester – which were open daily: the usual arrangement was to open for two hours in the middle of the day on two days a week. At Bristol, Chester, Lincoln, and St. Paul's, in 1852, the library was restricted to the use of the clergy, and the same was true even of Westminster, which had once been so readily open to "the professors of Learning".[1] Elsewhere the library was usually available, at least for reference, to "respectable persons" other than the clergy, but admission was not always easy to arrange. At Hereford, for example, the commissioners of 1852 reported: "accessible by order from dean or canon residentiary; applicant to be accompanied by an officer of the church." At Canterbury, owing to past losses, the books were guarded with "draconic vigilance".[2] Only about half the libraries had any form of heating, and few had artificial lighting.

It would be wrong, however, to paint too black a picture. The "obsolete divinity" which appalled Beriah Botfield in the mid-nineteenth century was probably less forbidding to the general reader in the seventeenth and eighteenth centuries, and in spite of all the difficulties these libraries did frequently provide an additional resource for the scholar in or near a cathedral town. Dr. Johnson borrowed from the cathedral library at Lichfield, and Coleridge from that at Carlisle. Most libraries included classics and ecclesiastical history as well as theology, and some, for example Durham, Exeter, and York, had collections on British history and topography which would be invaluable to the local antiquarian.

As books became more plentiful, and the practice of chaining was abandoned, it became possible to borrow books from the cathedral libraries, and eight cathedrals still have loan registers going back to the eighteenth century.[3] It must be confessed that

[1] Washington Irving in his *Sketch-Book* (1819), described the Westminster library as "a kind of literary catacomb, where authors, like mummies are piously entombed, and left to blacken and moulder in oblivion" – E. Edwards, *Memoirs of Libraries*, Vol. I (1859), p. 688.

[2] Botfield, *op. cit.*, p. 8.

[3] Canterbury, Carlisle, Durham, Exeter, Gloucester, St. Paul's, Winchester and York. See Bibliographical Note at end of Chapter.

the number of loans was very small – one or two a week at
Canterbury and Durham, one or two a month elsewhere. None
the less these registers are full of interest. The first of the York
registers, which runs from 1716 to 1778, includes the names of
a number of non-clerical readers. A local antiquary, Dr. Francis
Drake, borrowed Dugdale's *Monasticon;* another, Dr. John
Burton, Rymer's *Foedera;* a surgeon, Clifton Wintringham,
borrowed a book on physic; a doctor, Dr. Alexander Hunter,
borrowed Columella's *De re rustica;* a York bookseller, John
Hildyard, borrowed the *Monasticon* and the works of Theodoret
(a fifth-century church historian) for clients in the country;
three ladies borrowed books of history or divinity, and a fourth,
William Turner's *Herball.* Nor should it be supposed that the
borrowings of the local clergy were invariably restricted to
religious books. The most famous of them, at this time, was
Laurence Sterne, the author of *Tristram Shandy,* who became
a prebendary of York in 1741. His miscellaneous borrowings
included Ralph Thoresby's *Antiquities of Leeds,* John Speed's
History of Great Britain, three volumes of the *Biographia
Britannica,* two little books about China, and three volumes of
music.

SCOTTISH CATHEDRAL LIBRARIES

In Scotland cathedral libraries played no significant part in
the development of public library provision. The episcopal form
of church government, overthrown at the Reformation, and
thrice restored by the Stuart monarchs, was again abolished at
the accession of William III, and it was not until the repeal of
the penal laws in 1792 that it was re-established on a more
limited scale. The present cathedral and diocesan libraries,
therefore, are nearly all of relatively modern foundation.

The one exception is the library founded in 1688 at Dunblane
Cathedral under the will of Robert Leighton, formerly Bishop
of Dunblane and Archbishop of Glasgow. Leighton bequeathed
his own library of some 1,400 books (including a splendid
collection of Hebrew works) for the use of the clergy of the
diocese, and his executors provided a building and the sum of
£300 to be invested for maintenance and for the salary of a
librarian. Regulations drawn up in 1688 provided that the
librarian should be a student of divinity, and should be in

attendance daily from 10 to 12 and 2 to 4. He was to keep a fire in the library at least once a week in the winter, "for the better preservation of the House", and was to "sufferr no persones to haunt the Library but such as come with a purpose to read, &c.".[1] Students as well as clergy seem to have been permitted to use the library, and apparently books might be borrowed by persons living within the city, for the regulations laid down that no books should be lent outside the city except with the Bishop's consent.

After the abolition of episcopacy in 1689 the library was placed under the control of trustees, including the minister of Dunblane and other clergy of the presbytery. It seems to have continued in active use throughout the eighteenth century; at any rate more than 1,700 books were added during this period, including many dealing with Scottish history and literature, and also – an unusual feature in a library of this period – many items about North and South America. The library still exists, and has recently been restored with assistance from the Pilgrim Trust.[2]

[1] R. Douglas, "An Account of the Foundation of the Leightonian Library", in *Bannatyne Miscellany*, Vol. III (Bannatyne Club, Edinburgh 1855), pp. 258–9.
[2] G. Davidson, *Catalogue of Selected Volumes from the Leighton Library* (Dunblane 1960), Introduction.

Bibliographical Note

A useful introduction to the development of the university libraries in this period is to be found in F. Wormald and C. E. Wright, *The English Library before 1700*, Chs. x and xi. G. W. Wheeler, *The Earliest Catalogues of the Bodleian Library* (Oxford 1928), is a detailed and illuminating study.

For the cathedral libraries see B. Botfield, *Notes on the Cathedral Libraries of England* (1849); *Report from Select Committee on Public Libraries* (1849) (especially the table at pp. 228–30); *First Report of the Royal Commission on the State and Condition of the Cathedral and Collegiate Churches of England and Wales, 1852* (1854); E. Edwards, *Memoirs of Libraries* (2v. 1859) Vol. I, Bk. III, Ch. xii; H. E. Reynolds, "Our Cathedral Libraries", and appended table, in *Transactions and Proceedings of the First Annual Meeting of the Library Association, 1878* (1879). J. W. Clark, *The Care of Books* (Cambridge 1901, 2nd edn. 1902), and B. H. Streeter, *The Chained Library* (1931), are again useful, the latter especially for its detailed account of the reconstruction of the Hereford Library. P. Kaufman, "Reading Vogues at English Cathedral Libraries of the Eighteenth Century", in *Bulletin of the New York Public Library*, Vols. 67–8 (1963–64), is based on a study of borrowers' books at eight cathedrals. For the Welsh cathedrals see M. Tallon, *Church in Wales Diocesan Libraries* (Athlone 1962). Accounts of individual libraries include:

Canterbury: M. Beazeley, "History of the Chapter Library of Canterbury Cathedral", in *Bibliographical Society Transactions*, Vol. VIII (1904–06).

Dunblane: A. B. Barty, *The History of Dunblane* (Stirling 1944), Ch. xv; "Robert Leighton, his Family and his Library", in *Society of Friends of Dunblane Cathedral*, Vol. VIII, Pt. ii (1959).

Exeter: L. J. Lloyd, *The Library of Exeter Cathedral* (Exeter Univ. 1954).

Hereford: F. C. Morgan, *Hereford Cathedral Library* (Hereford, 3rd edn. 1963); M. Tallon, *Hereford Cathedral Library* (Athlone 1963).

Lichfield: H. E. Savage, *Lichfield Cathedral; a Cathedral Library* (Lichfield 1934).

London, St. Paul's: W. M. Atkins, "St. Paul's Cathedral: a Short History of the Library and Archives", in *A Record of the Friends of St. Paul's* (1954).

York: J. Raine, *A Catalogue of the Printed Books in the Library of the Dean and Chapter of York* (York 1896), Introduction; F. Harrison, "The Dean and Chapter Library", in A. H. Thompson (ed.), *York Minster Historical Tracts* (1927); E. Brunskill, *18th Century Reading* (York Georgian Society, Occas. Papers No. 6, 1950).

CHAPTER IV

Early Endowed Libraries

In the absence of assistance from public funds, there are three ways in which a library may be provided. One is by gift or endowment; another is by subscription; and the third is by attaching a library to an institution which exists also for other purposes. In an endowed library the cost is borne by the donor or donors; in a subscription library it is borne by the users; in an institutional library the cost may or may not be borne by the users, according to the nature of the institution. There are, of course, various ways in which these methods may be combined, e.g. a library may be created by endowment and subsequently maintained by subscription, or by an institution. But the broad distinction is worth bearing in mind.

Until the Reformation, libraries were almost all institutional in character. The fifteenth-century libraries at the London Guildhall and in Worcester and Bristol were indeed endowed, but all were attached by their founders to ecclesiastical institutions, and this feature was characteristic also of most of the endowed libraries which were established, primarily for the use of the clergy, in the two centuries following the Reformation. These libraries became numerous, especially in England from the late seventeenth century onwards, and deserve much more careful study and analysis than they have so far received. As time went on they became increasingly accessible to the public, and less exclusively religious in character, so that they came to form a bridge between the mediaeval libraries and the modern public library system which had its beginnings in the mid-nineteenth century. In some respects, moreover, for example in the development of municipal control and the introduction of lending services, they anticipated important features of the later public system.

Altogether, excluding what are known as the Bray and Kirkwood libraries, described later, over two hundred endowed libraries are known to have been established in England alone

between the Reformation and the end of the eighteenth century.¹
They owed their origins either to individual benefactors, or
more rarely, to groups of benefactors. A parson would bequeath
his library to his successors; a bishop would leave books to the
parish church of his native town; a country gentleman, or a
wealthy burgess, would demonstrate his piety or his civic pride
by a gift of books, and perhaps a building to house them in.²
These initial benefactions often became the nucleus for further
gifts and bequests, and books were sometimes added also by
churchwardens or civic authorities.

The overwhelming majority of the libraries were attached to
parish churches and under the control of the local clergy. They
were usually kept either in the vestry, in the parvis over the
south porch, in the parsonage, or in some convenient adjoining
building. Frequently they were chained. The score or so of
libraries which did not conform to this pattern included a small
but important group which were either from the beginning or
from an early stage under the control of municipal corporations.
Some of these were associated with churches, others not. The
remaining libraries were either attached to schools or under the
control of trustees.

In the development of the libraries it is possible to distinguish two periods. The first, embracing rather more than a
quarter of the total number, extends to about the year 1680.
The libraries founded during this period were, for the most part,
in the market towns. Though they were sometimes stated to be
for the use of laymen as well as clergy, they were in practice
almost exclusively theological in character, and largely in Latin.
Most of the municipally-controlled libraries belong to this
period. After 1680 there came a sudden change of emphasis,
and attention was turned to the needs of the rural parishes.

¹ For a full list of the libraries described in this chapter, see Appendix II.
² The library at Milton Abbas in Dorset was founded by John Tregonwell
(d. 1680), "as a thankfull acknowledgment of God's wonderful mercy
in his preservation, when he fell from the top of this church". It appears
that at the age of five he fell from the church tower, but his frock acted
as a parachute and bore him safely to earth. – J. M. J. Fletcher, "Chained
Books in Dorset and Elsewhere", in *Proc. Dorset Nat. Hist. and Antiq.
Field Club*, Vol. XXXV (1914), p. 21.

ENGLISH ENDOWED LIBRARIES BEFORE THE CIVIL WAR

We have referred in a previous chapter to traces of the existence of parochial libraries in villages in Yorkshire and Wiltshire in the middle of the sixteenth century,[1] but with these two exceptions all the early libraries were in the corporate towns. There can be no doubt that in a number of instances this movement was connected with the desire of the Puritan party in the Church to secure a "preaching ministry". Placing, as they did, supreme emphasis on the Bible as the foundation of religion, the Puritans naturally regarded the preaching of the word as the Church's chief function. Following Scottish and continental examples, they introduced in the 1560s what were known as "exercises" or "prophesyings", i.e. meetings of the clergy for the exposition and discussion of Biblical texts. These are first heard of at Norwich in 1564, and for a few years they were very popular, especially in the north and east of England. Strype tells us:

> "At these assemblies were great confluxes of people to hear and learn. And by this means the Ministers and Curates were forced to read authors, and consult expositors and commentators, and to follow their studies, that they might speak to some purpose when they were to appear in public. . . . "[2]

Elizabeth, who distrusted popular preaching, peremptorily forbade the prophesyings in 1577, and from this time onwards the Puritans concentrated their efforts on the development of a system of preaching lectureships, supplementary to the normal services of the Church. These lectureships, supported by private endowments or often by town corporations, were founded in increasing numbers in the late sixteenth and early seventeenth centuries, and although Archbishop Laud did his best to suppress them they continued in many places until the Civil War brought the triumph of the Puritan cause. It was against this background that the first town libraries were established.

The earliest to be recorded, at Ludlow, clearly had nothing to do with Puritanism, for it was in existence in 1557, in Mary's

[1] See above, p. 50.
[2] J. Strype, *Life and Acts of Edmund Grindal, Archbishop of Canterbury* (1710, new edn. 1821), p. 326.

reign. It is known only by the survival of two books bearing the inscription *ad librariam ecclesie ludloiensis*.[1] With this exception the two earliest town libraries were associated with grammar schools. One was at Guildford, where in 1573 John Parkhurst, Bishop of Norwich, bequeathed books "to the Lybrarie of the same Towne ioyning to the schole".[2] This library, however, had been appropriated to the School by the end of the century. At Shrewsbury School the library was founded in 1596: there is no specific evidence that it was designed as a public library, but there are many indications that this was in fact the case, not least the character of the books acquired. A former librarian has pointed out that purchases during the first thirty years included not only the classics, history and geography but many learned works which could be of little value as adjuncts to school work, e.g. new editions of Ambrose, Clement, Jerome, Tertullian, Anselm, Calvin, Spelman's *Concilia*, Grotius, *Corpus Iuris Civilis*, *Lexicon Juridicum*, and Vesalius's *Anatomy*, besides various incunabula and even some mediaeval manuscripts.[3]

The main movement for town libraries, however, was linked with the Church, and must be regarded as beginning with Norwich, where a library is said to have been founded at St. Andrew's Church in 1586, and Leicester, where a library is first mentioned in the churchwarden's accounts of St. Martin's for 1587. Others founded before 1600 were Bury St. Edmunds (1595), Newcastle upon Tyne (by 1597), Grantham (1598), and Ipswich (1599).

All these were initially church libraries, but the only ones which remained under parochial control throughout their history were those at Norwich and Bury St. Edmunds. The

---

[1] Central Council for the Care of Churches, *The Parochial Libraries of the Church of England* (1959), p. 88.

[2] J. W. Clark, "On chained libraries at Cesena, Wells, and Guildford", in *Proc. of the Cambridge Antiq. Soc.*, Vol. VIII (1891–94), p. 14.

[3] J. B. Oldham, "Shrewsbury School Library", in *The Library*, 5th Ser., Vol. XIV (1959), p. 82. The present librarian, Mr. D. S. Colman, informs me that he has since found indications that the library continued to be regarded as public until the early nineteenth century. In the seventeenth century it is twice referred to as *Bibliotheca Salopiensis*, and in the eighteenth century, when the books began to be unchained, it evidently became a lending library for the whole county: "the Public Library of Shrewsbury Schools" is the description found in a book presented in the 1790s. Borrowing was under the control of the Headmaster, and registers of loans were kept from 1737 to 1826.

early existence of the library at St. Andrew's, Norwich, is
known only from a record preserved by the eighteenth-century
Norfolk antiquary John Kirkpatrick, who tells us that at the
time he wrote there was in the vestry

"a Library of some of ye first Reformers, Commentaries, etc., such
as Gualter, Masculus [i.e. Musculus], Calvin, Erasmus, Henry 8th's
Bible: ye most were given by Tho. Beamond alderman in 1586; and,
among other books, an ancient MS. of Wickliff's translation of ye
New Testam^t. into English (wth some other things at ye end of it)."[1]

In 1628 the library consisted of 26 works (including an
English MS. New Testament), but one of the 26, Theophy-
lactus on the Gospels, is recorded as belonging to the City
library which by this time had been established in an adjoining
building.[2] Whether this indicates any association between the
two libraries is not clear, but the St. Andrew's library seems to
have remained in the church until at least 1806.[3] In 1883 there
were still "eight old books" in the vestry,[4] but as far as is
known none of these has survived.

The library at Bury St. Edmunds, created by the combined
efforts of a number of donors (both lay and clerical) in 1595,
was a much more substantial affair: by 1599 it already contained
nearly 200 volumes. It ultimately became part of the cathedral
library when a bishopric was established in 1914, and now
numbers about 475 volumes.

The element of municipal control first appears in post-

---

[1] J. Kirkpatrick, *Extracts from MSS. relating to Norwich* (MS. Norwich
City Library, *c.* 1725).

[2] F. R. Beecheno, *Notes on the Church of St. Andrew, Norwich* (MS.
Norwich City Library 1883). For the old City Library, see below,
pp. 74–5.

[3] See Vol. IV (1806), p. 313, of F. Blomefield, *An Essay Towards a
Topographical History of the County of Norfolk* (1739–75, 2nd edn.
1805–10), which refers to a MS. of Trevisa's translation of parts of
the New Testament and other old books. The supposed New Testament
by Trevisa is probably the Wycliffite translation referred to above.

[4] Beecheno, *op. cit.*

[5] The early existence of this library was lost sight of until brought to
light by Mr. N. G. Wiltshire, of the Norwich City Library, in an
unpublished F.L.A. thesis on *The Continuity of the Library Tradition in
English Provincial Town* (1957), pp. 18–23. It is possible that some of
the books found their way into the old City Library, but there is no
certain evidence of this.

Reformation England at Grantham, where Francis Trigge, Rector of the neighbouring parish of Welbourne, gave books to the value of about £100 to the alderman and burgesses and the clergy of St. Wulfram's. They were to be chained in a room over the south porch "for the better encreasinge of learninge . . . by such of the cleargie and others as well beinge inhabitantes in or near Grantham and the soake thereof as in other places in the said Countie".[1] A further substantial bequest was made to this library by Professor John Newcome, of Cambridge University, in 1765.

The first post-Reformation library to come under full municipal control was that at Ipswich, which had its origins in a bequest by Alderman William Smart, draper, of some thirty Latin books and manuscripts to the church of St. Mary Tower, for the use of "the common preacher of the Town for the time being, or any other preacher minded to preach in the said parish church".[2] The Corporation seems to have taken charge almost immediately, and in 1612 deposited the books in Christ's Hospital, which also housed the Grammar School. By the end of the eighteenth century the library had grown to eight or nine hundred volumes.

The libraries at Leicester and Newcastle remained for some time parochial. The foundation of the library at St. Martin's, Leicester, is attributed to Henry, third Earl of Huntingdon, who was a zealous Puritan and maintained a public lecturer at this church. The Corporation, which interested itself in the matter almost from the beginning, appointed a librarian in 1628, and in 1632, at the instance of John Angel (afterwards public lecturer at St. Martin's) seems to have taken over complete control. The library was now moved from its original home in the belfry to a building adjoining the church and was considerably augmented by gifts from various sources.

The library at St. Nicholas' Church, Newcastle, after being pillaged by the Scots during the Civil War, was restored as the result of a bequest from Alderman John Cosins. At this time, if not before, it was under the control of the Corporation, which

[1] Copy of indenture of 20th October, 1598, Grantham Public Library. Trigge was himself the author of a number of works of divinity, and also of an address "To the King's Most excellent Majestie" protesting against the enclosure movement – see E. I. Carlyle in *D.N.B.*
[2] *Times Literary Supplement*, Vol. XLIX (1950), p. 524.

in 1677 appointed the curate of St. Nicholas' as librarian. In the following century a gift of 4,600 volumes by a neighbouring clergyman, Dr. Robert Thomlinson, and the provision of new accommodation, made the library for a time "a place of great resort for the literary gentlemen of the town",[1] but the Corporation now lost effective control, and after 1750 the library fell into neglect and disuse. Thomlinson's books are now in the Public Library, but the "old library" remains at the Church.

The library established by the Corporation in the Grammar School at Coventry, in 1602, seems to have been designed for clergy and scholars rather than for the boys. It was described later in the century as "your publique library at the Free School",[2] and the books were mainly theological. The Corporation retained an interest in it until at least 1830, but the remnants were eventually absorbed into the school library, and sold by the Governors in 1908.

The first municipal foundation independent of either church or school was at Norwich in 1608. Though a cathedral city, Norwich had at this time no effective cathedral library, and the small library at St. Andrew's Church was evidently regarded as inadequate. The civic authorities therefore resolved to convert three rooms in the house of Jerrom Goodwyn, sword-bearer, into "a lybrary for the use of preachers, and for a lodging chamber for such preachers as shall come to this cittie".[3] In 1655, perhaps as a result of the religious changes following the Civil War, it was reported to be locked up, and the books "devoted to the wormes, dust, and rotteness";[4] and in the following year it was converted into a subscription library, for reference only, on the basis of a subscription of 12d. per quarter. The donation book begun in 1659 describes it as "a public library for the common good of students" (*Bibliotheca publica Norvicensis communi studiosorum bono*), and the early list of members does include some who were not ministers, but in essence it was and remained a clerical library. After many vicissitudes, including more than half a century in the hands of

---

[1] E. Mackenzie, *A Historical and Descriptive Account of . . . Newcastle upon Tyne* (Newcastle 1827), Vol. II, p. 493. For Thomlinson's library see also below, pp. 96–7.
[2] "The School Library", in *The Coventrian*, April 1963.
[3] G. A. Stephen, *Three Centuries of a City Library* (Norwich 1917), p. 4.
[4] *Op. cit.*, p. 5.

a private subscription library, it passed in 1862 into the possession of the new Public Library.

Another independent municipal library was that at Bristol, established in 1615 in a house near the town wall which had been given by Robert Redwood, gentleman, "to be converted to a Librayre, or place to put bookes for the furtherance of Learninge".[1] Its clerical character is indicated by the appointment of the Vicar of St. Leonard's as librarian at a salary of 40s. per annum. The 186 chained volumes recorded in 1640 included some bequeathed by Tobias Matthew, Archbishop of York, "for the benefit of his native city by the dissemination of knowledge, and for the purpose of founding a Library of sound divinity and other learning, for the use of the Aldermen and Shopkeepers".[2] This reference to aldermen and shopkeepers was optimistic, for the catalogue shows that nearly all the early books were in Latin or Greek.

Redwood's house, having fallen into a ruinous condition, was splendidly rebuilt in 1740, but the library does not seem to have been extensively used at this time, and books and building alike were transferred to a private subscription library thirty-three years later. They did not return into public possession until 1853.

The movement for the establishment of town libraries continued in full swing until almost the eve of the Civil War, but only two other municipal libraries are recorded. That at Colchester was founded in 1631 by a bequest from Samuel Harsnett, Archbishop of York, for the use of the clergy of the town and other divines. That at St. Margaret's, King's Lynn, founded in the same year, was a church library under municipal control; it absorbed a parochial library established at St. Nicholas' in 1617. Many other towns had libraries under purely parochial control: the list includes Oakham (1616), Totnes (1619), Bath (*c.* 1619), Stamford (by 1626), Halifax (*c.* 1626), Boston (*c.* 1634, Manchester (1636), Spalding (1637), possibly also Southampton and Great Yarmouth.[3] Norwich, by 1629, had added to its two existing libraries a

[1] C. Tovey, *The Bristol City Library* (1853), p. 1.
[2] *Op. cit.*, pp. 11–12. Matthew, who died in 1628, was a Bristol man.
[3] At Southampton books and a book-cupboard were given some time before 1646. The date of the Great Yarmouth library is unknown, but the character of the collection suggests the early seventeenth century.

parochial library at the church of St. Peter Mancroft. The large number of libraries in the eastern counties reinforces the association with Puritanism which has been mentioned earlier.

At Bury in Lancashire, Henry Bury, clerk, some time before 1634 gave more than 600 books "to certain ffeffoes in trust for the use of Bury parish and the cuntrie therabouts of ministers also at ther metinge and of schole maisters and others that seek for learninge and knowledge".[1] This library seems to have passed to the grammar school which Bury had founded in 1625.

London, it will be observed, was very ill provided for. Indeed, apart from the library created in the 1620s at Westminster Abbey, and the indifferent collection at St. Paul's, the only library which was in any sense public was that established in 1630 at Sion College – a college and almshouse for clergy founded on London wall four years earlier. This library, which should perhaps be classed as institutional rather than endowed, was in part destroyed by the Great Fire, but became in time an important collection.[2]

Village libraries were rare at this stage, and were all parochial in character. The earliest recorded (except for the two sixteenth-century libraries mentioned above[3]) was at Tankersley in Yorkshire, where books were bequeathed by Robert Booth, in 1615, to the rector "and his successors for ever" – a common formula in later parochial foundations. Others before the Civil War were at Swaffham in Norfolk (1622?), Langley Marish in Buckinghamshire (1623), and Hurley in Berkshire (by 1634).[4] Langley Marish is of special interest because of the beautiful library room adjoining the church which was built by the donor, Sir John Kederminster, and still survives.

FROM THE CIVIL WAR TO THE RESTORATION

During the Cromwellian epoch, as might be expected, few libraries were founded. At Lewisham the vicar, Abraham Colfe,

---

[1] R. C. Christie, *The Old Church and School Libraries of Lancashire* (Chetham Soc. N.S. Vol. VII, Manchester 1885), p. 139.
[2] The Middle Temple had a library bequeathed in 1641 by Robert Ashley, "to be a publick library from which he desired no student might be excluded whether of our own or any foreign nation", but how far the founder's intent was carried out is not clear. See *Master Worsley's Book*, ed. A. R. Ingpen (1910), p. 107.   [3] See above, p. 50.
[4] For a library for parishioners at Repton (1622), see below, pp. 82–83.

in 1652, persuaded the Worshipful Company of Leathersellers to establish in the new grammar school a library similar in purpose to that at Bury; and he himself afterwards bequeathed the best of his books to be chained in the upper room over the school, to form a public library for the ministers and gentlemen of Blackheath, and "all the godly students that will frequent it".[1] The parish church of Wootton Wawen, in Warwickshire, acquired a library in the same year.[2] At Wisbech, in 1653 or 1654, a number of burgesses and gentlemen contributed books and money for a library founded by the town council in the parish church of St. Peter.[3] At Frisby-on-the-Wreak, in Leicestershire, the parish church acquired a small collection of books from a bequest about 1655.

By far the most important library formed in this period – indeed the greatest of all the early town libraries – was Chetham's Library, Manchester, founded as the result of a bequest by Humphrey Chetham, the first great pioneer of public libraries in this country. Chetham, a prosperous woollen and linen merchant of the town, died in 1653, leaving the bulk of his large fortune to be disposed of for charitable purposes. Part of it was used to endow Chetham's Hospital, for the maintenance and education of forty poor boys; part for the establishment of popular libraries (of which more hereafter) in a number of local churches; and the sum of £1,000, together with the residue of the estate after other charitable bequests had been fulfilled, was left for the establishment of a chained library of reference in Manchester "for the use of schollars and others well affected to resort unto . . . the same bookes there

---

[1] W. H. Black (ed.), *Bibliothecae Colfanae Catalogus* (1831), Introduction.
[2] See below, p. 85.
[3] Historical MSS. Commission, *IXth Report* (1883), pp. 293–4, misleadingly refers to this library as a book club, and lists two works, *Tractatus Spagyricus* and *Collectionum Hermeticarum*, as "Given to the Wisbech Book Club by John Swayne of Leverington" in 1643 and 1646 respectively. These and other works, eight volumes in all, are MS. notes, in Latin or German, on medical and scientific topics, and are inscribed simply, "The gift of Mr. John Swayne of Leverington". They bear on the covers dates between 1642 and 1649, which are presumably the dates of compilation or binding. They do not, therefore, provide any evidence for the existence of a library before 1653–54. I am indebted to Mr. W. L. Hanchant, Curator of the Wisbech and Fenland Museum, for assistance on this point.

Macmillan and

8. LIBRARIES MEDIAEVAL AND MODERN

The sketch on the left, from B. H. Streeter, *The Chained Library*, shows the rather elaborate lecterns used in the mediaeval library of Lincoln Cathedral. The bookplate of John Peace, on the right, shows the interior of the eighteenth-century subscription library at Bristol, with free-standing bookcases and an ornate chimney piece attributed to Grinling Gibbons.

to remaine as a publick library forever". A further £100 was allocated for the equipment of the library building.[1]

The Library and Hospital were accommodated in buildings which had formerly housed the college attached to the parish church, and the combined institutions were incorporated by charter of Charles II in 1665. It was not, however, a parochial library, nor, since Manchester was not at this time a corporate town, was it a municipal library. It was, and remains, in the hands of a body of trustees. Very wisely they decided, in 1661, to invest the residue of the estate in land to provide an income for the purchase of books.

This decision was crucial. While most other early libraries, lacking endowments, sank gradually into decay, Chetham's Library was enabled to grow steadily over the years and to adapt itself to changing needs. From the beginning, moreover, it benefited from the care of a full-time librarian. The first was appointed in 1656. He was to have a salary of £10 a year, together with food and accommodation; and in return was to be in attendance for six hours daily in the winter and seven in the summer, "and to require nothing of any man that cometh into the Library".[2]

Chetham's Library was at the outset, and long remained, predominantly theological in character. It should be noted, however, that it was founded for the use of "scholars", and not specifically of the clergy. From the very beginning, moreover, the books purchased included some works other than theology, and as time went on the book selection was steadily widened. By 1684 there were already nearly 3,000 volumes, including fairly substantial sections on history, travel, topography, law, medicine, and science. It seems clear that the trustees, who in the early years included clergy, landed gentry, business men, an apothecary and a physician, had in mind the professional needs and leisure-time interests of all the educated people of the town.

Chetham's Library was, in fact, rapidly developing into a public library in the modern sense. In the mid-eighteenth century,

[1] The will is printed in Vol. II of the *Life of Humphrey Chetham* by F. R. and C. W. Sutton (Chetham Soc., N.S. Vols. XLIX–L, Manchester 1903).

[2] A. F. Maclure, "The Minute Books of Chetham's Hospital and Library, Manchester", in *Trans. of the Lancs. and Ches. Antiq. Soc.*, Vol. XL (Manchester 1922–23), p. 21.

during the librarianship of Robert Thyer, it was frequented by a group of friends, among them John Byrom the poet, "who not only came as readers but also met in the Librarian's rooms for discussion".[1] About this time, in 1745 apparently, the practice of chaining was abandoned in favour of locked gates at the entrance to each alcove – a unique feature of this library.

The twenty years following the Restoration saw the foundation of another cluster of libraries, still mostly in the towns: Birmingham (1661), Barnstaple (1664), Hull (1665), Durham (1669), Ottery St. Mary (by 1672), Marlborough (1678), and Chelmsford (1679). Smaller centres which acquired libraries at this time included King's Norton in Warwickshire (1665), Marske near Richmond in Yorkshire (1666), North Grimston in the same county (1671), and Chirbury in Shropshire (1677). Most of these libraries were parochial, but those at Barnstaple and Marlborough were also under municipal control, while that at Durham was neither municipal nor parochial but a special foundation endowed by Bishop John Cosin for the use of the diocesan clergy.[2] At King's Norton the library was housed in the Grammar School in the churchyard.

King's Norton offers an interesting example of how these libraries came to be founded. Thomas Hall, curate of King's Norton from 1640 until his ejection in 1662, and master of the Grammar School there, was a well-known Puritan divine, whose influence in the Midlands, it has been said, was second only to that of Richard Baxter. Though not a wealthy man, he accumulated a substantial library, which before his death in 1665 he divided into three portions. To Birmingham (apparently to St. Martin's Church), he allocated 300 of his best books to form a library for the ministers of that town; a further 750 were given "for a Library at Kingsnorton for the Use of the Minister of Kingsnorton, Mosely and Withal etc. and of the Two Schoolmasters there"; and finally 270 volumes of "Schoole bookes and Phylosophy" were assigned to the Grammar School.[3]

---

[1] H. Lofthouse, "Unfamiliar Libraries: I. Chetham's Library", in *Book Collector*, Vol. V (1956), p. 324.

[2] It is now in the care of the University Library.

[3] J. E. Vaughan, "The Former Grammar School of King's Norton", in *Trans. Worcs. Archaeol. Soc.*, N.S. Vol. XXXVII (1960). Cf. W. S. Brassington, "Thomas Hall and the Old Library Founded by him at King's Norton", in *Library Chronicle*, Vol. V (1888), pp. 61–71.

"THE EDIFICACION OF THE COMMON PEOPLE"

The provision of books in churches for the lay reader goes
back, as we have seen, to Thomas Cromwell's injunction of 1536
for the chaining of the Bible in churches.[1] As time went on, other
books were added, e.g. the two books of *Homilies*, the *Para-
phrases* of Erasmus, John Jewel's *Apology in Defence of the Church
of England*, and John Foxe's *History of the Acts and Monuments
of the Church*, popularly known as the *Book of Martyrs*. By the
mid-seventeenth century nearly every parish church had a few
books of this kind chained to lecterns or a reading-desk, and in
about a hundred churches one or more volumes have survived
to this day.[2] Those mentioned above are the ones most frequently found, and the others are mostly theological works, but
secular works are not unknown. In London the church of St.
Andrew Undershaft had a chained copy of Raleigh's *History of
the World*;[3] and at Alkley, near Doncaster, Rev. T. Sylvester
bequeathed in 1615 his copy of Cooper's *Dictionary* to be chained
in the church for the use of poor scholars in the neighbouring
grammar school at Rossington.[4] This latter example is reminis-
cent of mediaeval practice.[5] At Easton-in-Gordano, near Bristol,
one Captain Samuel Sturmy, in 1669, presented a copy of his
folio volume on mathematics, *The Mariner's or Artizan's
Magazine*, for the use of this and neighbouring parishes. It was
to be chained, but might be borrowed on a security of £3.[6]

In some instances books for the use of parishioners were included in libraries intended primarily for the clergy. This seems
to have been the case at St. Martin's, Leicester, and St. Nicholas,
Newcastle. At Leicester the library included not only Foxe's

[1] See above, p. 48.
[2] An admirable example of parish expenditure on such books, in the
sixteenth and seventeenth centuries, is to be found in the Churchwardens' Accounts for Wimborne Minster – see J. M. J. Fletcher,
"Chained Books in Dorset and Elsewhere", in *Proc. Dorset Nat. Hist.
and Antiq. Field Club*, Vol. XXXV (1914), pp. 15–17.
[3] Still in the possession of the church, though no longer chained.
[4] This would be the *Thesaurus linguae Romanae et Britannicae*, by Thomas
Cooper, Bishop of Lincoln and afterwards of Winchester, first published
1565.   [5] See above, p. 25.
[6] The details are given in a very curious inscription, painted on a wooden
board inside the church, of which the Rector, Rev. J. Ramsay, has kindly
supplied me with a copy. The burial register of the church shows that
Sturmy died a few months later, in September 1669.

Book of Martyrs, presented in 1598, and Jewel's *Works*, purchased in 1614, but seven books, "Written in the English tongue for the good and benefitt of the volger and not so well learned sort of people", given by Symon Craftes in 1593–94.[1] A volume of the Homilies in the Newcastle library is inscribed:

"This booke was given by Bulmer the Apothicary unto the Librayrie in the Church of St, Nicholas of Newcastell upon Tine, and their to be kepte for any well disposed persone who have a minde to read one it, but not to be lent, nor taken out of the Librayrie, so long as this said booke shall last. Maye the 8th Anno Domini 1628."[2]

A number of other early town libraries, as we have seen, purported to serve lay as well as clerical readers, but the character of these libraries was such that their use was restricted to a small minority of scholars. The same may be said of the library bequeathed in 1677 by Edward Lewis, Vicar of Chirbury in Shropshire, to be chained in the schoolhouse in the churchyard, for the use of the schoolmaster or any other of the parishioners who should desire to read them: apart from a Chaucer, a Pliny's *Natural History* and a few other works, the 207 volumes were nearly all theology or Biblical commentaries.[3]

At the parish church of Repton, in Derbyshire, in 1622, we have a very interesting example of a small collection of unchained books deposited with the vicar and churchwardens for loan to the parishioners. These books, according to the churchwardens' accounts, were given by a Mr. William Bladon, "to be emploied for the use of the parrishe, and to be disposed of at the discretion of Mr. Thomas Whiteheade", the recently appointed Headmaster of Repton School. Fifteen volumes are listed, including a Bible, "two bookes of Martters", and various

[1] F. S. Herne, "The Town Library, Leicester", in *Trans. Leic. Lit. and Phil. Soc.*, N.S. Vol. III (1891–95), pp. 249–50. The books given by Craftes are described as "cheynedd in the Church", but Herne thinks they were in fact chained in the belfry along with the rest of the library. The other two books appear in the catalogue compiled by C. Deedes, J. E. Stocks and J. L. Stocks, *The Old Town Hall Library of Leicester* (Oxford 1919).

[2] E. B. Hicks and G. E. Richmond (eds.), *Catalogue of the Newcastle Chapter Library and of the Churchwardens' or Old Parish Library* (Newcastle 1890), p. 43.

[3] See the catalogue in W. Wilding, "On a Library of Chained Books at Chirbury", in *Trans. Shrops. Archaeol. and Nat. Hist. Soc.*, Vol. VIII (1885, reprinted from *Journ. of the Brit. Archaeol. Assoc.*, 1883).

English theological works such as Elton on the Colossians, Perkins on the Creed, Dod and Cleaver on the Commandments, Brinsley's *True Watch*, and Dent's *Plain Man's Pathway* and *Sermon of Repentance*. The regulations governing their use were surprisingly liberal:

" . . . the said minister and Churchwarddens, or anye of them, shall have authoritie to lend any of the said bookes to anie of the parrishe of Reptoun for the space of one 2 or 3 moneths, as they in their discrecione shall see fittinge one this Condicione that the parties borrowinge anye of the bookes afornam[ed] eyther fowly bruisinge tearinge defacinge or embez[ellinge] the said booke borrowed, shall make good the said bo[oke] thus defaced, tourne, bruised or embezelled into the parrishe.

"Alsoe that the said bookes kept by the minister and Churchwarddens in some convenient place, shall [not] be lent out more than one at a time to anye of the parrishe.

"Alsoe that everye person borrowing any of [the said] bookes shall subscribe his name . . . "

At this point a corner of the page is torn away, but from the words that remain it appears that the minister and churchwardens were required to keep a list of the borrowings.[1]

If a collection of fifteen volumes may be called a library, this is, as far as is known, the earliest free lending library in Great Britain. Humphrey Chetham of Manchester, who was the first to attempt a systematic provision of libraries for parishioners, kept to the older tradition of the chained library. On his death in 1653 he bequeathed not only funds for the establishment of a library for scholars but also £200 to be spent on "godly English Bookes, such as Calvins, Prestons and Perkins workes, comments or annotacions uppon the bible or some partes thereof", or such other books as his executors should think "most proper for the edificacion of the common people, to be chained uppon deskes, or to bee fixed to the pillars or in other convenient places", in the parish churches of Manchester and Bolton and the chapels

---

[1] Churchwardens' Accounts, Repton, 1622, f. 365. This document is printed in R. Bigsby, *Historical and Topographical Description of Repton* (1854), pp. 147–8, and the list of books is reproduced in J. C. Cox, *Churchwardens' Accounts* (1913), p. 121, but in both cases there are errors in the transcription of the names, e.g. *Doe* for *Dod*, *Bellymy* for *Basting*, *Yonge* for *Gouge*. I am indebted to Rev. P. R. W. Tomlinson, Vicar of Repton, for assistance in this matter.

of Turton, Walmsley and Gorton.[1] Some years elapsed before
these instructions were fulfilled, but between 1658 and 1668 a
collection of some 200 volumes was chained in the parish church
of Manchester, and smaller collections at Bolton, Gorton and
Turton – the collection destined for Walmsley seems to have
been diverted to increase the stock at Turton. The books were
all formidably theological, but at least they were in English.
The remains of the libraries at Gorton and Turton are still to
be seen, and fifty-six volumes from the Bolton collection are
now in the library of Bolton School.

How far books provided for the use of parishioners were
actually read by them must remain a matter for speculation, but
it would be wrong to judge the question in the light of modern
reading tastes. We must not forget the zeal for the reading of
the English Bible which was revealed at the time of the Reformation, nor the passionate interest in religious reading of all kinds
which persisted throughout the sixteenth and seventeenth centuries, and to a lesser extent into the eighteenth century. Of the
Elizabethan period a distinguished American scholar has written:

"No phase of Elizabethan literary interest seems stranger to-day
than the inordinate appetite of that age for 'good Books'. The zeal
for collections of pious aphorisms, books of prayers and religious
guidance, printed sermons, adaptations of the Psalms, and moralized
allegories was limited only by the ability of the printers to pour out
such works. Nor was the zeal for godly reading confined merely to a
few Puritan fanatics; in every rank of society from the dissolute
courtier to the ribald apprentice, pious books found their place."[2]

In the late seventeenth century the same spirit is seen in the
inscription in a copy of the *Book of Martyrs* chained to the pulpit
in the church of Standon in Staffordshire:

"William Lovatt [a churchwarden] gave this book to the church of
Standon, there to be kept for the use of the parishioners, to read in
before and after prayers on Sundays, holidays and other convenient
times. That they may see the great happiness they enjoy in having
the free exercise of religion. . . . "[3]

[1] For the reference see above, p. 79, note 1.
[2] L. B. Wright, *Middle-Class Culture in Elizabethan England* (North
    Carolina Univ. Pr. 1935, repr. Cornell Univ. Pr. 1958), p. 228.
[3] W. S. Brassington, "Additional Notes to Blades' 'Bibliographical
    Miscellanies' ", in *The Library*, Vol. III (1891), p. 273.

About the same time the parishioners of Wootton Wawen in Warwickshire, to whom the vicar, George Dunscomb, had bequeathed a number of volumes forty years earlier, insisted that the books should be brought forth from the vicarage where they had hitherto been kept, and "chained to a Desk in the South Isle of the Church, April 11th, 1693".[1] The desk and eleven books remain to this day. We may, therefore, reasonably suppose that what seem to us rather forbidding tomes were actually read, or at least dipped into, by the yeomen, the craftsmen, the shopkeepers and other literate members of society.

THE EARLY ENDOWED LIBRARIES OF SCOTLAND

Information concerning endowed libraries in Scotland is scanty, but sufficient is known to make it clear that developments there paralleled to some extent those in England, and considering that the population in 1700 (estimated at one million) was only about one-fifth that of England and Wales, the record is not unimpressive. In particular, Scotland can boast the earliest post-Reformation libraries in Great Britain under municipal control.

The first of these (though in the light of our present information it is impossible to assign an exact date for its origin) may have been at St. Mary's Church, Dundee, a church which from 1443 onwards was controlled and maintained by the Town Council. The library here seems to have been founded by William Christison, who was the Protestant minister from 1560 to 1598. In a catalogue of 1724 it is recorded that four volumes of the works of St. Augustine contained an inscription stating that they had been given by Christison, and afterwards bequeathed by him "for the use of the common library of the church of the aforesaid town". This inscription was presumably written soon after Christison's death in 1599. The existence of a library in 1599 is also attested by the gift of a volume in that year by James Anderson, a neighbouring Protestant Minister.

It seems safe to say, therefore, that the library came into existence some time during Christison's ministry. It was under the joint control of the minister and the Town Council, but the ultimate authority of the Council was firmly asserted in 1636,

[1] B. H. Streeter, *The Chained Library* (1931), p. 292.

when it was decreed that an inventory of the books should be drawn up, that they should be inspected yearly by the magistrates and Council, that the Kirkmaster (a Council officer) should have one of the keys of the library, and that no books should be lent out without his advice and upon sufficient pledge deposited in his hands. This limited provision for lending is notable at this early date, though it does not substantiate the claim that Dundee had "the earliest free lending library in Britain".

The library evidently continued in active service throughout the seventeenth and early eighteenth centuries, and received many gifts, so that the catalogue of 1724 is able to list the very large total of 1,676 works (78 of them published since 1700), in about 4,000 volumes. Unfortunately all but six were destroyed by fire in 1841.[1]

Apart from Dundee the earliest town libraries were those of Edinburgh and Aberdeen. The former was founded in 1580 by Clement Little, advocate, who bequeathed his theological library, to the number of 76 volumes, to the town and church of Edinburgh, for the use of "sik personis knawin of honest conuersation and guid lyfe (and na vtheris) quhilkis ar and sall be willing to travell and be exercised in the estait and vocatioun of the ministerie, or vtherwayis of dewitie desyrous".[2] They were first lodged in a special room attached to the manse of St. Giles, but on the death of the then minister, James Lawson, in 1584, they were transferred to the "Town's College", i.e. to the University of Edinburgh, of which Lawson had been the principal founder. For more than half a century, however, outsiders were still permitted under certain conditions to read in the library, and the Town Council continued to appoint the librarian until 1854.

The Aberdeen library, which comprised mainly theology and law, was founded in 1585 by a group of ministers, lawyers, and burgesses, and was known as the Common Library of New Aberdeen, or alternatively, since it was kept in the session house of St. Nicholas' Church, as the Kirk Library. It was removed in

---

[1] On the supposed mediaeval origin of the Dundee library see Note at end of Chapter.
[2] The documents, and a list of the books, are printed in Maitland Club, *Miscellany*, Vol. I (1833–34), Pt. II, pp. 285–301.

1632 to Marischal College, and 93 volumes now remain in the University Library.

Only one other library is known to have been established in Scotland in the period before 1680. This was the parochial library of Saltoun in East Lothian, founded in 1658 by Norman Leslie, minister of Gordon in Berwickshire. The famous Gilbert Burnet, afterwards Bishop of Salisbury and chaplain to William III, was minister of Salton at this time: it was his first living. He himself added to the collection, and at his death in 1715 left a substantial legacy for its augmentation.

NOTE—*The Origin of the Town Library of Dundee*

Dr. A. H. Millar, a former Librarian of Dundee, in an unpublished address of 1920 (MS. in the Dundee Central Library), traced the origin of the public library back to the fifteenth century. He pointed out that the agreement by which the Town Council took over the control of the church from the Abbey of Lindores in 1443 specifically mentions "vestments, books, challices, palls, and linen cloths of the Great Altar, and other ornaments . . . ", and he believed that the books here referred to were those of the Franciscan friars of Dundee, who as a result of the English invasions had been obliged to take refuge in St. Mary's about a century earlier. Dr. Paul Kaufman, who has contributed so much to the study of these early libraries, prints the story in his article, "The Earliest Free Lending Library in Britain" (*Library Association Record*, Vol. LXIII, 1961, pp. 160–2).

Unfortunately for this theory, J. M. Bryce, in *The Scottish Grey Friars* (1909), Vol. I, Ch. viii, makes it clear that whatever may have happened in the fourteenth century the Franciscans were still in their own building at the time of the Reformation. Moreover they still had their library, which was put into pawn during the famine of 1481 and redeemed in the following year. An inventory of 1454 shows that the books referred to in the agreement of 1443 were in fact service-books, and there is no evidence that the pre-Reformation church ever possessed much more than this (cf. A. Maxwell, *The History of Old Dundee* (Dundee 1884), pp. 555–85).

There has been misunderstanding, also, regarding the inscription in Christison's books, referred to by Dr. Kaufman, as "the inscription of 1559". This inscription is known only from a copy in the 1724 catalogue, which reads:

> *Hunc Librum Dono dedit, piae Memoriae Vir Gulielmus Christi-*
> *sonus, quadraginta annis Ecclesiae Taodunanae Minister, qui & moriens*

16 *Calend: Maij Anno Dom.* 1559 *Testamento legavit in Usum communis Bibliothecae praedictae Urbis Ecclesiae.*

Such an inscription can only have been penned after Christison's death. The date 1559 does not make sense, and is probably a slip for 1599. Dr. J. H. Baxter, *Dundee and the Reformation* (Abertay Hist. Soc., Dundee 1960), p. 26, has shown that the date of Christison's death was not 1603, as stated in H. Scott (ed.), *Fasti Ecclesiae Scoticanae*, Vol. V (Edinburgh 1925), p. 315, but 16th October, 1599. 16 Kal. May, i.e. 16th April, is presumably the date of the will. It will be noted that the reference is to the common library of the Church, and not the common library of the town. (*Taodunanae* is from *Taodunum*, a mediaeval form of the name of Dundee.)

I am greatly indebted to the present City Librarian of Dundee, Mr. W. S. Taylor, for assistance in my researches on this point. In view of the early date of this library, it seemed important to establish the facts as accurately as possible.

Bibliographical Note

The standard work on parish libraries in England and Wales is that published by the Central Council for the Care of Churches on *The Parochial Libraries of the Church of England* (1959), with a historical introduction by N. R. Ker. This does not, of course, include town libraries unless they were also parochial. Some others are dealt with in E. Edwards, *Memoirs of Libraries* (2v. 1859), Bk. III, Chs. xi, xv, xvi, xxii. See also the lists in *Report from the Select Committee on Public Libraries* (1849), pp. 221–6, and in the appendix to T. W. Shore's article on "The Old Parochial Libraries of England and Wales", in *Transactions and Proceedings of the First Annual Meeting of the Library Association, 1878* (1879). B. H. Streeter, *The Chained Library* (1931), has brief accounts of some libraries. R. C. Christie, *The Old Church and School Libraries of Lancashire* (Chetham Society Publications, N.S. Vol. VII, Manchester 1885) is admirable within its limits; and the historical introduction to R. A. Rye, *Students' Guide to the Libraries of London* (1908, 3rd edn. 1927), has notes on some early London libraries. A valuable recent study is J. A. Fitch "Some Ancient Suffolk Parochial Libraries", in *Proceedings of the Suffolk Institute of Archaeology*, Vol. XXX (1964).

Satisfactory histories of individual libraries are few, but the following contain useful information:

> Bristol: C. Tovey, *The Bristol City Library* (Bristol 1853).
> Colchester: G. Godwin (ed.), *A Catalogue of the Harsnett Library at Colchester* (1888), Introduction.

Halifax: T. W. Hanson, "Halifax Parish Church under the Commonwealth", in *Transactions of the Halifax Antiquarian Society,* 1909, and "Halifax Parish Church Library", *ibid.,* 1951.

King's Lynn: T. E. Maw, "The Church Libraries of King's Lynn", in *The Antiquary,* Vol. XL (1904).

Leicester: F. S. Herne, "The Town Library, Leicester", in *Transactions of the Leicester Literary and Philosophical Society,* N.S. Vol. III (1892–95).

Manchester: F. R. Raines and C. W. Sutton, *Life of Humphrey Chetham* (Chetham Society Publications, N.S. Vols. XLIX–L, Manchester 1903); H. S. A. Smith, "Readers and Books in a Seventeenth-Century Library", *in Library Association Record,* Vol. LXV (1963).

Marlborough: E. G. H. Kempson, "The Vicar's Library, St. Mary's Marlborough", in *Wiltshire Archaeological and Natural History Magazine,* Vol. LI (1945–47).

Newcastle: E. Mackenzie, *A Descriptive and Historical Account of . . . Newcastle upon Tyne* (2v. Newcastle 1827), Vol. II, pp. 490–6.

Norwich: G. A. Stephen, *Three Centuries of a City Library* (Norwich 1917).

On books chained in churches see the lists in W. Blades, *Books in Chains* (1892); J. C. Cox and A. Harvey, *English Church Furniture* (1907), Ch. xi; J. C. Cox, *Churchwardens' Accounts* (1913), Ch. viii; and *Notes and Queries,* 12th Ser., Vol. XII (1923), pp. 493–5. The two former also include many chained libraries, and the same is true of J. M. J. Fletcher, "Chained Books in Dorset and Elsewhere", in *Proceedings of the Dorset Natural History and Antiquarian Field Club,* Vol. XXXV (1914).

For Scotland there is no general account in print, but W. R. Aitken, *A History of the Public Library Movement in Scotland* (Ph.D. thesis, Edinburgh University 1956), Ch. i, provides a useful survey. The *Report from the Select Committee on Public Libraries* (1849), pp. 303–5, has lists of parochial and non-parochial libraries; and Edwards's *Memoirs* (see above), Ch. xx, includes some Scottish libraries. For Dundee see the references in the note appended to this chapter; for Aberdeen W. S. Mitchell, "The Common Library of New Aberdeen", in *Libri,* Vol. IV (1953–54); and for Edinburgh "Catalogus librorum quos. . . . Magister Clemens Litill Edinburgene ecclesie et ministris ejusdem obiens legavit et consecravit", in Maitland Club, *Miscellany,* Vol. I (1833–34), Pt. II, and A. Grant, *The Story of Edinburgh University* (2v. 1884), App. O.

CHAPTER V

The Later Development
of Endowed Libraries

IT is a surprising fact that more than one-third of the total number of endowed libraries were founded in the years between 1680 and 1720. Whereas in the period before 1680 the main concentration had been on the establishment of libraries in the larger towns, most of the new libraries were in small towns and villages. The Bray library movement, which also had its beginnings during this period, and which will be described hereafter, also focused its attention on the needs of the rural areas. The impulse which gave rise to this sudden outburst of activity was both religious and educational. It can be linked with that new spirit of piety – a reaction, perhaps, against the laxity of the Restoration period – which manifested itself at this time in the formation of religious societies, and led on in the eighteenth century to Methodism and evangelicalism. It can also be linked, quite unmistakably, with the movement for popular religious education which found its expression in the thousands of charity schools established during the eighteenth century for the education of the children of the poor.

The lead in this work was taken by the greatest of the religious societies – the Society for Promoting Christian Knowledge, founded in 1699, and its sister organization the Society in Scotland for Propagating Christian Knowledge, and it is significant that Thomas Bray, the founder of the Bray libraries, was also the principal architect of the S.P.C.K. In this narrative, for the sake of clarity, I have dealt with the Bray libraries separately, but this separation is quite artificial and to some extent misleading. The Bray organization systematized the provision of libraries for the clergy just as the S.P.C.K. systematized the provision of charity schools, but there was nothing essentially new about either.

CHARACTERISTICS OF THE LATER ENGLISH
ENDOWED LIBRARIES

Between 1680 and 1720 libraries were being founded at the rate of about two a year. After 1720 the pace slackened, probably because most of the more obvious needs had been met, and although libraries continued to be founded here and there well into the nineteenth century, comparatively few can be assigned to the period after 1770. Altogether about 160 libraries were founded between 1680 and 1800.[1]

Of this total twenty-nine only were founded in corporate towns, and of these only Preston (1761) and possibly Gainsborough (1696) were under independent municipal control.[2] Newark (1698) had a church library under municipal control; so also had Harwich, for at least a brief period *c.* 1710;[3] Leeds (1692), Maldon (1704), Nottingham (1744), and Tamworth (1786) had libraries in schools; Bedford (1700) and Lewes (1717) had church libraries in the hands of trustees; Huntingdon (by 1716) had a special library, lodged in a room in the town, for the clergy of the archdeaconry. All the others[4] were parochial libraries of the ordinary kind.

One of the earliest and best-known of these latter was Archbishop Tenison's Library at St. Martin's in the Fields, founded in 1684 by the vicar, Thomas Tenison, afterwards Archbishop

---

[1] For further details see Appendix II.

[2] For Gainsborough we have only a statement by the vicar, in a return to an inquiry made in 1705, that "A Lending Library is settled in the said Town by the voluntary subscriptions of severall persons which was begun A.D. 1696" (*Notitia Parochialis*, no. 879, Lambeth Palace MSS. 960–5), and a note of a subscription by Dr. Bray to what was probably the same library (Bray Accounts 1695–99, MS., U.S.P.G. Archives – cf. below, p. 106, note 3). It seems to have been short-lived, for another library was founded in 1731 by Nathaniel Robinson, who bequeathed 350 volumes to be placed in the schoolmaster's house for the use of the inhabitants. This still survived in the 1820s (see below, pp. 196–7), but appears to have been transferred to a subscription library in 1837.

[3] See Appendix II, *s.v.*

[4] Hull, St. Mary Lowgate (by 1682); London, St. Martin's (1684); Beverley (1699); Durham, St. Oswald's (1701); Reigate (1701); Warwick (1701); York, St. Mary's (*c.* 1705); London, St. George the Martyr (early 18th cent.?); Doncaster (1714); Liverpool (1715); Tiverton (1715); Maidstone (by 1716); Whitchurch, Hants. (1731); Crediton (1721); Bridgnorth (1743); Stockton-on-Tees (by 1750?); London, St. Leonard, Shoreditch (1763); Northampton (1777).

of Canterbury. It was housed in a special building designed by Wren and erected in the churchyard, and was for public use, but especially for the use of the clergy of St. Martin's, the schoolmaster and usher, and neighbouring clergy. In spite of this addition the library resources of the capital at this period remained exceedingly scanty. John Evelyn complained in a letter to Pepys in 1689 that "this great and august city of London, abounding with so many wits and lettered persons, has scarce one library founded or endowed for the public". Tenison's library he described as "a charity . . . worthy his generous spirit".[1]

The situation did not greatly improve in the early part of the eighteenth century. One or two small parochial libraries were formed, and Dr. Williams's Library, founded under the will of a Presbyterian divine, Daniel Williams, in 1729, developed into a rich storehouse of Nonconformist history and theology, but its use was reserved mainly for Dissenters until 1841. In 1747 Thomas Carte, in his *General History of England*, declared: "there is scarce a great city in those parts of Europe where learning is at all regarded, which is so destitute of a good publick library as London."[2] Gibbon testified to the same effect: "The greatest city in the world is destitute of that useful institution, a public library; and the writer who has undertaken to treat of any large historical subject is reduced to the necessity of purchasing for his private use a numerous and valuable collection of the books which must form the basis of his work."[3]

The great majority of these post-1680 libraries were in the smaller centres of population, especially in rural areas such as East Anglia and the North of England. Such libraries were almost invariably parochial in character, but an interesting exception is found at Bamburgh in Northumberland. Here, in 1778, a library was established in the castle, which as a result of a generous bequest earlier in the century by Lord Crewe, Bishop of Durham, had become the centre for a number of charitable enterprises, including schools and a dispensary for

---

[1] J. Evelyn, *Diary and Correspondence*, ed. W. Bray (new edn. 1902), Vol. III, pp. 305, 307.
[2] Vol. I, p. vi. Cf. J. Nichols, *Literary Anecdotes of the Eighteenth Century*, Vol. II (1812), pp. 509–12.
[3] E. Gibbon, *Miscellaneous Works*, ed. John, Lord Sheffield (1796, new edn. 1814), Vol. IV, pp. 591–2.

the poor. By the mid-nineteenth century this library numbered about 6,000 volumes – a large collection by the standards of that time.

The contents of the libraries of this period varied according to the origins of the collection, but since most of them were founded by the clergy themselves – very often by an incumbent for the benefit of his successors – theology was always well represented. The chained library still existing at Wimborne Minster in Dorset (1685) is fairly typical. Its 240 volumes include a few classics, numerous lexicons, five Bibles, some general and ecclesiastical history, the Fathers, and large quantities of post-Reformation divinity. There is also one manuscript, a copy of the *Regimen Animarum*, a fourteenth-century manual for priests. Quite a number of these libraries possessed a manuscript or two, and many possessed early printed books which are now great rarities – only a few years ago a unique *Sarum Legenda*, printed for Caxton in 1488, was discovered at St. Mary's, Warwick.[1]

A high proportion of the Wimborne books are in Latin. This was common before 1700, and even as late as 1764 the rector of Wendlebury in Oxfordshire stipulated, on bequeathing his library to the church, that no book in any modern language should be admitted. By this date, however, English books were common in most libraries, and the scope of their subject matter had also broadened, for the library of the cultivated eighteenth-century gentleman or clergyman could usually be counted upon to include not only theology and the classics but works of general literature, history, topography, travel and natural science. The library bequeathed to the parish of Henley-on-Thames by the rector, Dr. Charles Aldrich, in 1737, included all these subjects, and also mathematics, astronomy, medicine, agriculture, philosophy, education, poetry, and the fine arts.[2] Few collections showed so catholic a taste as this, but many others reflected some special interest on the part of their former owner: for example, Rougham in Norfolk (1714), had valuable oriental

---

[1] P. Morgan and E. H. Painter, "The Caxton *Legenda* at St. Mary's, Warwick", in *The Library*, 5th Ser., Vol. XII (1957), pp. 225–7. For other interesting examples of early printed books see E. G. H. Kempston, "The Vicar's Library, St. Mary's, Marlborough", in *Wilts.Archaeol. and Nat. Hist. Mag.*, Vol. LI (1945–47), pp. 194–215.

[2] See *The Catalogue of the Old Library at Henley-on-Thames* (1852).

books which came from the library of Roger North; and the
5,000 volumes presented by Dr. William Shepherd to his native
town of Preston in 1761 included a splendid collection of medical
books.

INCREASING EMPHASIS ON PUBLIC USE

This broadening of the scope of endowed libraries is particularly significant because it was accompanied by an increasing
emphasis on public use. As we have seen in the case of Bristol,
a library of Latin theology was not of much value to the general
public even if it were available to them, but a library such as
that at Henley could be of real service to the more educated
parishioners, and when it came into use in 1777 it was in fact
thrown open for reading and borrowing by all parishioners
liable for church rates. At More in Shropshire (1680) the books
were given "for the use and benefit of the inhabitants of the
same, and especially for the encourageing of a Preaching
Minister there".[1] At Newark (1698), the library was for the
use of the mayor, aldermen and vicar, "and of the inhabitantes
of that towne and the gentlemen and clergy of the adjacent
countrey". The library at Reigate, founded in 1701, was constituted in 1708 as a public lending library for "the Freeholders,
Vicar and Inhabitants of Reigate, and the gentry and clergy of
the neighbourhood". Rotherham (1704) had a library for
"clergy and parishioners"; and the library at Maldon, founded
in the same year, was open to "any gentleman or scholar". At
Ashby-de-la-Zouch (by 1714), the library was for "parishioners
and others"; at Lewes (1717), "for the benefit of the inhabitants"; at Corbridge (1729), "for the use of the parishioners
in common for every person"; at Halton in Cheshire (1733), *pro
communi literatorum usu sub cura curati*; and at Nottingham
(1744), "for the use of the Clergy, Lawyers, Phicitians, and
other persons of a liberal and learned education".[2] The Shepherd Library at Preston (1761) was given, rather more
cautiously, for the use of the Mayor and Corporation and such
others as they or any of them might permit.

[1] County Record Office, Shrewsbury, MS. 1037/More. Mr. N. R. Ker has
kindly drawn my attention to this entry.
[2] For references see the alphabetical list in Central Council for the Care of
Churches, *The Parochial Libraries of England and Wales* (1959), and
below, Appendix II.

It is true that the majority of parochial libraries continued to be founded for the use of the clergy, but probably most incumbents, like that Rector of Whitchurch in Shropshire whose evidence is quoted in the *Report from the Select Committee on Public Libraries* (1849), would "always rejoice in the circulation of the books among those who would make a careful and proper use of them".[1] Certainly by the mid-eighteenth century the practice of chaining books in church for the use of parishioners had fallen into disuse: the last book known to have been chained in this way was a copy of William Burkitt's Commentary on the New Testament, a very popular eighteenth-century work which was chained in the church at Grinton, in Yorkshire, "for the use of the inhabitants", in 1752.[2]

It will have been noted that the library at Henley-on-Thames offered facilities for borrowing books as well as consulting them. This development is also found elsewhere, and is another sign of increasing public use. Its origins go back to the early seventeenth century: Repton, as we have seen, had a parishioners' lending library as early as 1622;[3] and St. Margaret's, King's Lynn, seems to have been a lending library from its inception in 1631 until 1657, when lending was forbidden on account of the number of volumes lost. A more limited arrangement operated from 1637 at Spalding, where those who gave books to the library were permitted to borrow.[4] Gainsborough had a lending library in 1696.[5]

In the eighteenth century the lending of books became much

---

[1] p. 225.

[2] J. C. Cox and A. Harvey, *English Church Furniture* (1907), p. 339. John Nelson records in his *Journal* (1767), p. 74, that on a visit with Wesley to St. Ives in 1743 he had to sleep on the floor, with Burkitt "for my Bolster". *John Wesley's Journal*, ed. N. Curnock, Vol. V (1938), pp. 212–13, has a fantastic story of Ellen Stanyers, a young woman of Macclesfield, who fell into such a state of melancholy as a result of an unfortunate love affair that her father, having consulted the clergy in vain, "ordered one to read to her Burkitt upon the New Testament, till she cried, 'Take it away; I cannot bear it ' and attempted to run away. But her father held her; and when she struggled, beat her, and told her she should hear it, whether she would or no." As a result of this treatment the poor girl completely lost her wits, but eventually the ministrations of a Methodist preacher restored her to sanity.   [3] See above, pp. 82–3.

[4] Other instances of borrowing at this period, e.g. Halifax Parish Church, where certain volumes borrowed in 1645 were not returned till 1659, do not necessarily imply a regular system of lending.

[5] See above, p. 91, note 2.

more common. This was undoubtedly due in part to the vigorous propaganda and active example of Dr. Thomas Bray, who was the great pioneer in the establishment of lending libraries for the clergy.[1] The fact that books no longer needed to be chained was also a great help: the latest instance of a chained parish library is that established at All Saints, Hereford, in 1715.[2] Lending was facilitated too by the gradual abandonment, about this time, of the old folio format, which by the middle of the century was used only for substantial works of reference.

As might be expected, however, lending was still commonly hedged round with a variety of precautions and restrictions. At Bedford (1700), Reigate (1701), Maldon (1704), Tiverton in Devon (1715), and Whitchurch in Hampshire (1731), books might be borrowed on payment of a deposit. At Bedford and Reigate, as an alternative to the payment of a deposit, the borrower might give a written undertaking to return the book within a specified time; at Tiverton, in default of a deposit, an oath was required. At Wisbech a seventeenth-century MS. catalogue has entries of loans from 1715, but on what terms is not stated.

The regulations for borrowing prescribed by Dr. Robert Thomlinson at Newcastle upon Tyne in 1745 were particularly stringent. The library was to be open for reading daily except on Saturdays and Sundays, feast days and fast days, in the mornings from 7, 8, or 9 (according to the season) until 1, and in the afternoons from 3 to 6, "if the sun do not set before"; but "No book is to be *lent out* of the said Library, but only to one that is going to publish a Book of at least 300 Pages in Octavo".[3] Such a borrower might have up to six books for two months, or in special cases up to ten books for ten weeks, but only by special licence signed by the Archdeacon of Northumberland, the Vicar of Newcastle, and the Lecturer of St. Nicholas. He must, moreover, deposit twice the value of the books borrowed, half the deposit to be forfeited if the books were

---

[1] See below, pp. 104 seq.
[2] The library of over 300 volumes of "Divinity, Morality and History" bequeathed by Dr. William Brewster, physician, is still *in situ* in its original chains, though it narrowly escaped being sold off to America by a bookseller-churchwarden in 1858.
[3] W. J. Haggerston, "The Thomlinson Library, Newcastle-upon-Tyne". in *Monthly Notes of the Library Association*, Vol. III (1882), pp. 71, 90.

[Country Life

10. CHETHAM'S LIBRARY

The South Range, looking east into the reading room.
The gates were erected when chaining was abandoned
about 1745.

Chetham's Library

9. HUMPHREY CHETHAM

An engraving by Charles Pye from a drawing by Henry
Wyatt. The original painting (artist unknown) is in
Chetham's Library.

11. ONE OF THE TREASURES OF THE OLD NORWICH CITY LIBRARY
A page of the Wyclif Bible, now at the St. Peter Hungate Church Museum.

returned damaged, and the whole if they were not returned on time. Finally he must present to the library a well-bound copy of his book when published. Whether any would-be author ever took advantage of these privileges does not appear, but this and other instances of special concessions to authors[1] were clearly an attempt to provide for what was regarded as an important problem.

Witham in Essex had a church lending library as early as 1751, and Maidstone by 1755.[2] At King's Cliffe in Northamptonshire the library was founded in 1752 by William Law, author of the *Serious Call* and a native of that place: it was in a house in the village which still bears the inscription: "Books of Piety are here lent to any Persons of this or ye Neighbouring Towns." At Bamburgh Castle the library established in 1778 was open to readers (according to the rules drawn up in 1810) on Saturdays from 10 to 1, and books might be borrowed by any well-known housekeeper living within twenty miles of the castle, and any clergyman of any denomination holding a benefice within the same area.

Another means by which town and parochial libraries became available to a wider public was through the formation of subscription libraries. This device was sometimes adopted by groups of clergy to improve the library stock and keep it up to date, but in several instances the laity also participated. All the early examples come from the East of England. The arrangement just mentioned at Spalding, in 1637, was an approach to the idea of a subscription library, and the conversion of the Norwich town library to a subscription basis in 1656 marks the emergence of the idea in an almost fully developed form, though at this stage it was mainly the clergy who took advantage of it, and it was not until 1716 that subscribers were permitted to borrow books.[3] In the meantime the Spalding plan was carried a stage further at St. John's, Bedford, where a library was founded in 1700 by the contributions of gentry and clergy for the use of the rector and his successors, and it was provided that

---

[1] See below, pp. 98, 111.

[2] The Maidstone parish library was founded in or before 1716, and greatly augmented in 1735 by books from the library of Dr. Thomas Bray. A borrowers' book, still surviving, begins in 1755 and ends in 1871, four years after the transfer of the books to Maidstone Museum, where they now are.   [3] See above, p. 74.

all present and future contributors to the value of 10s. should be entitled to borrow. At Spalding itself, in 1712, a Gentlemen's Society was formed "for the supporting of mutual Benevolence, and their Improvement in the Liberal Sciences and Polite Learning".[1] This Society, which met weekly for discussion and the reading of papers, had resort for books to the old parochial library, and every new member was required to present a book by way of entrance fee.

An almost identical arrangement was adopted at Wisbech, where the town library, founded in 1653 or 1654, was "in a Manner quite neglected, till the Year 1712, when some of the Neighbouring Clergy and Gentlemen, considering the Advantage of Parochial Libraries, formed themselves into a Club or Society, and agreed annually to contribute Twenty Shillings each to buy Books".[2] At Doncaster a similar society, the Society of the Clergy of Doncaster, which was founded in 1714 and included some of the local gentry among its members, established a library in the parish church with the Vicar of Doncaster as librarian. In 1726 this was erected into "a common public library", and any person contributing to the value of 20s. was permitted to use the books, but books might be borrowed only on deposit of a sum equal to their value. Three months were allowed for reading a folio, two months for a quarto, and one month for smaller books, but anyone engaged on literary work might borrow up to six books for four months.[3] Just about the same time, on the initiative of a local member of Parliament, Charles Gray, the old Harsnett Library at Colchester was moved to the castle and made the nucleus of a clerical subscription library, on book club lines, with the title Castle Society Book Club.[4]

It should be emphasized that the examples here given of new

---

[1] J. Nichols, *Literary Anecdotes of the Eighteenth Century*, Vol. VI, Pt. I (1812), p. 28.
[2] *A Catalogue of Books in the Parochial Library at Wisbech* (1718), Preface, quoted in *Report from the Select Committee on Public Libraries* (1849), p. 225.
[3] These rules are very similar to those adopted a few years earlier for the S.P.C.K. diocesan lending libraries in Wales. See below, p. 111.
[4] T. Cromwell, *History of Colchester* (1825), Vol. II, p. 344, says the Club was at that time "nearly of a hundred years' standing". For the foundation of the Harsnett Library see above, p. 75, and for the book club type of organization, below, p. 136.

developments concerned only a small number of libraries, mostly in the towns. The majority of endowed libraries continued along traditional lines, and by the end of the eighteenth century the older ones were mostly in a state of decay. None the less it is interesting to observe how some at least of these old libraries were steadily evolving in the direction of public libraries. They were becoming lending libraries, they were ceasing to be exclusively religious, they were ceasing to be exclusively for the use of the clergy. The trouble was, of course, that most of them were still clerical libraries, or at best scholars' libraries, and not suited to the use of a wider public.

THE LATER ENDOWED LIBRARIES OF SCOTLAND

In Scotland, as in England, in spite of the very different religious setting, we find signs of renewed activity in the formation of endowed libraries from the late seventeenth century onwards, though the number of such libraries continued to be relatively small.

The first example is to be found in far-away Kirkwall, capital of Orkney. In spite of their remoteness, the Orcadians of this period were far from uncivilized. Kirkwall had a grammar school, an English school, a commercial school, a music school, and a dancing school, and through its trading contacts with the Continent was familiar with such luxuries as tea and wine. William Baikie, a landowner on the island of Stronsay, and a burgess of Kirkwall, was a graduate of the University of Edinburgh and a great reader and collector of books. On his death in 1683 he bequeathed the bulk of his library, to the number of eight score volumes, to the minister of Kirkwall and his successors, "to be keepte and used be him for a publick liberarie as said is, within the Town of Kirkwall".[1] The books were, as usual, mainly religious in character, but the value attached to the library is attested by the fact that in 1738 at least one neighbouring parish (Stenness, about ten miles away) was contributing to its support from the "burse money", i.e. from

---

[1] It was in these terms that the minister presented the books to the Presbytery in 1684. The will merely states that the books shall be for the use of the minister and his successors. See Introduction to J. B. Craven, *Descriptive Catalogue of the Bibliotheck of Kirkwall* (Kirkwall 1897), pp. vii–viii, x.

an assessment on the local landowners. "Burse money to the Bibliotheck of Kirkwall for the year 1738, 10s.", reads the entry in the Kirk Session Register of the parish. This is an interesting early instance of support for a library from public funds.[1]

At Lord Madertie's estate at Innerpeffray, in Perthshire, was a library which, though not parochial, was similar in purpose. It was founded and endowed, "for the benefit and encouragement of young students",[2] under a bequest by David Drummond, the third Lord Madertie, who died in 1694 or soon after; and in the middle of the following century it was enriched and housed in a special building by Robert Hay Drummond, afterwards Archbishop of York. From at least 1747 it was a lending library, and although the number of loans was not large at this period (an average of twenty-eight per annum for the years 1747–1800), the variety of occupations referred to in the loans register shows that it was used not only by students but by people from a great variety of occupations. A list compiled by Dr. Kaufman includes: "barber, bookseller, army captain, cooper, dyer, dyer apprentice, factor, farmer, flaxdresser, gardener, glover, mason, merchant, miller, minister, quarrier, schoolmaster, servant, shoemaker, student (of humanity, divinity, philosophy), smith, surgeon, surgeon apprentice, tailor, watchmaker, weaver, wright."[3] It seems unlikely that such a list could be matched anywhere south of the Border at this time, and it is interesting to note that eleven of the borrowers were women.

The most popular work was William Robertson's *History of Charles V*, which is not surprising since this work by the Principal of Edinburgh University was a best-seller of the day. Other works in considerable demand included sermons by various authors, Mosheim's *Ecclesiastical History*, Locke's *Works*, Buffon's *Natural History*, the *Universal History*, and the *Monthly*

---

[1] The County Librarian of Orkney, Mr. Evan McGillivray, who has given me much assistance in my inquiries, has kindly drawn my attention to this entry. He points out that the local lairds, who had to be merchants as well because their rents were paid in kind, were all burgesses of Kirkwall, and many of them maintained a house in the town.

[2] W. M. Dickie, "Innerpeffray Library", in *Library Association Record*, N.S. Vol. VI (1928), p. 101.

[3] P. Kaufman, "A Unique Record of a People's Reading", in *Libri*, Vol. XIV (1964), p. 231.

Review.[1] No deposit seems to have been called for, but each borrower had to give a written undertaking to return the borrowed volume within a specified period.

In the first half of the eighteenth century libraries are recorded at Rothesay, where the minister had a small collection of books bequeathed in 1702 by Archibald Graham, the last Bishop of the Isles;[2] at Lochmaben in Dumfriesshire, where in 1726 James Richardson of Reading (a native of the nearby village of Hightae) bequeathed £100 for the maintenance of a house and library he had provided for the master of the Grammar School; at Haddington, which in 1729 acquired a valuable library of over 1,300 volumes bequeathed by John Gray, an ejected Presbyterian minister; and at Logie near Cupar, where about 1750 Walter Bowman, laird of the parish, left a library for the benefit of the gentlemen of the parish, with the stipulation that "a bason of water and a towel" should be provided in the library room for their use.[3] In 1711 the town council of Dunfermline put forward a proposal for a burgh library, and voted £10 "for the encouragement of so good and pious a design",[4] but nothing seems to have come of it.

There may well have been other Scottish libraries of which the story has not yet come to light, but that wonderful parish-by-parish record, the *Statistical Account of Scotland*, edited by Sir John Sinclair and published during the years 1791–99, does not suggest that even at that period parochial libraries were very numerous. From Campbeltown, in Argyllshire, we have an account of a recently established parish subscription library:

"A library, consisting of religious tracts and sacred writings, has also lately been set on foot by one of the clergymen, who expects much good from his institution. The books are, with little trouble, handed to such persons as attend for the purpose of reading between sermons. Every reader, or sharer in this compilation, pays only 1s. *per annum*; and it is intended, when the institution can afford it, to give the use of the books, that have been for the greatest length of time in the circle, to such of the poor, as may wish to read them, *gratis*. Books

---

[1] *Op. cit.*, p. 229.
[2] The books were available for the use of all in the parish.
[3] A. Anderson, *The Old Libraries of Fife* (Fife County Library 1953), p. 2. The library was lodged in the laird's house.
[4] *Op. cit.*, p. 1. Cf. E. Henderson, *The Annals of Dunfermline*, (Glasgow 1879), p. 388.

of controversy (which are read with such avidity by the common
people in Scotland) are carefully excluded from this collection, as the
fruit which they produce is bitter. The ancient martyr said, he could
either live or die for Christ, but could not dispute for him. In our
times the reverse of this is more commonly the case."[1]

From Tranent, in East Lothian, it was reported that a library
had recently been founded for the use of the parish. It had fewer
than 200 volumes, and "the increase, in great measure, depends
on the countenance and support of the more opulent ranks".[2]
At Wilton in Roxburghshire the parson had found it useful to
lend books to his parishioners, and thought parish libraries
would meet a great need.[3] None of these late eighteenth-
century enterprises survived long enough to be recorded in the
New Statistical Account of 1845.[4]

The closing decades of the century also saw, however, the
foundation of two town libraries. At Glasgow, in 1791, Walter
Stirling, merchant, bequeathed to the Lord Provost and his
successors, the sum of £1,000, and certain property, "for the
sole and only purpose of purchasing a Library, and supporting
a Librarian for taking charge of the books which may belong to
me at my death, as well as those which may be purchased in
future, from the fund above-mentioned". The Lord Provost and
twelve other Directors, chosen by the Town Council, the
Presbytery, the Merchants' House, and the Faculty of Medicine,
were empowered to make regulations, provided that no regulations should be made inconsistent with the primary purpose of
the gift, "viz. the constant and perpetual existence of a Public
Library for the Citizens of Glasgow".[5]

The Select Committee on Public Libraries, in 1849, commented that Glasgow had a free public library, "to which it
appears that the public, for some not very easily discoverable
reason, do not resort".[6] The reason, however, is not very far to
seek, for the sum bequeathed was not really sufficient to

---

[1] *Statistical Account*, Vol. X (1794), p. 561.
[2] *Op. cit.*, Vol. X, p. 99.
[3] *Op. cit.*, Vol. XV (1795), p. 641.
[4] A parish subscription library at Holywood, Dumfriesshire, however,
finds a mention there (Vol. IV, Dumfriesshire, p. 566). It seems to have
been founded about 1796.
[5] The will is printed in T. Mason, *Public and Private Libraries of Glasgow*
(Glasgow 1885), pp. 36–43.
[6] *Report*, p. vi.

maintain a librarian and provide for the increase of the library, and the Directors accordingly restricted its use to those paying a substantial life subscription – a subscription which began at £3 3s. but at one time rose as high as £10 10s. The result was that although by the mid-nineteenth century a library of over 11,000 books had been assembled, it was not up to this time extensively used. From the reminiscences of one who knew the library in its early days, however, we have an interesting impression of two of its early librarians. The first, Dr. William Taylor, a local minister, used "to give out books by armfuls, and he was not very particular about the period when they were returned, for the longer they were kept out so much less trouble was it to him".[1] Rev. James Pate, who succeeded him, was by contrast exceedingly conscientious: he used to examine every returned book leaf by leaf, and proceed at once to the repair of any damage. "I have seen ladies stand trembling from top to toe under the scolds of Mr. Peat [*sic*], for having returned valuable books a little soiled, or with a slight spot of ink upon them."[2]

The Stirling Library was united in 1871 with the Glasgow Public [Subscription] Library, formed in 1804.

Linlithgow also had a collection of books, bequeathed to the Town Council and Presbytery in 1790 by Dr. Robert Henry, an Edinburgh minister, in the hope that in course of time "a Library might at last be created, which should contribute to the diffusion of knowledge and literature".[3] The terms of the bequest were, however, rather peculiar. Members of the Council and Presbytery were to enjoy the use of the library for a subscription of 5s. per annum, and members of the Presbytery were to have the first reading of all new books. Others were to pay 10s. per annum, and take their turn. "Such a constitution", as the minister of Linlithgow remarked in the *New Statistical Account* in 1845,[4] "could scarcely be expected to insure prosperity", and in fact by that time the library was "completely neglected,

---

[1] Mason, *op. cit.*, p. 62.
[2] J. S. Paterson, *Stirling's and Glasgow Public Library, 1791–1907* (Glasgow 1907), p. 7. This and the previous quotation are from the reminiscences of "Senex" (Robert Reid).
[3] Edwards, *Memoirs of Libraries* (1859), Vol. II, p. 43.
[4] Vol. II, Linlithgowshire, p. 185.

the books being left to decay on the shelves, without one single reader". It was destroyed by a fire at the Town Hall in the same year.

One other library of this period does not fit into any of the established categories. It was founded by that eccentric Scottish judge, Lord Gardenstone, in a new village which he established, from 1765 onwards, at Laurencekirk in Kincardineshire. Here he erected, we are told, "an elegant inn, with a library of books adjoining it, chiefly for the use of travellers who may stop there".[1] Evidently the villagers were also intended to have the use of it, for Gardenstone referred to it as "the Public Library of Laurencekirk".[2] Dr. Johnson, who visited the inn in 1773, "praised the design, but wished there had been more books".[3] After Gardenstone's death in 1793 the project was allowed to lapse, but 200 volumes found their way in 1870 to the Brechin Diocesan Library, and thence eventually to the library of University College, Dundee.

THE BRAY LIBRARIES

From the beginning of the eighteenth century a very substantial addition to the number of parish libraries was brought about on the initiative of Dr. Thomas Bray. Most of these Bray libraries, as they are called, were exclusively for the clergy, but within their limits they were very important, and by the end of the century they were, in England and Wales, very nearly as numerous as all the other parish libraries together. A notable feature of Bray's work, moreover, was the special encouragement he gave to lending libraries: in 1700, as we have seen, such libraries were still rare.

Bray was Rector of Sheldon in Warwickshire from 1690 to 1729, and of St. Botolph's Aldgate, from 1706 until his death in 1730. In 1695 he was asked by the Bishop of London to undertake the organization of the Anglican Church in Maryland, and it was in this connection that he first became aware of the

---

[1] Sir J. Sinclair (ed.), *Statistical Account of Scotland*, Vol. V (1792), p. 178.
[2] *New Statistical Account of Scotland* (1845), Vol. XI, Kincardineshire, p. 150.
[3] J. Boswell, *Journal of a Tour to the Hebrides* (3rd edn. 1786), 21st August, 1773.

overriding need for the clergy to be adequately supplied with books. His first efforts were directed towards provision for the clergy of Maryland, but it was not long before he turned his attention nearer home.

In his *Essay towards promoting all Necessary and Useful Knowledge, both Divine and Human, in all parts of his Majesty's Dominions* (1697), Bray set out a plan for providing a lending library in each deanery in England, with books to the value of £30 paid for by local subscriptions. These libraries were to be located in market towns, for the use of both clergy and gentry. Later he made proposals for smaller libraries of catechetical works for country clergy, and for laymen's libraries to be administered by the clergy for the use of the parishioners. All these ideas, in Bray's mind, were linked together as part of a general plan for reviving the pastoral activity of the Church. In 1699, as we have observed above, he was largely instrumental in founding the Society for Promoting Christian Knowledge, for missionary work at home and abroad, and this body proved a powerful ally in the implementation of his library schemes.

There was nothing absolutely new in Bray's proposals, but his propaganda and his powers of organization undoubtedly gave a new impetus and a new direction to the movement for the establishment of religious libraries. He probably did more than any other man to popularize the idea of lending libraries, and he did a valuable service in drawing attention to the special needs of the poorer country clergy. There were, he pointed out, 500 parishes in England and Wales in which the annual income was less than £10, and 2,000 in which it was less than £30. In such cases the need for books was urgent, but apart from a small-scale effort in the diocese of Carlisle, where in 1685 Rev. Barnabas Oley bequeathed money to provide sixteen volumes of divinity for each of ten poor vicarages, nothing specific had been done to meet it.

The so-called "Bray Libraries" were founded by a variety of different agencies, including Bray himself, and this has given rise to a good deal of confusion. It is essential, in order to get a clear picture, to distinguish these agencies, and also to distinguish between lending libraries, strategically situated so as to be within reach of the clergy of a region, and fixed or parochial libraries, designed for the use of a single incumbent and usually located in the remoter rural areas.[1]

Bray's own first efforts were directed towards the formation of lending libraries. In the course of collecting funds for libraries for the clergy in Maryland, he found many people who were more interested in providing for the needs of the clergy at home. He at once seized the opportunity, and immediately after the publication of his *Essay* of 1697 he seems to have set to work to implement the scheme there adumbrated for a lending library in every deanery.[2] In his accounts for 1695–99 he records grants totalling £107 10s. towards the establishment of thirty-six lending libraries in Montgomeryshire and sixteen English counties.[3] The sums mentioned, however, ranging from £1 to £10 per library, can only have been grants in aid, and we must suppose that the bulk of the funds came from local resources. His activities in this direction are illustrated by his auto-biographical account of his voyage to Maryland in 1699–1700. Leaving London in December 1699, he travelled by way of Gravesend and Deal to Plymouth, and in each of these places he provided books for a lending library, and made arrangements for a subscription to be raised for its enlargement. At Plymouth there was already a small library, with some excellent books, but "covered with dust and overwhelmed with rubbish". Bray enlisted the help of the Mayor to have it cleaned up and rendered serviceable again.[4]

[1] In my study of the early history of the Bray libraries I have been particularly indebted to the generous assistance of Mr. A. E. Barker of the S.P.C.K. and Mrs. Belle Pridmore of the U.S.P.G.
[2] See *Publick Spirit illustrated in the Life and Designs of the Reverend Thomas Bray* (2nd edn. 1808), pp. 17–19.
[3] *Dr. Bray's Accounts*, (MS. in the archives of the United Society for the Propagation of the Gospel), Copy A, ff. 46–50. Among the more important English towns listed are Carlisle, Nantwich, Warwick, Coventry, Ludlow, Bromsgrove, Andover, Gravesend, Deal, Huntingdon, Northampton, and Gainsborough. Most of these libraries have vanished without trace, but some can apparently be identified with libraries listed in Central Council for the Care of Churches, *Parochial Libraries of England and Wales* (1959). See for details below, App. III(b).
[4] The relevant parts of this account, which survives in MS. at Sion College, are printed in G. Smith, "Dr. Thomas Bray", in *Library Association Record*, Vol. XII (1910), pp. 250–2. Cf. H. P. Thompson, *Thomas Bray* (1954), pp. 44–45, and for Plymouth the letter of John Gilbert, 23rd April, 1700, in S.P.C.K. MSS., *Correspondence*, File I, f. 88. Plymouth

From 1699 onwards Bray's efforts were reinforced by the creation of the S.P.C.K., many of whose correspondents, as the early records of the Society show, took an active interest in the promotion of lending libraries, e.g. at Reigate.[1] In 1702 the S.P.C.K. appointed a committee "to consider of Dr. Bray's Proposals . . . for the more effective promotion of Lending Libraries".[2] In the event the Society limited its official activity in this field to the promotion of lending libraries in Wales. This was done through a Standing Committee which was set up in 1705, and which was responsible for the establishment, during the years 1708 to 1711, of a clerical lending library in each of the four Welsh dioceses, namely at Bangor, St. Asaph, Carmarthen (for St. David's), and Cowbridge (for Llandaff).

Bray was equally active in promoting the establishment of fixed parochial libraries. Five or six parishes, including his own parishes of Sheldon and St. Botolph's, received libraries through his personal gift or bequest, and another twenty-two, in addition to sixteen in the Isle of Man, were aided with grants ranging from 15s. to £6.[3] Not surprisingly, he paid particular attention to the parishes he knew in his native county of Shropshire and the neighbouring county of Montgomeryshire. The main task of creating parochial libraries, however, was committed by Bray to a special committee, established in 1705, known as the

---

is not among the thirty-six lending libraries listed in Bray's accounts.

The Associates of Dr. Bray later advanced the claim that he had founded sixty-seven catechetical lending libraries in England and Wales, besides sixteen in the Isle of Man, but apart from the exaggeration involved in the use of the word "founded", the figures are suspect. The libraries in the Isle of Man, certainly, were not lending libraries but fixed parochial libraries (see below). The statement appears in *An Account of the Design of the Associates of the late Dr. Bray* (1762), and is repeated in subsequent reports.

See above, p. 94, and for Bray's personal interest in Reigate, G. Smith, "Dr. Thomas Bray", in *Library Association Record*, Vol. XII (1910), pp. 254–5. The Minutes of the S.P.C.K. for 1698–1704 have been edited by E. McClure under the title *A Chapter in English Church History* (1888).

[2] *Minutes of General Meeting*, 2nd February, 1702.

[3] *Dr. Bray's Accounts*, Copy A, ff. 51–52. See below, App. III(b). The history of libraries in the Isle of Man does not form part of this study. Bray's work there was carried out in collaboration with his friend Bishop Thomas Wilson, and the Convocation of the Diocese officially recorded its thanks to him in 1725. See the life of Wilson by John Keble prefixed to his *Works* (1863), Vol. I, pp. 148–9 and Vol. II, p. 642.

13. LEWISHAM LIBRARY BOOKPLATE

12. BRAY LIBRARY BOOKPLATE

Trustees for Erecting Parochial Libraries and Promoting other Charitable Designs. Many of the members were also members of the S.P.C.K., and this overlap of membership, together with the fact that Henry Newman was Secretary of both bodies, has led to the mistaken belief that the Trustees formed a standing committee of the Society. Newman himself explained the situation in a letter to a correspondent in Lewes, 2nd July, 1713:

"I must acquaint you that the Design of Paroch. Libs, is not carried on by the Society at Bartlet's Buildings [i.e. the S.P.C.K.], but by another Body of men, most of whom are indeed of the Society but act in this thing independently."[1]

By the time of Bray's death in 1730 the Trustees had established at least fifty-six libraries in England, and ten in Wales and Monmouthshire.[2] All these went to livings of less than £30 per annum. In 1725, for example, the curate of Flookburgh, an obscure village in North Lancashire, received an oak cupboard containing some seventy calf-bound volumes of divinity, sent to him at the request of Sir Thomas Lowther. "I wish", wrote Newman, "You may long enjoy the Effect of Sir Thomas's Kindness to You, which must be an agreeable Companion to a Man of Letters destitute of Books in a Solitary Country. . . . "[3]

These libraries cost rather more than £20 apiece, and of this sum the incumbent was expected to raise £5 from local sources. Very often, as in the case just quoted, the money was contributed by a single benefactor.

After Bray's death the work of promoting both lending and parochial libraries was transferred to a trust known as the Associates of Dr. Bray, originally formed in 1723 to administer a bequest for work with negroes in the British plantations. It was not until mid-century that the Associates began to interest themselves actively in this branch of their work, but in a sudden

---

[1] S.P.C.K. MSS., *Correspondence.* A similar letter from Newman to another correspondent, 26th January, 1713, adds that the Society has limited its activities to the provision of four diocesan lending libraries in Wales.

[2] These are the libraries referred to in Central Council for the Care of Churches, *op. cit.*, pp. 23–24, and incorrectly described as "S.P.C.K. libraries" in the alphabetical list that follows. There may have been more, e.g. the library at Oxford referred to on p. 112 of the same work. See below, App. III(d).

[3] Central Council for the Care of Churches, *op. cit.*, p. 32.

outburst of activity between 1753 and 1768 they founded a dozen lending libraries and more than seventy parochial libraries – the latter for the most part in the rural parishes of Wales and the north of England. After 1768 the work went on at a slower pace, with the Associates concentrating their main attention on lending libraries, which they considered more extensively useful.[1] By the end of the century they had established, in all, more than one hundred libraries, and the total number of Bray libraries in Great Britain, including those established by Bray personally, by the S.P.C.K., by the Trustees for Parochial Libraries, and by the Associates, was nearing the 200 mark, besides nearly sixty others which Bray had assisted with grants.

THE BRAY LIBRARIES IN WALES

The Bray libraries were particularly important for Wales, where the clergy were poor and often ill educated, and the majority of the people, until Rev. Griffith Jones of Llanddowror launched his great charity school movement in the 1730s, were still quite illiterate. At the beginning of the century there were no parochial libraries of the English type, and as we have seen no cathedral libraries of any consequence either. Bray himself had made a beginning in the 1690s, by grants in aid of nine lending or parochial libraries in the border county of Montgomeryshire, but there is little evidence that anything came of these projects,[2] and the first Welsh library of any kind established in Wales seems to have been that at Presteigne, in Radnorshire, which according to the records of the S.P.C.K. was founded about 1707.[3]

The subsequent fate of this library is unknown, and it may be that it was superseded by the four diocesan lending libraries established by the S.P.C.K. itself in 1708–11.[4] These libraries

---

[1] See *An Account of the Designs of the Associates of the late Dr. Bray* (1762), pp. 6, 16–17, 22. According to the Rules here printed the lending libraries were to be "for the Use and Benefit of such Clergymen as shall be nominated thereto by the Trustees". Folios might be borrowed for six months, other books for three months, on deposit of the value of the book.

[2] See below, App. III(b).

[3] See below, App. II.

[4] See above, p. 107.

were especially valuable because they were larger than the ordinary Bray parochial libraries and the books could be borrowed by anyone living within ten miles who was either a clergyman, a schoolmaster, a trustee, or a contributor to the library of money or books to the value of 10s. Loans were normally for a month at a time (folio volumes two months), but those engaged in the production of "some useful book" might borrow up to six books for two months. Loans had to be accompanied by a deposit of a quarter more than the value of the books.[1]

At Cowbridge, in 1736, the local clergy formed a Book Society, with an annual subscription of 5s., to procure additional books for the diocesan library. After a decade of useful activity this seems to have faded out, and in 1764 a new Society was formed on a wider basis, "for the benefit of the Free-School and Town of Cowbridge and for the accommodation and entertainment of the Clergy, Gentlemen, and others of the County of Glamorgan willing and desirous to promote those purposes".[2] Even ladies were admitted to the use of this library, though not to membership. The subscription was one guinea for three years, and the Society had a spasmodic existence until 1817, when it was in effect replaced by an independent body, the Cowbridge Clerical Book Club.

During the decade 1710–20 the Bray Trustees also gave some attention to Wales, founding six or seven parochial libraries in various parts of the country besides four in neighbouring Monmouthshire.[3] After this, however, there was a long gap until in the 1750s the Associates of Dr. Bray at last began to interest themselves actively in library provision. By this time the educational and religious revival resulting from Griffith Jones's work was at its height so the ministrations of the Associates were doubly welcome. In all, between 1757 and 1800, they established in Wales and Monmouthshire sixteen lending libraries and thirty-six parochial libraries, their period of greatest activity being during the years 1765 to 1768, when

---

[1] The arrangements for these libraries are described in detail in M.
[2] Tallon, *Church in Wales Diocesan Libraries* (Athlone 1962), pp. 9–19.
[3] E. Lewis, "The Cowbridge Diocesan Library, 1711–1848", in *Journ. of the Hist. Soc. of the Church in Wales*, Vol. VII (1957), p. 84.
  See below, App. III(d).

through the agency of Howell Howell, Vicar of Llanboldy in Carmarthenshire, thirty-four libraries of about thirty-six volumes each were distributed to poor clergy in Carmarthenshire, Pembrokeshire and Cardiganshire.[1]

John Vaughan of Derllys in Carmarthenshire, one of the leading Welsh supporters of the S.P.C.K., was not satisfied with the distribution of books for the clergy. In July, 1706, he wrote to the Society to desire "that the Inhabitants of every parish may have the perusal of the Books in the Welsh Libraries, as well as the Clergy and Schoolmasters, and more especially Housekeepers, they giving sufficient pledges to return all they borrow without damage".[2] This forward-looking policy was not adopted, but the need for a wider provision was real. Later in the century John Griffith or Griffiths, vicar of Llandyssilio on the border of Carmarthenshire and Pembrokeshire, found an answer to the problem by lending books from his own library. Griffiths received a Bray library in 1766, but he already had a private library of over 800 books and pamphlets, and in 1770 he threw this open to borrowers and commenced a list of "Books lended" which continues to 1796. During these years he made many hundreds of loans; on 16th February, 1774, he recorded that "106 books, or more", were out on loan. Where the borrowers are identifiable they are often ministers, schoolmasters, or gentry, but there were many humbler people, men and women, to take advantage of his generosity, as the following entries indicate:

" 'Gospel Sonnet', with Wm. Harry's maid."
" 'The Welchman's Candle', with Griffith, ye taylor."
" 'Hanes y ffyd', with Thomas Jenkin; and a book with his journeyman."[3]

---

[1] U.S.P.G. MSS., *Catalogues of Books for Home and Foreign Libraries A.D. 1753 to A.D. 1817.*

[2] M. Clement (ed.), *Correspondence and Minutes of the S.P.C.K. relating to Wales, 1699–1740* (Cardiff 1952), p. 260. Three years later Vaughan was urging the Society to encourage all parents, "and especially those of estate and abilitie", to bestow a small library of "good practical books" on each of their children (*op. cit.*, p. 21).

[3] G. E. Evans, "John Griffiths, Clericus: his Curious Register and Diary", in *Trans. Carmarthenshire Antiq. Soc. and Field Club*, Vol. II (1906–07), p. 193.

14. THOMAS BRAY

From a portrait by an unknown artist.

15. A LADY COMING FROM THE CIRCULATING LIBRARY
From a London print of 1781.

THE KIRKWOOD LIBRARIES

The Bray library scheme did not extend to Scotland,[1] but a similar scheme was operated for the Highlands at the instance of James Kirkwood, an ejected episcopalian minister. Taking refuge in England, Kirkwood served for a time as rector of Astwick in Bedfordshire, was again ejected, this time as a non-juror, in 1702, and became in the following year Scottish correspondent of the S.P.C.K. His first plan for libraries, propounded in his *Overture for Founding and Maintaining of Bibliothecks in every Paroch throughout this Kingdom* (1699), was even more ambitious than the original proposals of Bray, for it envisaged a free public lending library in each parish, furnished "not only with all the valuable and useful Old Books in any Art or Science, but also with all the valuable New Books, so soon as even they are heard of or seen in the World'.[2] The scheme had many impracticable features, and it is not necessary to enter into all the details, but it is of interest to note that it was to be financed by an annual levy on the minister and the heritors (landholders) of the parish; that the schoolmaster or reader was to act as librarian; and that the books were to be available on loan up to one month to ministers of the presbytery, heritors of the parish, and such other parishioners as could find sufficient caution.

Kirkwood has been called "the father of free libraries", and although it will be seen that his proposals differ in scale rather than in principle from what was already being done in England, it is probably true that he was the first to set out the case for such libraries on grounds of general public utility. It was, he argued, God's will that we should "search out and know all his wonderful Works". The pursuit of knowledge, however, was beset by many difficulties, for "books are so vastly multiplied, and do so encrease dayly", and the difficulty and cost of procuring them are so great, that no student can hope to procure

---

[1] An exception was Ballachulish, where a Bray library was founded in 1840 (see below, p. 202). In 1728 a library was conditionally allocated to Edinburgh University, and another to the Scottish Highlands, but there is no record that these proposals were implemented.

[2] *Overture*, p. 5. The original of this work is exceedingly scarce, but there is a reprint in a limited edition, with a preface by William Blades, privately printed in 1889.

all the books he needs. "Therefore", he concludes, "compleat and free Libraries are absolutely necessary for the Improving of Arts and Sciences, and for Advancing of Learning amongst us."[1]

Kirkwood's first plan was ignored by the Church Assembly, but a more modest scheme for the Highlands only met with a better reception, especially as Kirkwood succeeded in collecting, with the help of his S.P.C.K. friends in England, books and contributions to the value of over £650 towards putting it into practice. The upshot was that in 1704–08 the Assembly distributed seventy-seven libraries among the presbyteries and parishes of the Highlands and Islands. These were small but well-chosen collections, scholarly but not exclusively theological in character, and the books might be borrowed by any Protestant on deposit of one quarter more than their value. Unfortunately the matter ended there. Kirkwood himself died in 1709, and although the Assembly in that year urged all presbyteries which had not received libraries to raise a public subscription for the purpose, no further official assistance was given, with the result that the libraries gradually became out of date and fell into disuse. By 1826 most of them had disappeared.

One Kirkwood library at least found its way to the Lowlands. This was at Dumfries, where a presbytery library was received in 1706. Augmented in 1712 by the bequest of the library of Dr. John Hutton, M.P. for Dumfries, and housed from 1730 in its own building, this library continued in active use throughout most of the century, and from 1736 at least laymen were permitted to use it for a small fee. It is now in Edinburgh.[2]

THE FIRST LIBRARY ACT

An interesting by-product of the activity of Bray and the S.P.C.K. was an Act for the Preservation of Parochial Libraries, passed in 1709. This is the first example of library legislation in this country, and begins:

" 'Whereas in many Places . . . the Provision for the Clergy is so mean, that the necessary Expense of Books for the better Prosecution

[1] *Op. cit.*, pp. 5–6.
[2] G. W. Shirley, "Dumfriesshire Libraries", in *Scottish Adult Education*, No. 26 (August 1959), p. 17.

of their Studies cannot be defrayed by them; and whereas of late Years, several charitable and well-disposed Persons have by charitable Contributions erected Libraries within several Parishes and Districts in *England* and *Wales;* but some Provision is wanting to preserve the same, and such others as shall be provided in the same Manner, from Embezilment'; Be it therefore enacted . . . that every Parish or Place where such a Library is or shall be erected, the same shall be preserved for such Use and Users, as the same is and shall be given, and the Orders and Rules of the Founder and Founders of such Libraries shall be observed and kept."[1]

This Act, which went on to make provision for the care of the libraries and for their transfer on a change of incumbent, was clearly intended to cover not only the Bray libraries but all parish libraries for the clergy; and with a minor amendment in 1938 it is still on the statute-book.[2]

[1] 7 Anne c. 14, reprinted in Central Council for the Care of Churches, *op. cit.,* pp. 48–50. Cf. p. 60.
[2] A good instance of how the act was used in the case of a non-Bray library is to be found in the rules of the Henley Parochial Library, 1777, in J. S. Burn, *History of Henley-on-Thames* (1861), pp. 104–7.

Bibliographical Note

In addition to the general references given at the conclusion of the last chapter, the following accounts of individual town and parish libraries may be consulted:

Bamburgh: A. I. Doyle, "The Bamburgh Library", in *Book Collector,* Vol. VIII (1959).

Bedford: H. M. Walton, "The Old Bedford Library", in *Library Association Record,* 4th Ser., Vol. II (1935).

Doncaster: J. Ballinger, "An Old Doncaster Library", in W. Smith (ed.), *Old Yorkshire,* Vol. III (1882).

London: Dr. Williams's Trust, *A Short Account of the Charity and Library established under the Will of the late Rev. Daniel Williams* (1917); P. A. Hoare, *Archbishop Tenison's Library* (Dip. Lib. thesis, Univ. Coll. London 1963).

Maldon: S. G. Deed (ed.), *Catalogue of the Plume Library* (Maldon 1959).

Newcastle: W. J. Haggerston, "The Thomlinson Library, Newcastle-upon-Tyne", in *Monthly Notes of the Library Association,* Vol. III (1882).

Preston: J. A. Downton, *Dr. Shepherd's Library, Preston* (Harris Library, Preston 1961).

Skipton: P. S. Baldwin, *The Petyt Library, Skipton* (F.L.A. thesis 1957, Lib. Assoc.); *A Catalogue of the Petyt Library* (Coulthurst Trust, Gargrave 1964).

Spalding: J. Nichols, *Literary Anecdotes of the Eighteenth Century* (6 v. 1812), Vol. VI, Pt. I.

Tong: J. E. Auden, "The Minister's Library in Tong Church", in *Transactions of the Shropshire Archaeological Society*, 4th Ser., Vol. XII (1929–30).

The thesis by W. R. Aitken cited at the end of the previous chapter gives a general account of the Scottish libraries, and many interesting details are to be found in Sir John Sinclair (ed.), *Statistical Account of Scotland* (21 v. Edinburgh 1791–99), and the *New Statistical Account of Scotland* (15 v. Edinburgh 1845). For individual libraries see:

Glasgow: T. Mason, *Public and Private Libraries of Glasgow* (Glasgow 1885), Ch. i; W. J. S. Patterson, *Stirling's and Glasgow Public Library* (Glasgow 1907).

Haddington: W. J. Couper, *The Gray Library, Haddington* (Haddington 1916); W. F. Gray, *Catalogue of the Library of John Gray, Haddington* (Haddington 1929).

Innerpeffray: Innerpeffray Library and Chapel: a Historical Sketch (1916, 3rd edn. Innerpeffray 1960); W. M. Dickie, "Innerpeffray Library", in *Library Association Record*, N.S. Vol. VI (1928); P. Kaufman, "A Unique Record of a People's Reading", in *Libri*, Vol. XIV (1964).

Kirkwall: J. B. Craven, *Descriptive Catalogue of the Bibliotheck of Kirkwall* (Kirkwall 1897), Introduction.

There is no satisfactory general account of the Bray libraries, the records of which are in the archives of the Society for Promoting Christian Knowledge and the United Society for the Propagation of the Gospel. They are included in the lists of parochial libraries cited at the end of the last chapter, and those established in Bray's lifetime are fully dealt with in Central Council for the Care of Churches, *Parochial Libraries of the Church of England* (1959) (but see above p. 109, note 2). The most comprehensive list, to 1807, is in *Publick Spirit illustrated in the Life and Designs of the Reverend Thomas Bray* (1746, 2nd edn. 1808). See also G. Smith, "Dr. Thomas Bray", in *Library Association Record*, Vol. XII (1910); H. P. Thompson, *Thomas Bray* (1954); and E. Lewis, "The Cowbridge Diocesan Library", in *Journal of the Historical Society of the Church in Wales*, Vols. IV (1954) and VII (1957).

J. Minto, *History of the Public Library Movement in Great Britain and Ireland* (1932), Ch. ii, gives a useful short account of James Kirkwood. See also D. Maclean, "Highland Libraries in the Eighteenth Century", in *Records of the Glasgow Bibliographical Society*, Vol. VII (1918–20). Extracts from Kirkwood's writings are printed in J. L. Thornton, *A Mirror for Librarians* (1948), Ch. iv.

CHAPTER VI

Early Subscription Libraries

THE CHANGING SOCIAL BACKGROUND

THE religious libraries described in the last three chapters – cathedral libraries, and endowed libraries designed mainly for the use of the clergy – were the only form of public library provision until the close of the seventeenth century, and continued to dominate the scene well into the eighteenth. This is not perhaps so surprising as might at first sight appear, for although the names of Shakespeare and Milton, Bacon and Newton, Hobbes and Locke, Clarendon and Fuller, bear witness to the striking development of secular literature in the seventeenth century, religious books still formed the largest single category of published works. Moreover, although thanks to the spread of education the ability to read was already in mid-century common in all but the humblest ranks of society,[1] only a very small minority of people, and that chiefly in London and the university towns, was really conversant with books and in the habit of regular reading. For the average country parson or schoolmaster a parish library of the kind described was probably more than adequate, and the occasional cultivated provincial gentleman or merchant would probably have a library of his own. The really surprising thing is that library provision was so utterly inadequate in London.[2]

The latter part of the seventeenth century, however, brought changes which prepared the way for a different attitude towards libraries in the following century. Education was advancing apace: by 1700 there were in England and Wales no fewer than 500 grammar schools, and 460 charity schools providing a more elementary education; while the dissenting academies, which

[1] In 1651 Parliament agreed to despatch to Cromwell's soldiers in Ireland "four thousand Bibles, or to every six men one . . . to reade in their tents or quarters" – C. H. Firth, *Cromwell's Army* (1902, 2nd edn. 1912), p. 314.
[2] See above, pp. 91–2.

came into existence after the Act of Uniformity of 1662, provided for the education of Nonconformist students excluded from the universities. Scotland had no need of dissenting academies, but it had its burgh schools (the equivalent of the English grammar schools) and in 1696 the Act for Settling of Schools laid the effective foundation for a system of parish schools which became justly famous.

Newspapers had their origins during the Civil War, and increased rapidly in number when government censorship was allowed to lapse in 1694. The first English provincial papers, the *Worcester Postman* and the *Norwich Post*, appeared in 1690 and 1695 respectively. The first Scottish newspaper to achieve any degree of permanence was the *Edinburgh Gazette*, which appeared in 1699. Coffee-houses, which were introduced during the Commonwealth and rapidly spread throughout the country – there were 2,000 in London alone by the end of the century – were also important agents for the dissemination of news and information; and public lectures on science made a modest beginning in London in the 1690s.

All these developments tended to encourage the growth of the reading public and an interest in secular subjects. In the eighteenth century the trend was accentuated. Charity schools, established in hundreds by the S.P.C.K. and allied agencies, increased the provision for elementary education; new grammar schools continued to be founded; and the dissenting academies became a powerful intellectual influence. Public lectures, literary, scientific and antiquarian societies, and debating clubs, all contributed to the diffusion of knowledge.

Newspapers and periodicals, in spite of heavy taxation, multiplied on every hand, and were widely circulated through the coffee-houses. Addison and Steele, first in the thrice-weekly *Tatler* (1709–11) and then in the daily *Spectator* (1711–14), introduced a new kind of literature, light, amusing, instructive, and immensely popular. The *Gentleman's Magazine* (a kind of eighteenth century *Reader's Digest*) started by Edward Cave, a journeyman printer, in 1731, was an immediate success, and was followed by the *Scots Magazine* in 1739. The novel, in the hands of Defoe, Richardson and Fielding, emerged for the first time as an important literary form, and quickly attracted many readers, especially among women of the leisured middle classes.

Johnson, in his wholesale way, remarked in 1781 that the English had become "a nation of readers",[1] and James Lackington, the London bookseller, declared ten years later: "all ranks and degrees now READ".[2] These statements cannot be taken literally, for the book-reading public was still small by modern standards, but it was certainly true that reading had increased to such a degree that authorship had now at last become a profession by which a man might make a living. It was also true that although London continued to dominate the cultural scene its dominance was no longer so marked as in earlier times. The dissenting academies were to be found not only in and around London but in places such as Bristol and Exeter, Manchester and Warrington, Abergavenny and Carmarthen. The lecture-courses in mathematics, chemistry and natural philosophy which became so popular in the capital, the literary, scientific and antiquarian societies, the debating clubs, had their counterparts in Manchester, Birmingham, Newcastle, Edinburgh, Glasgow, and other centres. By the end of the century all the important provincial towns had their local newspapers (usually weekly), and the Scottish capital had several.

One factor in all these developments, of course, was the growing economic importance of the provinces. The population of towns such as Manchester, Liverpool, Leeds, Sheffield, Birmingham, Nottingham, and Glasgow grew many-fold during the century – that of Manchester, to give just one example, jumped up from 8,000 to 95,000 – and the commercial and industrial middle classes, as they increased in wealth, came more and more to demand the cultural amenities of civilized life. "The several great cities", remarked the *Annual Register* of 1761, "and we might add many poor country towns, seem to be inspired with an ambition of becoming little Londons of the part of the Kingdom wherein they are situated."[3]

The emergence of women readers was a social phenomenon of the first importance. Lackington wrote:

[1] S. Johnson, *Lives of the Poets*, ed. G. B. Hill (Oxford 1905), Vol. III, p.19.
[2] J. Lackington, *Memoirs* (1791, 9th edn. 1794), p. 243.
[3] Quoted in A. S. Collins, *Authorship in the Days of Johnson* (1927), p. 247. This was so even in Wales, where the county towns "became in their own way little models of 'the town'" – C. Price, "Polite Life in Eighteenth-Century Wales", in *Yr Einion*, Vol. V (Cardiff, July 1953), p. 98.

"Ladies now in general read, not only novels, although many of that class are excellent productions, and tend to polish both the heart and the head; but they also read the best books in the English language, and many read the best works in various languages; and there are some thousands of ladies, who frequent my shop, that know as well what books to choose, and are as well acquainted with works of taste and genius, as any gentleman in the kingdom, notwithstanding they sneer against novel readers, etc."[1]

It was in these circumstances, and against this background, that the demand arose for secular literature, a demand which the old town and parish libraries, in spite of the broadening of their scope at this period, were quite unable to meet. Unfortunately books, though smaller in format than in the seventeenth century, were still expensive, and became more expensive still as time went on. In the last two decades of the century, especially, prices were practically doubled, so that a quarto work cost a guinea, an octavo 10s. or 12s., and a duodecimo 4s. per volume. This was not only because of the general rise in prices, but because most publishers preferred small editions at high prices to larger editions at cheaper rates.[2] Price apart, moreover, books were difficult to procure outside London, since local booksellers could not afford to carry large stocks, and ordering from the capital was slow and hazardous.

PRIVATE SUBSCRIPTION LIBRARIES

The answer to the needs created by these developments was found in the private or commercial subscription library. Much labour has been devoted to establishing the exact date in the eighteenth century at which private subscription originated, but we have seen that the idea of clubbing together to buy books, which was the basis of the system, was frequently adopted in connection with religious libraries from the mid-seventeenth century onwards.[3] We have also noted that the same principle was in use among the gentlemen's societies of the eastern

---

[1] Lackington, *op. cit.*, p. 251.

[2] R. D. Altick, *The English Common Reader* (Chicago 1957), p. 52.

[3] R. T. Gunther, in *Notes and Queries*, Ser. XIII, Vol. I (1923), pp. 483–4, draws attention to what may have been a very early subscription library or book club among a small group at Oxford in the early years of Elizabeth's reign.

counties and Yorkshire in the early part of the eighteenth
century, and that some of these, for example Spalding and
Wisbech, actually took over former parish libraries as a nucleus
for their collections.[1] Some of these gentlemen's societies were
indeed virtually subscription libraries. Of that at Peterborough,
formed about 1730, its founder Dr. Timothy Neve, a minor
canon of the cathedral, wrote in 1741:

"Since I came to settle in this place, I have instituted a Society of
Gentlemen, most of university education, who meet every Wednesday
evening, whereof the Dean is president, and myself secretary. We are
near 20 regular members, and about 100 honorary. Each member is
obliged, upon his admission, to present us with some books to the
value of a guinea, by which we have raised already a considerable
library. Earl Fitzwilliam, one of our representatives in parliament and
lately elected a member, proposes to give us Rymer's Foedera, which
will greatly add to the number as well as the value of our collection."[2]

The gentlemen's subscription libraries, mainly theological in
character, organized by Rev. Samuel Fancourt, first at Salisbury
and later (from 1742 onwards) in London, also form a link in
the chain. They were semi-commercial in character, and will be
described later.[3]

It was not, however, among the gentlemen of England, but
among the miners of Scotland, that the first fully-fledged secular
subscription library came into being. The lead miners of Leadhills in Lanarkshire, employed by the Scotch Mining Company,
were a favoured class in that they were able to earn relatively
high wages for a six-hour day. "Having therefore", explains
the *Statistical Account*, "a great deal of spare time, they employ
themselves in reading, and for this purpose have been at the
expence of fitting up a library, out of which every one who
contributes to the expence receives books."[4] The Leadhills
Reading Society, as it was called, was founded in 1741 and had
a long and flourishing existence. It was supported by contributions from the local gentry, and by monthly contributions of a

[1] See above, pp. 97–8.
[2] J. Nichols, *Literary Anecdotes of the Eighteenth Century*, Vol. VI, Pt. I (1812), p. 136.
[3] See below, pp. 145–6.
[4] Sir J. Sinclair (ed.), *Statistical Account of Scotland*, Vol. IV (1792), pp. 511–12.

few pence from the miners themselves, and it evidently served a population wider than that of the village itself, for one of the rules was that every member not residing in Leadhills should be provided with a bag sufficient to keep out the rain.

The Leadhills library became rather famous, and references to it in nineteenth-century literature make it clear that its purpose was to provide for serious study, and not mere entertainment. Dr. John Brown, in one of his last essays, speaks of it in terms of the highest admiration:

"The people are thoughtful and solid, great readers and church-goers. They have a capital library. . . . We have been greatly struck with the range of subjects and of authors in this homely catalogue; and it is impossible to think with anything but respect of the stout-hearted, strong-brained men who, after being in the bowels of the earth all day, sat down to wrestle with John Owen or Richard Baxter, or dream of heaven and holiness with Scougall and Leighton, or refresh themselves with Don Quixote, the Antiquary, the Fool of Quality, and Daubuisson on 'The Basalts of Saxony' – besides eviscerating, with the help of Jonathan Edwards and Andrew Fuller, their own gloomy and masculine theology as mercilessly as they did the stubborn galena and quartz."[1]

The example of Leadhills was imitated in 1756 in the mining village of Wanlochhead, just over the border in Dumfriesshire. The existence of these two libraries, in a remote part of the Scottish Lowlands, is a reflection of the tremendous intellectual achievement of many Scottish working men at this period. This achievement is vividly illustrated in the career of Alexander Murray, a shepherd's son born in Kirkcudbrightshire in 1775, who became Professor of Oriental Languages in the University of Edinburgh. As a boy, with the help of the village schoolmaster of Minnigaff, he taught himself French, Latin, Greek and Hebrew. He scoured the countryside for books of learning, and it is astonishing what he was able to acquire: an ancient Latin dictionary, purchased from an old man for eighteen pence: Caesar and Ovid, borrowed from a tenant-farmer: *Paradise Lost*, lent by a housekeeper in a neighbouring village: a Hebrew lexicon, given by a cousin, and so forth. One of his benefactors, it is of interest to note, was a miner from Leadhills, who allowed

---

[1] J. Brown, *Horae Subsecivae*, 3rd Ser. (Edinburgh 1882), pp. 344, 360.

him the use of a number of books which had belonged to a
deceased brother: Lucian's *Dialogues* in Greek and Latin: a
Greek *New Testament;* the *Iliad*, in Greek and Latin; Buchanan's
Opera Poetica. It is an impressive list.[1]

The Leadhills and Wanlockhead libraries still survive, the
former serving as a centre for the county library service.

The first gentlemen's subscription libraries also belong to
Scotland. They were the Society Library of Dumfries, founded
about 1745, and the Public Library at Kelso, established in 1751.
Of the latter the *Statistical Account* reported:

"A public library, which has existed upwards of forty years, and can
now boast of a collection of the best modern authors, being regularly
supplied with every publication of merit; together with a coffee-house
supplied with the London, Edinburgh and Kelso newspapers, have
contributed to render them [the higher classes of inhabitants] not less
intelligent than agreeable. The proprietors of the library have lately
resolved to erect a neat elegant house for the books, and for the
accommodation of the librarian."[2]

The value of such a library in these times is illustrated by
the diary of George Ridpath, minister of the neighbouring
parish of Stitchell. Ridpath was one of the early presidents of
the Kelso Library, compiler of its catalogue in 1759, and a most
voracious reader. He read extensively in Scottish history; he
read Francis Home's *Principia Medicinae*, Musschenbroek's
Elements of Natural Philosophy, and other scientific works; he
enjoyed Sterne's *Tristram Shandy*, Swift's *Tale of a Tub*, and
Macpherson's *Fragments of Ancient Poetry*; Plato, Epictetus,
Horace, Virgil, Cicero, and other classical writers were his
bedtime reading. In all, in a period of six years, he read over
200 volumes, besides the *Critical Review*, the *Monthly*, the
London Magazine, and other periodicals.[3]

The phrase "every publication of merit" in the passage quoted
above is of interest, for it indicates the common ambition of all

[1] Murray's autobiography is incorporated in the Life prefixed to the
posthumous edition of his *History of the European Languages*, ed. D. Scot,
Vol. I (Edinburgh 1823).
[2] Sir J. Sinclair (ed.), *Statistical Account of Scotland*, Vol. X (1794), p. 597.
[3] See *Diary of George Ridpath, Minister of Stitchel, 1755–1761*, ed. Sir J. B.
Paul (Scottish Hist. Soc. Pubns., 3rd Ser., Vol. II, Edinburgh 1922),
and the article by P. Kaufman, "Library News from Kelso", in *Library
Review* (Glasgow), Autumn 1960.

the eighteenth-century subscription libraries. They did not aim at comprehensiveness: they excluded purely professional literature on the one hand, and ephemeral fiction on the other. The emphasis, therefore, was upon belles lettres, history, biography, travel, science, and such fiction as was regarded as of literary merit: in short what was commonly called "polite literature". The third of the Scottish gentlemen's subscription libraries, the Ayr Library Society (1762), included by the end of the century works by Adam Smith, Gibbon, Boswell, Paine, Godwin, Burke, and Burns, but Paine's *Rights of Man*, having been pronounced by the judicial authorities treasonable and seditious, was burnt in 1793 in the presence of the Committee.[1]

It will be noted that at Kelso the subscription library, providing books, and the coffee-house, supplying more ephemeral literature, were separate institutions, but we can have little doubt that the clientèle was largely the same, and it is clear that the dissemination of newspapers and periodicals was one of the factors contributing to the demand for secular libraries. The Spalding Gentlemen's Society, for example, had its origins in the meetings in a coffee-house to discuss the latest issue of *The Tatler*;[2] and the Liverpool Library, the first of the English gentlemen's subscription libraries, began in much the same way, except that in this instance three reading societies contributed to its formation. One had been in the habit of meeting in a private house "for the purpose of discussing literary subjects, and of reading a portion of the periodical publications of the day".[3] Another met at the Merchants' Coffee-house, and the third at the Talbot Inn. Each had accumulated a small collection

---

[1] J. Strawhorn, "Further Education in Burns's Ayrshire", in *Scottish Adult Education*, No. 26 (August 1959), pp. 11–12. Burns's brother Gilbert recalled that when he and Robert were boys their father borrowed books from this Society for their use. "He procured for us the reading of *Derham's Physico* and *Astro-Theology*, and Ray's *Wisdom of God in the Creation*, to give us some idea of astronomy and natural history. Robert read all these books with an avidity and industry scarcely to be equalled." – J. G. Lockhart, *Life of Robert Burns* (1828, Everyman edn. 1959), p. 8.

[2] See above, p. 98.

[3] P. Macintyre, "Historical Sketch of the Liverpool Library", in *Trans. of the Historic Soc. of Lancs. and Ches.*, Vol. IX (Liverpool 1856–57), pp. 235–6.

of books, and in 1758 they pooled their resources to launch a library, with an entrance fee, initially, of one guinea and an annual subscription of five shillings.

A natural sequel to this development came, in Liverpool, forty years later, with the erection of the Athenaeum, designed to combine a newsroom and coffee-room with a reference library of standard English and foreign works. Both the Library and the Athenaeum were supported, about this time, by the notable literary and scientific group which centred on William Roscoe, biographer of Lorenzo de'Medici and one of Liverpool's most famous citizens. Both institutions remain to this day, though the Library, known since 1803 as the Lyceum, survives only as a club, having unhappily parted with its books during the Second World War.

By the time the Athenaeum was founded the example of the original Liverpool Library had been followed in Manchester (1765), Leeds (1768), Sheffield (1771), Hull (1775), Newcastle (1787), and other northern towns.[1] In Scotland, too, the movement continued to advance, with libraries in Glasgow (1779), Greenock (1783), Perth (1786), Edinburgh (1794), and many smaller places.[2] Dumfries, in 1792, even acquired a second library, in the formation of which Robert Burns played an important part. In the English south and Midlands progress was much slower. Bristol led the way in 1772 with the establishment of the Bristol Library Society, which in the following year was permitted to take over the old city library.[3] A similar development took place a little later, at Norwich, where a Public Library on a subscription basis was founded in 1784, and took over the city library in 1801.[4] Birmingham's subscription

---

[1] E.g. Warrington (1760), Lancaster, Carlisle, and Halifax (1768), Rochdale and Settle (1770), Bradford (1774), Whitby (1775), Stockton-on-Tees (1791), Colne (1793), Kendal, Sunderland and York (1794), and Whitehaven (1797).

[2] E.g. Duns (1768), Selkirk (1772), Kirkcudbright (1777), Montrose (1785), Dunfermline (1789), Rothesay (1792), Cambusnethan (by 1794), Dundee (1796), Arbroath (1797), and Port Glasgow (1798).

[3] See above, pp. 74-5.

[4] The city rescinded the order four years later, on the ground that its books were not being adequately cared for, but in 1815 the authorities relented, and from that date until 1862 the books were in the possession of the Public Library. As might be expected, the use made of them was exceedingly limited.

library, which still exists, was founded in 1779, and libraries are also recorded at a number of other centres,[1] but there were not so many as in the north. Even London had only two – the London Library, founded in 1785, and the Westminster Library, founded four years later.[2]

All these were "gentlemen's" libraries, supported by the middle class of merchants, manufacturers, and professional men (and their wives). Working-class subscription libraries, in spite of their early appearance on the scene, remained quite exceptional, even in Scotland. Apart from the original pioneering institutions at Leadhills and Wanlockhead, only two such libraries are recorded in Scotland at this period. One was founded in 1792 in the little Dumfriesshire village of Westerkirk, for the use of the antimony miners: whether this was a subscription library from the beginning is not clear, but it was certainly such by 1843, when the entrance fee was 5s., payable if desired in annual instalments. The members met monthly for the exchange of books, at the time of the full moon.[3] The other example was at Langloan in Lanarkshire (now a suburb of Coatbridge), where a group of weavers and other working men established a subscription library in 1794.[4]

In England we find no examples of working-class subscription libraries until almost the end of the century. In 1797 there was established at Kendal what was known as the Economical Library, "designed principally for the use and instruction of the working classes". We are told that "the terms of this society were so extremely moderate, that the library never attained much usefulness", but it survived to be incorporated in the

---

[1] E.g. Lewes (1785), Bury St. Edmunds (1789), Leicester and Worcester (1790), Coventry (1790/91), Chesterfield and Ipswich (1791), Truro (1792), Wolverhampton (1794), King's Lynn (1797), and Tavistock (1799).

[2] The London Library should not be confused with the present library of that name, which is a nineteenth-century foundation. See below, p. 207.

[3] Westerkirk Library, *Catalogue* (Langholm 1925), pp. 3–6. The antimony mine at Westerkirk was the only one in Great Britain. Its miners, 40 in number, were well cared for by the mining company, and were even better paid than the lead miners – see Sir J. Sinclair (ed.), *Statistical Account of Scotland*, Vol. XI (1794), pp. 525–8.

[4] Janet Hamilton, *Poems, Sketches and Essays*, ed. Jas. Hamilton (1880, 2nd edn. 1885), p. 393; A. R. Thompson, "The Use of Libraries by the Working Class in Scotland in the Early Nineteenth Century", in *Scottish Historical Review*, Vol. XLII (1963), pp. 27–28.

Kendal Mechanics' Institute in 1825.[1] A more successful venture was the Artizans' Library established, on a subscription basis, at Birmingham in 1799. This grew out of a subscription library formed two years earlier in connection with a Sunday school at the works of Messrs. T. and S. Carpenter, and by 1825 had 1,500 volumes and 182 subscribers. It was open three evenings a week, the entrance fee being 3s. and the subscription 1s. 6d. per quarter. This was a library of general literature: novels, at first excluded, were afterwards admitted on condition that they did not account for more than one-tenth of the annual income.[2]

There are, however, two earlier instances of working-class libraries attached to mutual improvement societies. The first of these, a rather unusual one, was the Mathematical Society formed in 1717 among the Huguenot silk-weavers of Spital-fields, for the study of mathematics and natural philosophy. It flourished for more than a century, and is said to have accumulated a considerable library. The other society, likewise for the study of science, was formed in the 1780s by a group of Dissenting Sunday school teachers in Birmingham, who gathered for the purpose a collection of apparatus and a small lending library.[3]

The gentlemen's subscription libraries, sometimes known as proprietary libraries, were nearly all organized on a common pattern. Membership was restricted to the proprietors or shareholders, and ranged from a dozen or two to between four and five hundred. The entrance fee, i.e. the purchase price of a share, was in early days usually a guinea, but rose sharply as the century advanced, often reaching four or five guineas during the French wars; the annual subscription, during the same period, rose from about six shillings to ten shillings or more. The book-stock was, by modern standards, small (Liverpool, with over 8,000 volumes in 1801, seems to have been the largest), and was accommodated, at the outset, in makeshift premises – very often over a bookshop, with the bookseller acting as librarian and receiving an honorarium for his pains.

[1] C. Nicholson, *The Annals of Kendal* (1832, 2nd edn. 1861), p. 278.

[2] W. Matthews, *A Sketch of the Principal Means which have been employed to ameliorate the Intellectual and Moral Condition of the Working Classes at Birmingham* (1830), p. 16.

[3] On these two societies see T. Kelly, *History of Adult Education in Great Britain* (Liverpool 1962), pp. 79, 103–4, and authorities there cited.

As the stock grew, a move would be made to independent premises, usually rented. Only a few libraries, at this period, acquired buildings of their own. Bristol was lucky in securing a building along with the old city library, and Liverpool (1786) and Birmingham (1799) erected buildings on the "tontine" system, which was not uncommon in those days.

The day-to-day control of the library was in the hands of a committee of the proprietors, which was responsible for selecting the books (usually by ballot), managing the premises, and supervising the work of the librarian. The librarian, therefore, was merely a custodian of the books, and an ill-paid one at that. At Birmingham in 1782, when the library hours were from 2 to 5 p.m. on every day except Sunday, the salary was £10 per annum, and this was about average at this time. By the end of the century it had risen to 40 guineas, but by this time the library was open six hours daily – 11 to 1, 3 to 6, and 7 to 8.[1] The librarian was expected to enforce the library rules rigorously, and in many cases was subject to severe penalties for any failure in this respect.

The rules themselves were commonly very strict, and the fines for keeping books beyond the stipulated time were by our standards heavy. At Leeds, for example, in 1768, they were 1d. per day for a pamphlet, 2d. for an octavo or duodecimo, 3d. for a quarto, and 4d. for a folio, and similar rules applied at Birmingham and Hull. The time allowed for reading varied somewhat. At Leeds, at this period, it was fixed for each volume at the discretion of the president: for a volume entered in 1771, for example, it was two weeks during the first year, and three weeks thereafter.[2]

There can be no doubt that one of the factors contributing to the spread of subscription libraries, especially in the north of England and the Midlands, was the strength of the Dissenting influence in those parts, for throughout the eighteenth and nineteenth centuries the Nonconformists are regularly to be found associated with almost every form of educational activity for adults. Joseph Priestley, the scientist and Unitarian minister,

---

[1] At Sheffield, at this date, the librarian (a woman) was still receiving only twelve guineas per annum for rent and attendance, with disastrous consequences that will be seen in a later chapter (below, p. 206).
[2] Information from Mr. F. Beckwith, Librarian of the Leeds Library.

in his *Familiar Letters addressed to the Inhabitants of Birmingham* (1790), declared:

"It is a remarkable fact, that, in almost all places in which there are *public libraries* on such a liberal and open plan as that which has lately been established in this town, the Anglican clergy have, in the first instance, discountenanced them; and when that could not be done, they have endeavoured to get the controul of them, for the sake of keeping out such books as they wish the common people not to read; while the *Dissenters* have always been foremost to promote these libraries, and when they have been instituted, have been as ready to introduce into them books unfavourable to their opinions, as those in favour of them."[1]

This is an *ex parte* statement, in a context of controversy. It was not true, for example, of Sheffield, where both Dissenting and Church of England clergy are found among the early presidents. But it did reflect pretty accurately Priestley's own experience in Birmingham.

Priestley played an active role successively in the subscription libraries at Warrington (1763–67), Leeds (1768–72), and Birmingham (1780–91).[2] At Leeds he was the first secretary, and at Birmingham, where eighteen of the nineteen original subscribers of 1779 were Dissenters, it was from Priestley that the library received "that stability and method without which no institution can prosper".[3] In an advertisement which he prepared for the library in 1781 he expressed the conviction that

"As all books are bought by a committee of persons annually chosen by a majority of the subscribers, and every vote is by ballot, this institution can never answer the purpose of any party, civil or religious, but, on the contrary, may be expected to promote a spirit of liberality and friendship among all classes of men without distinction."[4]

His hopes, alas, proved ill-founded, for within a few years a bitter dispute arose on the question of the admission of books of controversial divinity. Priestley was at first opposed to the admission of such works until the funds should permit the purchase of works dealing with all sides of any disputed question,

[1] J. Priestley, *Works*, ed. J. T. Rutt (1817–32), Vol. XIX, p. 277.
[2] In the years between 1772 and 1780 he acted as librian to the Earl of Shelburne.
[3] J. A. Langford, *A Century of Birmingham Life*, Vol. I (1868), p. 286, quoting a contemporary, William Hutton.
[4] S. Timmins, *Centenary of the Birmingham Library, 1779–1879* (Birmingham 1879), p. 13.

but when in 1787, following a decision to purchase one of his own works, *The Corruptions of Christianity*, a motion was brought forward by the Church of England party to exclude for the future all works of religious controversy, he resisted it strongly. The proposal was defeated, but the Dissenting members became increasingly dissatisfied with the management of the library, and in 1793 a large number of them withdrew to form their own library, which maintained an independent existence until re-united with the parent body in 1860.

Priestley's association with the Leeds and Birmingham libraries also serves to illustrate another facet of the period, namely the growing interest in science. An emphasis on experimental science was characteristic of the dissenting academies, and Priestley himself is now far better known for his chemical researches than for his voluminous writings in theology. At Birmingham, naturally enough, he became an active member of the Lunar Society – which was formed in 1775 and was the precursor of the numerous provincial literary and philosophical societies of the late eighteenth and early nineteenth centuries.[1] It was no accident, therefore, that at Birmingham special provision was made in the early years, for members interested in procuring books on science. Such members paid an additional subscription of one guinea a year: the scientific books thus purchased were available to all for reference but might be borrowed only by those specially subscribing.[2]

The same combination of interests was to be found in the London Library, which was formed in 1785 by a group in which Dissenting ministers, medical men and scientists played a leading part. Many members were both ministers and Fellows of the Royal Society, and in the first catalogue books on science – anatomy, botany, chemistry, mathematics, natural history, natural philosophy, and physic – constituted nearly two-fifths of the total.

---

[1] The history of this Society, which included *inter alios* Matthew Boulton, James Watt, Erasmus Darwin, Richard Lovell Edgeworth, and Josiah Wedgwood, has recently been told in R. E. Schofield, *The Lunar Society of Birmingham* (Oxford 1963).

[2] J. A. Langford, *A Century of Birmingham Life*, Vol. I (1868), p. 287. A similar arrangement operated at Leeds in respect of foreign books, until 1814, when the Foreign Library was absorbed into the main collection.

The name of Priestley also suggests a connection with the Radicalism which became such a characteristic feature of English political life from the time of the French Revolution onwards. Priestley's Radical opinions were well known, and at Birmingham led to virulent controversy, culminating in the riots of 1791, in the course of which his chapel and house were burnt, and his library, manuscripts and laboratory destroyed. He himself luckily escaped, and after three years as a minister in London emigrated to join his three sons in America.

The associations of Radicalism, however, were as might be expected less with the gentlemen's subscription libraries than with certain working-class organizations, such as the book clubs to be described shortly, and the working men's libraries of the early nineteenth century. The only other example of a connection between Radicalism and a middle-class subscription library appears to have been at Leicester, where Richard Phillips, bookseller, founded a "Permanent Library" in 1790. It proved, unfortunately, far from permanent, for in 1793 Phillips was sent to prison for eighteen months for selling Paine's *Rights of Man* and other seditious literature, and in 1795, shortly after his release, his shop and library were destroyed by fire. Like Priestley, Phillips retreated to London, where he set up as a publisher of educational books, became Sheriff, and was knighted by George III.

One other subscription library deserving special comment is that in Bristol. It was in 1772 that a Library Society was formed in Bristol to establish a library on the lines of those already flourishing in Manchester and Liverpool. With the consent of the Corporation the Society took over the old City Library building and the books it contained, and the Corporation appointed the Society's nominee to the vacant post of librarian at the same salary as had originally been fixed in 1615, i.e. 40s. a year. Charles Tovey, the leader of the public library movement in Bristol in the nineteenth century, thought this was a shameful transaction, but it must have seemed reasonable enough at the time, for the old library was essentially a scholars' library, and the activity of the new Society seemed an excellent way of making it more useful and more extensively available.

The librarian's lot was not an enviable one. He lived in the basement of the library building, and was required to be in

attendance from 10 to 1 on Tuesdays and Thursdays, and from
6 to 9 on Mondays, Wednesdays and Fridays; to keep a catalogue of the books; and to keep a constant fire in the library
room during opening hours. Fortunately the decision regarding
his salary was later amended, and instead of forty shillings he
received ten guineas, which as we have seen was about average
for those days.

The Library Society continued to occupy the building (enlarged by an additional wing in 1785) until 1853, when the
Corporation resumed possession and the old City Library
became the nucleus for a new public library. This was opened
in 1856, though it was not till 1874 that the Public Libraries
Act was adopted. By an irony of fate the books of the subscription library also came eventually (1894) into public
possession.

A special feature of the Bristol Library Society is the survival
of a continuous record of borrowings (in seventy-seven folio
volumes) from 1773 to 1857. An analysis of the registers for
the first twelve years[1] provides some fascinating glimpses of
middle-class reading habits in a mercantile community at this
period. The largest and most popular sections of the library
were History, Antiquities and Geography, with 283 titles and
6,121 borrowings, and Belles Lettres, with 238 titles and 3,313
borrowings. Far below came Theology and Ecclesiastical
History, Natural History and Chemistry, Philosophy, Jurisprudence, Miscellanies, Mathematics, etc., and Medicine and
Anatomy, all with fewer than 100 titles.

The most popular single work was John Hawkesworth's
Account of Voyages . . . in the Southern Hemisphere (3 vols.),
which was borrowed on 201 occasions. Next in order came
Patrick Brydone's *Tour through Sicily and Malta*, Lord Chesterfield's *Letters to his Son*, David Hume's *History of England*,
Oliver Goldsmith's *History of the Earth*, Guillaume Raynal's
*History of the Settlements and Trade of the Europeans in the East
and West Indies*, William Robertson's *History of Charles V*,
Laurence Sterne's *Tristram Shandy*, Francis Grose's *Antiquities
of England and Wales*, Lord Lyttleton's *History of Henry II*,
and Henry Fielding's *Works*. All these had 120 or more borrow-

[1] P. Kaufman, *Borrowings from the Bristol Library, 1773–1784* (Bibliog.
Soc. of the Univ. of Virginia, Charlottesville 1960).

16. BRISTOL SUBSCRIPTION LIBRARY

Part of a page from one of the borrowers' books, showing a loan to S. T. Coleridge.

ings. Selecting almost at random other items in the list, we note with interest that Gibbon's *Decline and Fall* scored 96; Johnson's *Lives of the Poets* 92 and his *Journey to the Western Isles* 42; Shakespeare's *Plays* (in ten volumes) 62; Gray's *Poems* and Percy's *Reliques* 42 each; and Bacon's *Works* 5.

The borrowings of Coleridge and Southey in the 1790s have been recorded in detail,[1] and those of Coleridge in particular have been subjected to searching analysis.[2] Here we must be content to quote once more Coleridge's well-known letter to the librarian, which throws light not only upon Coleridge but also upon the functioning of the library:

Stowey, May, 1797.

"Mr. Catcott – I beg your acceptance of all the enclosed letters. You must not think lightly of the present, as they cost me, who am a very poor man, five shillings.

With respect to the *Bruck[eri] Hist[oria] Crit[ica]*, although by accident they were registered on the 23rd of March, yet they were not removed from the library for a fortnight after, and when I received your first letter, I had had the books just three weeks. Our learned and ingenious committee may read through two quartos, that is, one thousand and four hundred pages of close printed Latin and Greek, in three weeks, for ought I know to the contrary. I pretend to no such intenseness of application, or rapidity of genius.

I subscribe to your library, Mr. Catcott, not to read novels, or books of quite ready and easy digestion, but to get books which I cannot get elsewhere – books of massy knowledge – and as I have few books of my own, I read with a common-place book, so that if I be not allowed a longer period for the perusal of such books, I must contrive to get rid of my subscription, which would be a thing perfectly useless, except in so far as it gives me an opportunity of reading your expensive little notes and letters. –

Yours in Christian fellowship,

S. T. COLERIDGE."

---

[1] P. Kaufman, "The Reading of Southey and Coleridge", in *Modern Philology*, Vol. XXI (1923–24); G. Whalley, "The Bristol Library Borrowings of Southey and Coleridge, 1793–98", in *The Library*, 5th Ser., Vol. IV (1949–50). Cf. E. R. N. Mathews, "A Century Ago", in *The Library*, Vol. V (1893).

[2] Especially in J. L. Lowes, *The Road to Xanadu* (1927).

BOOK CLUBS

A humbler form of subscription library, which also became very popular in the latter half of the eighteenth century, was the book club or reading society. Characteristically, this differed from the ordinary subscription library in three respects. First, the membership was small, not usually more than a dozen or two people. In the second place, no attempt was made to build up a permanent collection, the books being either sold or divided among the members when they had served their turn. Finally, the club served a social as well as a literary purpose, great emphasis being placed on the periodical meetings (usually monthly) for the sharing out of books and decisions on new purchases. It would be a mistake, however, to make too sharp a distinction: there were book clubs which had permanent libraries, and subscription libraries which had regular monthly meetings. Everything depended upon local circumstances, and names such as book club, book society, reading society, literary society, were used more or less indiscriminately to cover a great variety of organizations.

The origin of book clubs in the sense above defined is to be found, like that of subscription libraries, among the clergy. The earliest references so far known occur in 1709 in the correspondence of the S.P.C.K. where we find a Mr. A. D. Frank of Cranfield in Bedfordshire reporting: "That formerly he knew a Society of Ministers that subscribed 20s. p. ann. each man towards raising a Fund for buying New Books, which after they had Circulated thro' all those hands that pleased to peruse 'em, were divided into Lotts and each person had his particular share."[1] In the same year a Mr. Robert Nelson communicated to the Society a proposal "concerning a Subscription made by some Clergyman in Pembrokeshire for buying of Books to be mutually read by them and afterwards dispers'd among themselves"; and Thomas Phillips, Vicar of Laugharne, reported that "the methods used in Pembrokeshire for circulating books are practis'd in Carmarthenshire with good success".[2] The same

[1] S.P.C.K. MSS., *Abstracts of Correspondence*, Vol. I, No. 1884, 23rd November, 1709.
[2] M. Clement (ed.), *Correspondence and Minutes of the S.P.C.K. relating to Wales, 1699–1740* (Cardiff 1952), pp. 24–25, 272.

system was used, as we have seen, at Colchester about 1730 when the Harsnett Library was converted into a subscription library for the local clergy.[1]

The book club was a very economical form of organization, since it did not involve either a salaried librarian or extensive premises: a few shelves in a private house, or in an inn or coffee-house, would suffice for the relatively small number of books in the possession of the society at any one time. Such an arrangement was particularly well suited to small towns and villages, and to working-class groups which could not afford the outlay required for a permanent library. Unfortunately, just because the clubs were so easy to organize, and involved so little commitment, they were often rather ephemeral, and records of their history are scanty and incomplete. Dr. Kaufman, in the fullest study of the subject to date,[2] identifies over 100 groups in twenty-nine English counties up to the year 1800, but the actual number may well have been twice this figure.

Apart from South Wales and Colchester only a handful of clubs are known from the period before 1750. One in the Cambridgeshire village of Caxton is said, on rather slender evidence, to have been in existence as early as 1712.[3] The well-known Nonconformist divine Philip Doddridge, as a young man in his first ministry at Kibworth in Leicestershire, was a member of what seems to have been a book club in the year 1725; and in the same year a group of clergy formed a club at Alford in Lincolnshire.[4] Other clubs are recorded at Sheffield in 1737 and at Halifax and Holmfirth about 1740.[5] The exact nature of many of these early clubs is not known: one suspects that most of them were clerical.

The first identifiable club not restricted to the clergy seems to have been founded at Leicester about 1740: it still exists today, under the name of the Leicestershire Book Society, and

[1] See above, p. 98.
P. Kaufman, "English Book Clubs and their Rôle in Social History", in *Libri*, Vol. XIV (1964).
[3] *Notes and Queries*, 11th Ser., Vol. IX (1914), p. 462.
[4] *Op. cit.*, 5th Ser., Vol. VIII (1877), p. 259.
[5] Sheffield (not listed by Dr. Kaufman) is a doubtful case. It is described in 1737 as a "Society for reading books", with a subscription of 5s. per annum – Sir G. R. Sitwell, *The Hurts of Haldworth* (Oxford 1930), p. 261.

still has half-yearly dinners at which new books are selected and books withdrawn from circulation are sold by auction.[1] Another early club, rather atypical, was the George Book Club at Huntingdon, formed by a group of clergy, lawyers, and medical men in 1742. It had its regular monthly meetings on the Tuesday before the full moon, with dinner on the table at three o'clock, but its membership, originally nineteen, had grown by 1790 to 75, and some at least of its books were kept as a permanent library.[2]

The only other clubs known to have been founded before 1750 were at Boston (date unknown) and Birmingham (about 1745).[3] Birmingham, which like Leicester has continued to the present day, offers a marked contrast to Huntingdon. It was a small club, with no more than twenty-four members at the time the surviving records begin in 1775; and its surplus stock was sold off annually. Unlike the Huntingdon Club, whose early members included four successive bishops of Lincoln, it seems to have been from the beginning a Dissenting venture, membership being drawn from that same Radical-Unitarian group which later played a prominent part in the establishment of the Birmingham Subscription Library.[4] Towards the close of the century it evidently served as a focus for Radical opinion in the town:

"While, in 1793, the effigy of Tom Paine was being carried in derision through the town, and afterwards consigned to the flames, the members of the club were reading his books. At a later date Cobbett's works, the Memoirs of H. Hunt, Bamford's Poems, Hall's Apology for the Freedom of the Press, Pearce on the Abuses of the Laws, and Bentham's works, were pretty well circulated, and it is fair

[1] See *Monthly Magazine*, Vol. LI (1821), p. 397; W. G. Corp, "An Historic Book Society", in *News Sheet*, No. 94 (National Book Council July 1937).

[2] The "Society of Clergy and gentlemen at Pembroke" which subscribed to Conyers Middleton's *Life of Cicero* in 1741 may have been another early example, perhaps a successor to the society of clergy formed in Pembrokeshire in 1709 (see above, p. 136). On the other hand it may be identifiable with the Pembroke Society recorded later in the century, which appears to have been a subscription library: a catalogue of its books was published in 1791.

[3] Boston, recorded by Dr. Kaufman under date 1750, was defunct by that date – see J. Nichols, *Bibliotheca Topographica-Britannica*, No. II, Pt. I (London 1781), p. 432.

[4] See above, pp. 130 seq.

to suppose, pretty well studied. These books as well as the list of members show the original character of the club."[1]

As the century advanced, the number of clubs rapidly increased – more than one-third of all the clubs listed by Dr. Kaufman were founded or first recorded in the '80s or '90s. Probably this was due to the political excitement engendered by the American and French wars, for periodicals and pamphlets formed a large part of the stock of most clubs. This can be illustrated from the case of the Cirencester Book Club, which was founded in 1782 or 1783 by R. D. Cumberland, a local Church of England parson. The Club's purchases, of which the records survive in the accounts of a local bookseller, include many books and pamphlets dealing with contemporary political issues, besides periodicals, books of travel, and a few works on history and belles lettres. If we look, for example, at the account for 1791, we find among other items the *Gentleman's Magazine*, the *European Magazine*, the *Monthly Review*, Priestley's *Letters to Burke*, Burke's *Reflections on the French Revolution*, Paine's *Rights of Man*, Rousseau's *Confessions* and Boswell's *Life of Johnson*.[2] A club at Ely, founded in 1766, was actually called the "Pamphlett Club", though its purchases were not in fact restricted to pamphlets.

In the main the book clubs were a male affair, but women were occasionally admitted to membership. The Society for Reading at Clavering, Essex (1786), which was a debating society as well as a book club, agreed in 1789 to admit ladies at half price. A separate Ladies' Book Club was formed at Penzance in 1770, and twenty years later there was another at Taunton.

In the village of Luddenden, near Halifax, was a rather unusual library serving the needs of a small group of local farmers, mill-owners and shopkeepers. It is said (the earliest records have now been lost) to have been founded in or before 1776, and to have originated in a bequest of books by the local parson, and this is likely enough since some of the books were of seventeenth-century date. In form it was a subscription library,

---

[1] J. A. Langford, *A Century of Birmingham Life*, Vol. I (1868), p. 58.
[2] P. Kaufman, "A Bookseller's Record of Eighteenth-Century Book Clubs", in *The Library*, 5th Ser. Vol. XV (1960).

based on proprietary shares, but the small membership –
twenty-three in 1781 – and the regular monthly meetings at the
White Swan Inn (renamed in due course the Lord Nelson) gave
it something of the character of a club. New books were purchased from a levy of 4d. per member at the monthly meeting,
and from fines imposed for various offences, such as returning
a book late, unseemly scrambling for books, drunkenness and
swearing. The books were distributed each month in a rotation
determined by lot, and afterwards went to form a permanent
library, amounting ultimately to upwards of 1,100 volumes.

A unique feature of this library was a provision by which
books could be borrowed by non-members through the medium
of a member, the rates fixed being 4d. for a folio, 3d. for a
quarto, and 2d. for smaller books. For a second month the
charges were increased by fifty per cent.[1] At a later stage in the
library's history this practice seems to have been abandoned.

This library has a special interest because of its later association with Patrick Branwell Brontë, who was a regular frequenter
of the Lord Nelson during his brief service as clerk in charge at
Luddenden Foot railway station in 1841–42. There is no evidence that he was ever a member of the library, but local
tradition has it that he availed himself of its books, which were
stored at the Inn, "at hours unsuspected by the prudent library
committee".[2]

The Luddenden Library continued in active operation until
1914. It was sold two years later, but thirty-one books which
remained at the Inn were rescued in 1958 and are now preserved,
together with the surviving records, in the Public Library at
Sowerby Bridge near by.

The social aspect of the clubs was clearly important. The
monthly meeting, even if it did not involve a dinner, was usually
an occasion for a drink, a smoke, and a gossip with friends. This
kind of gathering is illustrated in the sketch by Rowlandson,
reproduced herewith, which adorns the title-page of an anonymous satirical poem entitled *The Country Book-Club*, published
in 1788. The members of this "cottage Book-club on the village

---

[1] These rules, now lost, but apparently belonging to the earliest period
of the library's history, are printed in J. Walton, "An Eighteenth-
Century Village Library", in *The Librarian and Book World*, Vol.
XXVIII (1938–39), pp. 329–30.
[2] W. Gerin, *Branwell Bronte* (1961), p. 196.

green" met "to dispute, to fight, to plead, to smoke, to drink – do anything but read", and the books and periodicals piled on the table were used only as missiles in argument.[1] This no doubt hits off the tendency in some clubs, but it cannot be regarded as typical. At Luddenden in the early nineteenth century, though the ale circulated freely enough, the members regularly went off with four books or more apiece for the next month's reading.[2]

The *Country Book-Club* appears to have its setting in Essex. Over against it we must set a very different, if slightly nostalgic, picture given by a correspondent of the *Gentleman's Magazine* of a country book club in Norfolk in the opening years of the nineteenth century. This club, founded about 1760, provided some twenty-five to thirty families with "nearly all the new publications of English origin which were really worth having, in general literature and popular science". The emphasis, the writer notes, was on contemporary literature: authors before 1760 – even Shakespeare, Spenser, Bacon, and Hooker – were absent, but within its limits the collection was very comprehensive. In this instance the club had a permanent library, in a crowded room like a ship's cabin in the librarian's house.[3]

In Wales and Scotland book clubs seem to have been much less numerous. In Wales there was a Reading Society at Carmarthen by 1752, and Merthyr Tydfil may also have had one by the end of the century, since "several book societies" are recorded there in 1804.[4] In Scotland we have only two examples, both in Nithsdale, Dumfriesshire. The first, at Dunscore, was known as the Monkland Friendly Society, and was organized by Robert Burns in 1788–89, during his brief and unsuccessful spell as a farmer at Ellisland. Burns acted as its "treasurer, librarian, and censor". The second, at Closeburn a few miles

---

[1] Kaufman, "English Book Clubs" (*loc. cit.*), p. 3, reproduces the drawing and part of the poem, which is attributed to Charles Shillito and was published in London and Colchester. It was privately reprinted by G. K. Hall & Co., Boston, Mass., in 1964.

[2] I am indebted to Mr. S. Robinson, Librarian at Sowerby Bridge, for information on this point.

[3] "Country Book-Clubs Fifty Years Ago", in *Gentleman's Magazine*, N.S. Vol. XXXVII (1852), pp. 571–2.

[4] P. Kaufman, "Community Lending Libraries in Eighteenth-Century Ireland and Wales", in *Library Quarterly*, Vol. XXXIII (Chicago 1963), pp. 309–10.

away, was founded in 1789 in imitation of the successful venture at Dunscore. In a letter to Sir John Sinclair, editor of the *Statistical Account of Scotland*, Burns describes the Dunscore club as follows:

"To store the minds of the lower classes with useful knowledge, is certainly of very great consequence, both to them as individuals, and to society at large. Giving them a turn for reading and reflection, is giving them a source of innocent and laudable amusement; and besides, raises them to a more dignified degree in the scale of rationality. Impressed with this idea, a gentleman in this parish, Robert Riddell, Esq. of Glenriddel, set on foot a species of circulating library, on a plan so simple, as to deserve the notice of every country gentleman, who thinks the improvement of that part of his own species, whom chance has thrown into the humble walks of the peasant and the artisan, a matter worthy of his attention.

"Mr. Riddell got a number of his own tenants, and farming neighbours, to form themselves into a society, for the purpose of having a library among themselves. They entered into a legal engagement, to abide by it for 3 years; with a saving clause or two, in cases of removal to a distance, or of death. Each member, at his entry, paid 5s.; and at each of their meetings, which were held every fourth Saturday, 6d. more. With their entry money, and the credit which they took on the faith of their future funds, they laid in a tolerable stock of books at the commencement. What authors they were to purchase, was always to be decided by the majority. At every meeting all the books, under certain fines and forfeitures, by way of penalty, were to be produced; and the members had their choice of the volumes in rotation. He whose name stood, for that night, first on the list had his choice of what volume he pleased in the whole collection; the second had his choice after the first; the third after the second, and so on to the last. At next meeting, he who had been first on the list at the preceding meeting, was last at this; he who had been second, was first; and so on, through the whole 3 years. At the expiration of the engagement, the books were sold by auction, but only among the members themselves; and each man had his share of the common stock, in money or in books, as he chose to be a purchaser or not.

"At the breaking up of this little society, which was formed under Mr. Riddell's patronage, what with benefactions of books from him, and what with their own purchases, they had collected together upwards of 150 volumes. It will easily be guessed, that a good deal of trash would be bought. Among the books, however, of this little library, were, Blair's Sermons, Robertson's History of Scotland, Hume's History of the Stewarts, the Spectator, Idler, Adventurer,

Mirror, Lounger, Observer, Man of Feeling, Man of the World, Chrysal, Don Quixotte, Joseph Andrews, etc. A peasant who can read, and enjoy such books, is certainly a much superior being to his neighbour, who perhaps, stalks beside his team, very little removed, except in shape, from the brutes he drives."[1]

Another letter, from Burns to an Edinburgh bookseller, indicates that his tastes as librarian did not always coincide with those of the members:

"At a late meeting of the Monkland friendly Society it was resolved to augment their Library by the following books which you are to send us as soon as possible – The Mirror – the Lounger – Man of feeling – Man of the world (these for my own sake I wish to have by the first Carrier) Knox's History of the Reformation – Rae's History of the Rebellion 1715 – Any good history of the Rebellion 1745 – A Display of the Seccession Act & Testimony by Mr. Gib – Hervey's Meditations – Beveridge's Thoughts – & another copy of Watson's body of Divinity – This last heavy Performance is so much admired by many of our Members, that they will not be content with one Copy, so Captn Riddell our President & Patron agreed with me to give you private instructions not to send Watson, but to say that you could not procure a Copy of the book so cheap as the one you sent formerly & therefore you wait further Orders."[2]

Actually the library was not disbanded after the first three years, as Burns's account suggests: it was re-organized and continued in existence until 1931.[3]

CIRCULATING LIBRARIES

The growth of private subscription libraries and book clubs was paralleled by the development of commercial subscription libraries, run by booksellers for their private profit. These are generally known as circulating libraries, though this name is also occasionally used of private subscription libraries, e.g. at Manchester and Halifax.

From Restoration times onwards it seems to have been fairly common for booksellers in London to hire out surplus books. The bookseller and publisher Francis Kirkman announced at the

[1] Sir J. Sinclair (ed.), *Statistical Account of Scotland*, Vol. III (1792), pp. 598–600. The letter is signed, not untypically, "A PEASANT".
[2] J. de L. Ferguson, *Letters of Robert Burns* (Oxford 1931), Vol. II, p. 15.
[3] F. B. Snyder, *The Life of Robert Burns* (New York 1932), p. 325.

end of Webster and Rowley's comedy, *The Thracian Wonder*,
in 1661:

> "If any Gentlemen repair to my House aforesaid, they may be
> furnished with all manner of English, or French Histories, Romances,
> or Poetry, which are to be sold, or read for reasonable considerations."

In 1674 the Widow Page, at the Anchor and Mariner near
London Bridge, was advertising "All sorts of Histories to buy,
or let out to read by the week". A well-known later instance
occurs about 1725, when Benjamin Franklin made an arrangement with a bookseller named Wilcox, of Little Britain, "that,
on certain reasonable terms, which I have now forgotten, I
might take, read, and return any of his books".[1] "Circulating
libraries", remarks Franklin, "were not then in use", but it was
clearly only a short step from the hiring out of surplus volumes
to the formation of a separate collection of books for lending.

The first known circulating library, in fact, seems to have
been established in that same year 1725, not in London but in
Edinburgh, in the High Street shop of that well-known bookseller, poet, and wigmaker, Allan Ramsay. The first recorded
English libraries of the kind appear to have been at Bath and
Bristol in 1728, and within a few years there were libraries also
at Scarborough and Salisbury. London's first circulating library
was in existence by 1740, and there were half a dozen or more
by 1750. By that time there were also libraries in Beverley,
Cambridge and Newcastle.[2] At Birmingham a circulating library
was opened in 1751,[3] at Glasgow in 1753; Liverpool had a
library by 1757, Aberdeen by 1765.

Before long the bookseller's circulating library became a
commonplace in London, in the larger provincial towns, and in
the spas and watering-places. By the end of the century there

---

[1] B. Franklin, *Autobiography*, ed. J. Bigelow (1868, new edn. 1924), p. 58.
Cf. J. H. Shera, *Foundations of the Public Library* (Chicago 1949),
p. 130 n., where it is stated that in 1720 two London booksellers,
Robert Willoughby and A. Jackson, were advertising books for rent.
Unfortunately Shera does not give his authority. His reference (p. 130)
to a circulating library at Dunfermline in 1711 is incorrect.

[2] A copy of the bookseller's advertisement for the Beverley library (1740)
is to be found in *Book Auction Records*, Vol. VI (1909), p. iv.

[3] In 1729 Thomas Warren of Birmingham advertised "Books are Hired
out to Read or Exchanged" – J. Hill, *The Bookmakers of Old Birmingham*
(Birmingham 1907), pp. 39–40.

were reported to be not less than a thousand such libraries in the country,[1] including twenty-six in London. Bath even had a music library. Very often, in the provincial towns, the conduct of a library was combined not only with bookselling but with the sale of stationery, perfumes, patent medicines, even hats and haberdashery. The method of organization was very similar to that familiar in more modern circulating libraries, and need not be described in detail. A Birmingham advertisement of 1787 illustrates the kind of arrangement that was customary:

"March 19, 1787. – LITERATURE. – M. and S. Olds respectfully inform their Friends and the Public that they have opened a Circulating Library, No. 13, Suffolk-street, Birmingham, consisting of a variety of Books, in History, Voyages, Novels, Romances, Adventures, Poetry, Plays, etc., which will be lent to read on the following Terms: – Twelve Shillings per Year; Seven Shillings the Half Year; Four Shillings per Quarter; Six-pence per Week; or at Two-pence per Volume; and should their Endeavours meet the Support and Patronage of the Ladies and Gentlemen in or near Birmingham, they will annually make Additions to their Collection, so as to make it a general Repository of useful and entertaining Literature.

"N.B. Stationery and Perfumery of all Sorts."

Strangely enough, the man who seems to have invented the name "circulating library" was not a bookseller, but a Dissenting clergyman, Samuel Fancourt. His first venture was at Salisbury, where from 1735 to 1742 he conducted a subscription library on book club lines. The annual subscription was half a guinea, and the used books were disposed of by means of a periodical draw at half a guinea a lot. In 1741 he claimed that "Great Numbers of Gentlemen, particularly of the Law, Physick, and Divinity, are Subscribers to it, even sixty Miles round, and more. . . . "[2]

Later Fancourt transferred his activities to London, where from 1742 onwards he conducted what he called a Universal Circulating Library, in Crane Court, Fleet Street. At first he tried to run it on the same lines as his library at Salisbury, except that the subscription was a guinea a year instead of half

---

[1] *Monthly Magazine*, Vol. XI (1801), p. 238.
[2] *Daily Advertiser*, 11th April, 1741, quoted in A. D. McKillop, "English Circulating Libraries, 1725–50", in *The Library*, 4th Ser., Vol. XIV (1933–34), p. 480.

a guinea. By 1745, however, he worked out a new plan which closely resembled that of the later subscription libraries. The subscribers, under this scheme, were to elect a committee of trustees in whom the library was to be vested, and Fancourt himself was content to be appointed librarian, during good behaviour. This enterprise met with more success than might have been expected, and the library continued in active existence at Crane Court until at least 1759, by which time Fancourt was over eighty years of age. Eventually, however, he ran into financial difficulties, and became bankrupt.

The importance of Fancourt lies not in his actual achievement but in the fact that he was a link between the clerical subscription libraries of the seventeenth and early eighteenth centuries and the secular subscription libraries and book clubs of later times. His library in London, though run in some degree for his personal profit, bore a much closer resemblance to a private subscription library than to a commercial circulating library. This is seen not only in its organization but also in its contents, for one-third of the library or more consisted of books and pamphlets on theology, ecclesiastical history, and the like, and only about one-tenth of light literature.

Most ordinary commercial circulating libraries had a much higher proportion of light literature than this. Many, indeed, like the 2d. subscription libraries of our own day, concentrated almost entirely upon novels and romances, and some made their purpose quite plain by adopting the title "Entertaining Library". The great purveyor of lurid and romantic fiction in the latter part of the century was William Lane, proprietor of the Minerva Press in Leadenhall Street, who not only maintained a large circulating library himself but did much to stimulate the establishment of libraries in the provinces to provide an outlet for his products. In 1787 he was offering to supply complete libraries, "from Twenty to Five Hundred Pounds, properly arranged and classed with a Printed Catalogue", at a week's notice.[1]

The increase in the reading of fiction, particularly among women and amongst the lower classes, was of course denounced by the moralists as undermining the foundations of morality

[1] D. Blakey, *The Minerva Press, 1790–1820* (Bibliog. Soc. 1939), pp. 120–1.

and social order. In Edinburgh Robert Wodrow lamented in 1728 that "all the villanous profane and obscene books and playes printed at London . . . are got down by Allan Ramsay, and lent out, for an easy price, to young boyes, servant weemin of the better sort, and gentlemen, and vice and obscenity dreadfully propagated".[1] In England there were many who held similar views, and the opposition to the circulating library, on moral grounds, persisted well into the nineteenth century.[2] The burden of many complaints was summed up by Sir Anthony Absolute in Sheridan's *Rivals:*

"Madam, a circulating library in a town is an evergreen tree of diabolical knowledge! It blossoms throughout the year! – and depend on it, Mrs. Malaprop, that they who are so fond of handling the leaves, will long for the fruit at last."[3]

Lydia Languish, when Sir Anthony was announced, hastened to thrust all her novels out of sight, and make a show of more improving literature:

"Here, my dear Lucy, hide these books. Quick, quick! – Fling *Peregrine Pickle* under the toilet – throw *Roderick Random* into the closet – put the *Innocent Adultery* into *The Whole Duty of Man* – thrust *Lord Aimworth* under the sofa – cram *Ovid* behind the bolster – there – put the *Man of Feeling* in your pocket – so, so – now lay *Mrs. Chapone* in sight, and leave *Fordyce's Sermons* open on the table."[4]

This, of course, is satire. Lewis Bull's circulating library in Bath, from which Lydia is supposed to have drawn her novels, was a very respectable establishment and like most of the larger libraries probably included in its stock a substantial proportion of non-fiction, e.g. history, biography, travels, belles lettres and divinity. Southey used it in his schooldays, and afterwards recalled that "Bull's Circulating Library was then to me what the

[1] R. Wodrow, *Analecta* (Maitland Club 1842–43), Vol. III, pp. 515–16.
[2] Cf. J. T. Taylor, *Early Opposition to the English Novel* (New York 1943), Ch. v; R. D. Altick, *The English Common Reader* (Chicago 1957), pp. 123–4.
[3] Act I, Sc. ii.
[4] *Ibid.* The reference to *Mrs. Chapone* is no doubt to *Letters on the Improvement of the Mind*, by Hester Chapone, which was published in 1772 (three years before the appearance of *The Rivals*) and had already reached a third edition by 1774.

Bodleian would be now".[1] The better libraries usually sought
to cater for serious as well as for frivolous tastes, and since many
of them provided a service for country readers as well as local
residents, they were not without value to the scholar. Cowper,
for example, living in Olney, wrote in 1781, to his friend Joseph
Hill in London:

> "I shall be obliged if you will be so good as to subscribe for me to
> some well-furnished circulating library, and leave my address upon
> the counter written in a legible hand, and order them to send me down
> a catalogue."[2]

Before we leave the subject of circulating libraries, it is worth
mentioning that in the early days of the movement, at any rate,
some of the London coffee-houses provided books and pamphlets
for their patrons. William Shenstone, the poet, boasted in 1741
that at George's Coffee-House in the Strand, for a subscription
of a shilling, he could read "all pamphlets under a three shillings'
dimension"; and in the following year a writer in the *Champion*
complained of "a scandalous and low Custom that has lately
prevail'd amongst those who keep Coffee Houses, of buying one
of any new Book so soon as it is publish'd, and lending it by
Turns to such Gentlemen to read as frequent their Coffee
House".[3] How far this custom spread is not clear, but it was a
not unnatural development, for the coffee-houses had long been
in the habit of providing their patrons with newspapers and
periodicals.[4]

We may conclude with a comment from James Lackington,
writing in 1791:

> "I have been informed, that when circulating libraries were first
> opened, the booksellers were much alarmed, and their rapid increase,
> added to their fears, had led them to think that the sale of books would

---

[1] H. M. Hamlyn, "Eighteenth-Century Circulating Libraries in England",
in *The Library*, 5th Ser., Vol. I (1947), p. 207.

[2] *Op. cit.*, p. 215. Cf. W. Cowper, *Life and Works*, ed. R. Southey (1836–
37), Vol. XV, p. 102.

[3] A. D. McKillop, "English Circulating Libraries, 1725–50", in *The
Library*, 4th Ser., Vol. XIV (1933–34), pp. 481–2.

[4] H. M. Hamlyn, *The Circulating Libraries of the Eighteenth Century*
(M.A. thesis, London Univ. 1948), cites T. Warton, *A Companion to
the Guide* . . . [to Oxford] (2nd edn., 1762?), pp. 9–11, as evidence
that the Oxford coffee-houses even provided encyclopaedias, but this
is probably not to be taken seriously.

be much diminished by such libraries. But experience has proved that the sale of books, far from being diminished by them, has been greatly promoted, as from those repositories, many thousand families have been cheaply supplied with books, by which the taste for reading has become much more general, and thousands of books are purchased every year, by such as have first borrowed them at those libraries, and after reading, approving of them, become purchasers.

"Circulating libraries have also contributed greatly towards the amusement and cultivation of the other sex; by far the greatest part of ladies have now a taste for books."[1]

[1] J. Lackington, *Memoirs*, (1791, 9th edn. 1794), pp. 247–8.

Bibliographical Note

For the general background to this period of library history, see A. S. Collins, *Authorship in the Days of Johnson* (1927), espec. Ch. iv, and *The Profession of Letters* (1928), espec. Ch. i; I. Watt, *The Rise of the Novel* (1957), espec. Ch. ii; R. D. Altick, *The English Common Reader* (Chicago 1957), Chaps. ii and iii; T. Kelly, *A History of Adult Education in Great Britain* (1962), Chs. iii–vii.

The best general account of private subscription libraries is F. Beckwith, "The Eighteenth-Century Proprietary Library in England", in *Journal of Documentation*, Vol. III (1947–48). Details concerning particular regions may be found in A. Anderson, *The Old Libraries of Fife* (Fife County Library, Kirkcaldy 1953); G. W. Shirley, "Dumfriesshire Libraries", in *Scottish Adult Education*, No. 26 (August 1959); P. Kaufman, "Community Lending Libraries in Eighteenth-Century Ireland and Wales", in *Library Quarterly* (Chicago), Vol. XXXIII (1963); and the same author's "The Rise of Community Libraries in Scotland", published in *Papers of the Bibliographical Society of America*, Vol. LIX (1965) just as this volume was going to press.

Studies of individual subscription libraries include:

Birmingham: S. Timmins, *Centenary of the Birmingham Library, 1779–1879* (Birmingham 1879); C. Parish, *An Eighteenth Century Proprietary Library: Annals of the Birmingham Library* (F.L.A. thesis 1964, Lib. Assoc., to be published 1966.)

Bradford: W. Scruton, "The Bradford Library and Literary Society", in *Library Association Record*, Vol. VIII (1906).

Bristol: C. Tovey, *The Bristol City Library* (1853); P. Kaufman, *Borrowings from the Bristol Library, 1773–1784* (Bibliographical Society of the University of Virginia, Charlottesville 1960); G. Langley, "A Place to put Books", in *Library Association Record*, Vol. LXV (1963).

Colne: W. M. Spencer, "The Coln Book Society", in *Transactions of the Historic Society of Lancashire and Cheshire,* Vol. CX (Liverpool 1958).

Dundee: D. M. Torbet, *The Growth of Municipal Libraries in Dundee* (F.L.A. thesis 1953, Library Association).

Halifax: E. P. Rouse, "Old Halifax Circulating Library, 1768–1866", in *Halifax Antiquarian Society Papers* (1911).

Hull: History of the Subscription Library at Kingston-upon-Hull (Hull 1876).

Leeds: F. Beckwith, "The Beginnings of the Leeds Subscription Library", in *Thoresby Society Publications,* Vol. XXXVII (Leeds 1945).

Leicester: F. S. Herne, *History of the Town Library and of the Permanent Library, Leicester* (Leicester 1891).

Liverpool: P. Macintyre, "Historical Sketch of the Liverpool Library", in *Transactions of the Historic Society of Lancashire and Cheshire,* Vol. IX (Liverpool 1856–57); P. Cowell, "Origin and History of some Liverpool Libraries", in *Transactions and Proceedings of the Library Association,* 6th Annual Meeting, 1883; G. T. Shaw, *History of the Athenaeum, Liverpool, 1798–1898* (Liverpool 1898).

London: P. Kaufman, "The Eighteenth-Century Forerunner of the London Library", in *Papers of the Bibliographical Society of America,* Vol. LIV (1960).

Norwich: P. Hepworth, "Norfolk and Norwich Subscription Library", in *East Anglian Magazine,* Vol. XIV, No. 10, August 1955; see also G. A. Stephen, *Three Centuries of a City Library* (Norwich 1917), Pt. I; N. G. Wiltshire, *The Continuity of the Library Tradition in an English Provincial Town* (F.L.A. thesis 1957, Library Association).

Sheffield: T. A. Ward, *A Short Account of the Sheffield Library* (Sheffield 1825).

Whitby: H. B. Browne, *Chapters of Whitby History* (Hull 1946), Ch. xii.

P. Kaufman, "English Book Clubs and their Role in Social History", in *Libri,* Vol. XIV (1964), is a valuable pioneering study. On the Luddenden Library see J. Longbottom, "Ye Olde Luddenden Librarye", in *Yorkshire Notes and Queries,* Vol. III (Bradford 1907), and J. Walton, "Eighteenth-Century Village Library", in the *Librarian and Book World,* Vol. XXVIII (1938–39).

For the commercial circulating libraries see A. D. McKillop, "English Circulating Libraries, 1725–50", in *The Library,* 4th Ser., Vol. XIV (1933–34); H. M. Hamlyn, "Eighteenth-Century Circulating Libraries in England", in *The Library*, 5th Ser., Vol. I (1947); and E. McGill, "The Evergreen Tree of Diabolical Knowledge", in *The Bookman*, Vol. LXXIII (1931). The subject is also well dealt with in G. K. Scott, *English Public and Semi-Public Libraries in the Provinces, 1750–1850* (F.L.A. thesis 1951, Library Association). Two well-known London libraries are described in V. Rendall, *Day's Library* (1937), and D. Blakey, *The Minerva Press, 1790–1820* (Bibliographical Society 1939), Ch. vi; and catalogues of two Aberdeen libraries are analysed in J. and L. Gough, "Aberdeen Circulating Libraries in the Eighteenth Century", in *Aberdeen University Review*, Vol. XXXI (1945–46).

CHAPTER VII

The Beginnings of the National Libraries

THE ORIGINS OF THE BRITISH MUSEUM LIBRARY

T H E idea of a national collection of books and manuscripts goes back in England, as we have seen, to the time of the Reformation. In the minds of its first sponsors, Leland, Dee and Cotton, it was connected particularly with the need to preserve a record of English history and antiquities.[1] The poet and historian Edmund Bolton (or Boulton), in a scheme which he submitted to James I in 1617, was also concerned mainly with historical records.[2] It was not long, however, before the new scientific spirit of the seventeenth century made itself felt. Sir Francis Bacon, in his *New Atlantis* (1627), depicted under the name of "Solomon's House" an imaginary institution for scientific research, with twelve travelling Fellows ("Merchants of Light") whose duty it was to collect "the Bookes, and Abstracts, and Patternes of Experiments" from all other countries.[3] Near the close of the century the idea of an enlarged royal library was again put forward by Richard Bentley, the royal librarian. In a broadside of 1697 Bentley proposed the erection of a new library in St. James's Park, to be open freely to all scholars, English and foreign, and to include "all sorts of books", to the number of 200,000. A reference to the work of the Royal Society indicates that his view was not restricted to literary and historical subjects.[4]

In the eighteenth century Thomas Carte the historian, whose comments on the absence of public libraries in London have already been noticed, came forward with a suggestion of a different kind, designed in the first instance to secure possession of the Harleian manuscripts, which he thought might be pur-

---

[1] See above, pp. 44–7.
[2] See the article on him by T. Cooper in *Dictionary of National Biography*.
[3] *New Atlantis*, ed. G. C. Moore Smith (Cambridge 1909), p. 44.
[4] The broadside is reprinted in E. Edwards, *Memoirs of Libraries* Vol. I (1859), p. 423 n.

chased for £20,000. He proposed that the twelve great livery companies should combine in the expense of a library to be erected on top of the new Mansion House, to contain not only the Harleian manuscripts but also printed books in all languages, relating to trade, arts and sciences, history and antiquities.[1]

Carte's suggestion regarding the Harleian manuscripts did actually bear fruit, though not in the way he suggested. The event which turned the idea of a national library into reality was the death in 1753, at the advanced age of 92, of Sir Hans Sloane, the famous physician who had been Newton's successor as President of the Royal Society. Born into the age of the great collectors, Sloane had become the greatest of them all, his interests embracing natural history, art, antiquities, books, manuscripts, and as his will expressed it, "whatever could be procured either in our own or foreign Countries, that was rare and curious". The will directed that the entire collection should be offered to the Crown for the modest sum of £20,000.

The offer was accepted, and the result was the establishment, under an Act of Parliament of 1753, of the British Museum. The Act provided for bringing together in a single repository not only the Sloane collection but also the Cottonian Library, which was already in the possession of the Crown, and the Harleian manuscripts, which were to be purchased for £10,000 from the Countess of Oxford. The funds required were raised by a public lottery, and a home for the combined collections was found at Montagu House in Great Russell Street, which was at that time on the outskirts of the town, with an uninterrupted view to the hills of Hampstead and Highgate. Before the Museum was opened to the public in 1759, it was augmented by the splendid gift of the Royal Library, which was transferred to the trustees by George II in 1757.

THE FOUNDATION COLLECTIONS

The British Museum Library was thus built on the foundation of four great collections. It embraced, from the beginning, both printed books and manuscripts. The printed books were by no

[1] J. Nichols, *Literary Anecdotes of the Eighteenth Century,* Vol. II (1812), pp. 509–12, citing *A Proposal of the Rev. Thomas Carte, M.A., for erecting a Library in the Mansion-house of the City of London* (1743). Cf. above, p. 92.

means insignificant: they comprised some 40,000 from the Sloane collection, including all departments of literature, but particularly strong on the medical and scientific side; about 9,000 from the Royal Library, among them many very early works and others notable for their splendid bindings; and 2,000, mainly antiquarian in interest, bequeathed to the Cottonian Library by Major Arthur Edwards in 1743. In respect of printed books alone, therefore, the Museum Library far excelled any other library in the country at that time. It was, however, in the quality of their manuscript material that the chief glory of the foundation collections lay.

The Royal Library, the oldest of the four, contained some 2,000 manuscripts, including splendidly illuminated Flemish volumes of history and romance written for Edward IV (the first royal collector); monastic books acquired by Henry VIII at the time of the Reformation; and over 300 manuscripts, many of them of monastic origin, procured during the reign of James I from the library of John Lord Lumley.[1] Two special gems of the collection are Queen Mary's Psalter and the Codex Alexandrinus. The former is a beautifully illuminated fourteenth-century English manuscript which once belonged to the Earls of Rutland. Henry Manners, the second Earl, being of the extreme Protestant party, was imprisoned on Mary's accession in 1553, and the psalter was seized by a customs officer when an attempt was being made to carry it over to the Continent. The Codex Alexandrinus is a Greek Bible of the fifth century which came to this country in 1628 as a present from the Patriarch of Alexandria to Charles I. It was long thought to be the earliest surviving Greek text of the Bible, but earlier texts have since been discovered, among them the Codex Sinaiticus, which was acquired by the Museum in 1933.

The Cottonian Library was assembled by Sir Robert Cotton

---

[1] Lumley's Library, which at its greatest extent embraced 400 MSS. and 2,600 printed works, was in part inherited from his father-in-law Henry Fitzalan, Earl of Arundel (cf. above, p. 47), and included books and manuscripts from the library of Archbishop Thomas Cranmer, which had been acquired by Arundel when Cranmer fell from power on Queen Mary's accession in 1553. When Lumley died in 1609 his library passed (by gift it would seem, and not as was long supposed by purchase) into the possession of Henry, Prince of Wales, on whose premature decease three years later it was united with the Royal Library.

to illustrate the history and antiquities of his country.[1] It numbered less than a thousand volumes, but these included, among other treasures, the Lindisfarne Gospels, written about 700, the unique manuscript of *Beowulf*, the unique manuscript of Asser's *Life of Alfred*, two out of the five oldest texts of Bede's *Ecclesiastical History*, five early texts of the *Anglo-Saxon Chronicle*, the unique text of *Sir Gawain and the Green Knight*, one of three original texts of *Piers Plowman*, two of the four copies of Magna Charta, a great store of mediacval chronicles, registers, chartularies, and saints' lives, and more than ninety volumes of state papers from the time of Henry VIII onwards.

The later history of the Cottonian Library was rather curious. When Sir Robert Cotton fell into disgrace in 1629 owing to his associations with the Parliamentary party, his library was sealed and his house in Westminster placed under guard. After his death two years later the library was allowed to return into the possession of the family, but partly because it included so many valuable state papers it was regarded, as indeed it had been in Sir Robert's time, as in some sense a public library. A special Act of Parliament of 1700 placed the books, house and garden under trustees for the benefit of the public, and eventually in 1706 the property was acquired by the Crown for the sum of £4,500.[2] The Royal Library was now moved from St. James's Palace to Cotton House, and before long the Cottonian collection passed into the charge of the Royal Librarian. The damp and dilapidated condition of the house, however, made it necessary to move the two libraries, first in 1722 to Essex House in the Strand, and then in 1729 to Ashburnham House, Westminster. Here, two years later, a disastrous fire broke out. The Royal Library escaped almost unscathed, but of the 958 volumes of the Cottonian Library, 97 were completely lost, and more than a hundred others seriously damaged by fire or water. From this time until the establishment of the British Museum, the Royal Library and what remained of the Cottonian Library were stored in the dormitory buildings of Westminster School.

The Harleian manuscripts, amounting to nearly 8,000 volumes, were collected by Robert Harley, first Earl of Oxford,

[1] Cf. above, p. 47.
[2] The date is often given as 1707. The Act authorizing the purchase was 5 and 6 Anne c. 30, 1706.

and his son Edward, the second Earl, between 1700, when Robert succeeded to the family estates, and 1741, when Edward died. Their success in bringing together so vast a collection at such a late date was undoubtedly due in considerable measure to the knowledge and assiduity of the well-known antiquarian Humphrey Wanley, who acted as librarian from 1708 until his death in 1726 (two years after the death of the first Earl).

The Harleian Collection included important early Biblical texts in Greek, Latin and Hebrew, early texts of classical authors and the Fathers of the Church, records of Church Councils, papal bulls and registers, and liturgical books of the Christian Churches of both East and West. Even the field of English history, in which Cotton had already reaped so industriously, was made to yield another rich harvest of deeds, charters, chronicles, biographies, letters, literary texts, and state papers reaching to the Harleys' own time. The first Earl's political career, culminating in his service as chief minister to Queen Anne during the years 1710–14, put him in a specially favourable position for securing state papers, and like Cotton before him he did not hesitate to appropriate anything that came his way.

The Sloane manuscripts, though collected about the same time as the Harleian, were quite different in character. Like Sloane's printed books, they were mainly scientific in interest. About two-thirds of them were concerned with medicine or the related subjects of alchemy and astrology. Botany also was strongly represented, and there were many accounts of voyages and discoveries, e.g. the journal of the South Sea voyages of William Dampier. Sloane's interest in everything that was "rare and curious" is reflected in the presence of more than 250 Oriental manuscripts. A consignment despatched to him from China in 1703 is thus described:

"In the foresaid Box there's for yourself a Chinese Common Prayer, Book, which I procur'd from the Bonzes at Pǔ-tó, the Lords Prayer Belief and 10 Commandements translated into Chinese by the Jesuites, a description of Pǔ-tó in Chinese, a Draft of the River of Ning-po done by a French Father who resides there."[1]

[1] MS. 4039, f. 85, quoted in *Brit. Mus. Quarterly*, Vol. XVIII (1953) p. 7.

Altogether the Sloane manuscripts today number just over 4,000.

Unfortunately, having founded the British Museum, the Government left it for the next fifty years very much to its own devices, and expansion was consequently very slow. The total staff of the Library at the outset comprised a Principal Librarian at £160 a year and five part-time Keepers and Assistant Keepers – clergy and medical men who enjoyed free apartments in Montagu House and combined a few hours' work each week in the Museum with their professional duties. The total income of the Museum as a whole, from investments, Government grants, and other sources, was initially only £900 per annum and was still under £3,000 at the end of the century.

There were, indeed, a few notable gifts. The Thomason Tracts – over 22,000 pamphlets and newspapers of the Civil War period collected by George Thomason, a London bookseller – were presented by George III in 1762; David Garrick bequeathed a remarkable collection of playbooks in 1779; Rev. C. M. Cracherode, a wealthy private collector and a trustee of the Museum, bequeathed in 1799 4,500 volumes (including many early printed works) distinguished for their fine condition and fine bindings; and in the same year Sir William Musgrave, another trustee, gave a collection of printed books and manuscript material relating to British biography. Otherwise, however, accessions were few: very little money was available for new purchases, and although under the Press Licensing Acts of 1662 onwards the Royal Library was entitled to receive a copy of every English publication registered with the Stationers' Company, no attempt seems to have been made to enforce this.[1]

The first Statutes and Rules drawn up by the trustees, in 1757, set out the principles regarding public access to the Museum which have been adhered to ever since. The preamble states that

"altho it was chiefly designed for the use of learned and studious men, both natives and foreigners, in their researches into the several parts of knowledge; yet being founded at the expence of the public, it may be judged reasonable, that the advantages accruing from it should be

[1] See below, p. 167.

rendered as general as may be consistent with the several considerations above mentioned."[1]

The lending of books was, of course, strictly forbidden. Permission to read in the Library had to be sought from the trustees, and was granted for a period of six months, after which a fresh application was needed. The intending reader was also required to give notice in writing, on the day before his visit, of the book or manuscript he wished to consult. Since there was no artificial lighting, the hours of opening were from 9 to 3 only, except during the summer months when the hours on Mondays and Fridays were from 4 to 8. On Saturdays and Sundays the Museum was closed.

The first reading room was a narrow, dark, damp and draughty apartment on the ground floor of the building. It had a bare wooden floor and the walls were lined with cases of stuffed birds. After some years it was decreed that the floors should be covered with rush matting. In 1774, however, a new and much more attractive room was opened on the first floor – a well-lighted room with books round the walls instead of birds. The rule about giving a day's notice for books was now abandoned.

"Two long tables covered with green baize were placed on each side of the fireplace ... for the readers, who were supplied with book-rests, pens, ink and sand-boxes. (Blotting pads were not introduced until 1838). The window-seats were filled with books of reference, and the catalogues, such as they were and what there was of them, stood on open shelves. When a reader had put the necessary particulars on a slip, he pulled the long bell-rope at the side of the door and a messenger speedily obeyed the summons, and returned with the book as soon as he could find it."[2]

A record of the famous people who have used the reading room of the British Museum would be a roll-call of the scholars of England for the past two hundred years. Amongst those who read there during its first half century were Gray, Gibbon, Burke, Hume, Boswell, Isaac Disraeli, Scott, Southey, and Sydney Smith. Johnson too, had a ticket though there is no

---

[1] Quoted A. Esdaile, *The British Museum Library* (1946), p. 37.
[2] G. F. Barwick, *The Reading Room of the British Museum* (1929), pp. 42–43.

evidence that he ever used it. At this time, however, though the occupants of the room might be eminent, they were rarely numerous: "It had been difficult", declared Disraeli, "to have made up a jury of all the spirits of study which haunted the reading room."[1]

THE EARLY NINETEENTH CENTURY

It was the early nineteenth century that saw the beginnings of those developments which were to make the British Museum Library one of the foremost libraries of the world. The changes were particularly associated with the name of Antonio Panizzi, who became Keeper of Printed Books in 1837, the year of Queen Victoria's accession. Even before this date, however, considerable improvements had taken place. The general Government grant in aid of the Museum as a whole was gradually but substantially increased, and although the library received only a small share of this increase, there were on several occasions between 1807 and 1818 supplementary grants for book purchase amounting in all to over £35,000. From 1834 onwards *ad hoc* grants were replaced by a regular annual purchase grant to the Museum trustees.

The library was thus enabled not only to strengthen its holdings of British books but also to acquire a number of special collections: the Lansdowne MSS., rich in additional materials relating to English history, in 1807; the Hargrave collection of legal books and manuscripts in 1813; the Van Moll collection of works on natural history in 1815–16; the two Burney collections, one of books on music and one of classical books and manuscripts, in 1815 and 1818; the first two of the three Croker collections of French Revolution tracts in 1817 and 1831 (the third was added in 1856); and a portion of the Arundel MSS., a priceless collection of English, European, Hebrew and Oriental manuscripts assembled by Thomas Howard, second Earl of Arundel, in the seventeenth century, and afterwards given to the Royal Society, which sold them to the Museum in 1830.

There were, too, important gifts and bequests: the Banks library of books on natural history and travel, bequeathed in

---

[1] *Op. cit.*, p. 47.

1820; the King's Library, presented by George IV in 1823;[1] and the Egerton MSS., bequeathed in 1829 by Francis Egerton, eighth Earl of Bridgewater. These last were in the first instance relatively few in number, but thanks to the endowments left for their increase they have become, as the years have gone by, one of the most important collections in the Library.

Of the three gifts here mentioned, however, that of the King's Library was outstanding. This library had been brought together by George III and is so called to distinguish it from the old Royal Library which had been presented by his grandfather George II in 1757. George III was one of the few English monarchs to take a serious interest in book collecting. He spent about £2,000 a year on building up a new royal library, and this rate of expenditure was continued under the Regency during the period of his insanity. When his library was eventually transferred to the Museum in 1828, it was found to contain over 65,000 printed volumes and 19,000 unbound pamphlets, besides about 450 manuscripts. The Museum's own collection at this time amounted to some 125,000 volumes.

The King's Library was not a collection of rarities. The manuscripts were mostly of no great importance, and though there was a considerable number of early printed books the collection was chiefly valuable for other things: Elizabethan literature, playbooks, historical pamphlets, periodicals, and standard works of recent date covering a wide range of subjects. The geographical section was particularly strong and included many maps, charts and drawings.

Thanks to these accessions, to the special purchases mentioned above, and to an improvement after 1814 in the flow of copyright works,[2] the Library's stock of recent English books gradually improved, and this was undoubtedly one factor contributing to the increasing public interest in the Library, and the increasing use of the reading room. Four times between 1803 and 1838 it was necessary to move to a larger room: that of 1838 provided accommodation for 168 readers – a striking change from the

---

[1] It has been suggested that in return for the surrender of the library George IV received assistance from public funds towards the liquidation of his debts, but firm evidence on this point seems to be lacking. See *Notes and Queries*, Vol. IV (1851), p. 69; and R. Fulford, *George IV* (1935), p. 257.

[2] See below, pp. 169 seq.

position in the eighteenth century. The hours of opening were also extended. In 1803 they had been fixed at 10–4 daily except Saturdays and Sundays. Saturday opening during the summer was introduced in 1831, and five years later the time of opening was fixed at 9 a.m. throughout the year, and the time of closure was extended to 7 p.m. during the four summer months.

The reading room of 1838, and its immediate predecessor opened in 1829, were not in the original Montagu House but in the new quadrangular building in the Greek style (the present building) which was designed by Robert Smirke and began to be erected in 1823. In 1845 the old building was pulled down, and by 1852 the quadrangle was complete.

THE REIGN OF PANIZZI

Panizzi, whose dynamic personality dominated the development of the library in the middle years of the nineteenth century, was born in 1897 at Brescello in Modena. Trained as an advocate in the neighbouring University of Parma, he became involved in revolutionary activities, was forced to flee the country, and reached England in 1823.[1] After five years in Liverpool, where he maintained himself by teaching Italian, he was appointed through the influence of Lord Brougham as first Professor of Italian Literature in the University of London, and in 1831, again thanks to Brougham, he entered the service of the Museum as an Extra Assistant Librarian. On his appointment to the Keepership of Printed Books six years later he resigned his chair, and henceforth he devoted his abundant energies first and foremost to the task of reorganizing the Library. He served as Principal Librarian from 1856 to 1866, and was afterwards knighted as Sir Anthony Panizzi.

His success as a librarian was due not only to his tremendous capacity for work, his skill as an administrator, and his punctilious concern for detail, but above all to his vision of what the Museum Library could and should be and his determination to

---

[1] He was tried and sentenced to death in his absence, and the bill for his trial *and execution* was forwarded to him in exile. He replied, from Liverpool in 1824, "*Mors omnia solvit*" (death pays all debts) – L. Fagan, *Life of Sir Anthony Panizzi*, Vol. I (1880), p. 51.

translate this dream into reality. It is true that he was a difficult man to get on with, that he was a rigid disciplinarian, and that he was sometimes ruthless in the pursuit of his objectives, but these faults were in large measure the obverse of his virtues. Nor should we forget how much his personal difficulties were increased by his foreign birth. Though he was naturalized in 1832, and though through his concern for the cause of Italian unity and freedom he became the friend of many leading English statesmen, there were many who were jealous of his rise to power, and did not hesitate to denounce him as an Italian upstart.

Panizzi did not attain a position of authority until 1837, but he had an opportunity of making his influence felt in the two previous years, when a Select Committee of the House of Commons was sitting to examine the affairs of the Museum. In his evidence before this Committee Panizzi stressed two important points: first, that a sharp distinction must be drawn between a scholar's library, such as he conceived the Museum Library to be, and libraries of a more general kind, which he called "libraries for education"; and second, that if the Museum Library was to function efficiently as a scholar's library there must be a very large increase in public expenditure upon it. On the former point he remarked:

" . . . if I am to choose, I would say that it is of less importance for the library of the British Museum to have common modern books, than to have rare, ephemeral, voluminous and costly publications, which cannot be found anywhere else, by persons not having access to great private collections. I want a poor student to have the same means of indulging his learned curiosity, of following his rational pursuits, of consulting the same authorities, of fathoming the most intricate inquiry, as the richest man in the kingdom, as far as books go, and I contend the Government is bound to give him the most liberal and unlimited assistance in this respect. I want the library of the British Museum to have books of both descriptions; I want an extra grant for those rare and costly books which we have not, and which cannot be bought but upon opportunities offering themselves. Then, the annual grant should be increased for modern books, that is for books printed from about the beginning of the last century."

If, he concluded, the Government were prepared to spend, say, £100,000 over a ten or twelve year period, "then you will begin to have a library worthy of the British nation, but not if you continue to go on as hitherto".[1]

The Select Committee made one recommendation that was of great importance to the future of the Library, and of Panizzi personally. Hitherto the staffing of the Library had been, as in the eighteenth century, on a very amateur basis, many of the responsible officers combining the work, as Panizzi himself had done, with other appointments. This pluralism was now abolished: the salaries of the officers were put on a professional basis, and they were forbidden to hold other paid appointments. Rev. H. H. Baber, the Keeper of Printed Books, resigned and went off to his living in Cambridgeshire: Panizzi gave up his chair of Italian and succeeded Baber as Keeper.

At this time the printed books in the Library had reached the impressive total of 227,000 volumes, but owing to the way in which it had been formed it was a very haphazard collection, and in many branches of learning it was very inadequate. Panizzi, after a careful survey of the whole library, set to work systematically not merely to enlarge the collection but to strengthen it in those sections where gaps had been revealed. Through the trustees he negotiated a substantial increase in Government grants; he rigidly enforced the Museum's rights in the matter of copyright deposit; and through his personal influence he secured the bequest in 1847 of Thomas Grenville's splendid library of 20,000 volumes, a library particularly rich in Italian and Spanish literature. When Panizzi retired in 1866 the Museum Library had grown to nearly a million volumes.

The accumulation of books, however, was of no use without

---

[1] *Report from the Select Committee on the Condition, Management and Affairs of the British Museum* (1836), p. 391. At this time the money available to spend on books was on average about £1,000 a year. It was at this same Committee that the ill-starred Edward Edwards first made his mark in connection with the British Museum. As a result of a pamphlet he had published on the subject he was invited to give evidence, and submitted a whole programme of reform. He was taken on to the library staff in 1839, but was dismissed in 1850, partly as a result of his own irresponsible behaviour and partly as a result of a personal antipathy which had developed between him and Panizzi. He afterwards became first librarian of the Manchester Free Public Library, but is best known for his part in the events leading to the Public Libraries Act of 1850, and for his voluminous writings on library history.

space to shelve them, adequate accommodation for readers, and an efficient catalogue. The catalogue, of which more will be said shortly, caused Panizzi a great deal of trouble, largely because he did not see eye to eye with the trustees on the matter. The trustees, and many scholars who used the Museum, favoured a printed catalogue, of the type with which they were familiar in other institutions, for example the larger subscription libraries. Panizzi believed that for so large a library a printed catalogue was useless, since it was bound to be out of date long before it was printed. Printed catalogues had indeed been produced in 1787, and again, in seven octavo volumes, in 1813–19. The latter, expanded by manuscript additions in folio volumes, had become by 1836 so unmanageable that it had to be completely recopied. The solution eventually adopted by Panizzi and put into practice from 1847 onwards, was a catalogue made up of individual manuscript entries pasted into folio volumes, and capable of being rearranged when necessary.[1]

Accommodation for books and readers was a matter of serious concern in view of the very rapid expansion of the library and the growing demand for its services. When a Royal Commission was appointed in 1847 to make a new examination of the Museum and its administration, several witnesses gave evidence of the inadequacies of the 1838 reading room, and the difficulty of securing access to books. One of the most outspoken critics was Carlyle, who while paying tribute to the exemplary conduct of the attendants, complained that the room was noisy, badly ventilated, and above all overcrowded:

"The jostling you are subject to, and the continual want of composure, were entirely fatal to any attempt on my part to study there. . . . I have gone into that room when it has been quite crowded, and there has been no seat vacant, and I have been obliged to sit on the step of a ladder: and there are such bustle and confusion that . . . I never do enter the room without getting a headach – what I call the Museum headach – and therefore I avoid the room till the last extremity. I may add, that I am rather a thin-skinned sort of student,

---

[1] The sheer bulk of the entries, which by 1875 occupied 2,250 folio volumes, eventually made it necessary to use printed slips, and a printed catalogue, complete to the year 1900, was published in 1881–1905. The new printed catalogue at present in process of publication is produced by photolithography.

and sensible to these inconveniences more than perhaps most other students."[1]

Carlyle also complained bitterly about the lack of an adequate catalogue, especially of the Thomason Civil War Tracts, and urged the importance of having someone present in the reading room to advise readers on their needs. These were both valid points. He showed his usual intolerance, however, in characterizing other readers:

"I believe, there are several persons in a state of imbecility who come to read in the British Museum. . . . I remember there was one gentleman who used to blow his nose loudly every half hour. I inquired who he was, and I was informed he was a mad person sent there by his friends; he made extracts out of books, and fuddled away his time there. A great number of the readers come to read novels; a great number come for idle purposes – probably a considerable proportion of the readers. And, on the whole, a vast majority come to the reading room chiefly to compile and excerpt; to carry away something that they may put into articles for encyclopaedias and periodicals, biographical dictionaries, or some such compilation."[2]

Carlyle's is merely the best known of many descriptions of the reading room and its readers about this time. From another, written by E. L. Manchard in 1848, we extract a typically Victorian comment on women readers:

"At various intervals will be found, mingling with the groups, some literary ladies, chiefly occupied on works of botany and conchology; and as one of the features of the age, showing that women, equally with men, enjoy the pleasures and the toils of literary occupation, their presence must give rise to some gratifying reflections."[3]

In 1852, after various alternative schemes for securing additional space had been vainly explored, Panizzi turned his attention to the possibility, which had several times been canvassed, of utilizing the vacant central quadrangle of the new Museum building. His plans were rapidly completed and approved: the building was begun in 1854, and triumphantly

[1] *Report of the Commissioners appointed to inquire into the Constitution and Management of the British Museum* (1850), pp. 272–3.
[2] *Op. cit.*, p. 277.
[3] Quoted from the *People's Journal*, 1848, in G. F. Barwick, *The Reading Room of the British Museum* (1929), p. 85.

opened in 1857. Thereby at a single stroke Panizzi solved both his main problems. The great new circular reading room, its dome inferior in size only to that of the Pantheon in Rome, provided seating for over 300 readers (and ultimately, by the insertion of extra tables, for half as many again). Round its walls were ranged shelves for 60,000 volumes, and in the area outside the circle the "iron library" provided accommodation for a million more.

It is not surprising that this new building at once became one of the wonders of London. What is surprising, to the modern reader, is that the new buildings still had no artificial lighting. The Museum authorities steadfastly set their face against gas-lighting, as dangerous and also deleterious to the books, and it was not until 1879 that electric lighting was at last introduced. Otherwise, however, the central reading room, familiar now to so many generations of students, remains today essentially what it was in 1857.

We cannot leave this period of the Museum's history without referring to one rather unusual episode – the Chartist demonstration of April, 1848. This affair, which in retrospect looks rather ludicrous, was taken very seriously by the inhabitants of London at the time, and by none more than the authorities of the British Museum, since the official programme provided for a meeting of the Western division of the Chartists in Russell Square. On the fateful day the Museum was closed, every entrance except that in Great Russell Street was strongly barricaded, and a force of 59 regular troops, 20 Chelsea pensioners, and 250 special constables armed with muskets, pikes or cutlasses was assembled to guard the building and its treasures. The special constables consisted of the Museum staff and workmen engaged on the rebuilding, and although Sir Henry Ellis was at this time the Principal Librarian, it was, of course Panizzi who was the real commander-in-chief. "He was everywhere", writes an eye-witness, "looking personally into all that was taking place, and encouraging us all with the motto: 'England expects that every man this day will do his duty'."[1] After all this, the complete collapse of the demonstration must have come as something of an anti-climax, but honour at least had been saved.

[1] R. Cowtan, *Memories of the British Museum* (1872), p. 150.

COPYRIGHT DEPOSIT

This brief account of the early history of the British Museum Library opens up two topics of wider interest with which the Museum was particularly concerned – the system of copyright deposit, and methods of book classification and cataloguing.

The idea that a free copy of every book published should be deposited in a national library is said to have been imported from France, where it was introduced by Francis I in 1537 for the benefit of the royal library. In England the proposal first appears in Sir Humphrey Gilbert's scheme for a royal academy, which included a provision that

"All Printers in England shall for ever be charged to deliver into the Liberary of the Achademy, at their owne Charges, one Copy, well bownde, of euery booke, proclamacion, or pamflette, that they shall printe."[1]

A more practical step in the same direction was taken in 1610, when Sir Thomas Bodley, by what means of persuasion we do not know, negotiated an agreement with the Stationers' Company for the delivery to the Bodleian Library of a free copy of every book published by a member of the Company. Since the Company had an official monopoly of all printing except that undertaken by the two university presses, this was on the face of it a most important concession, but though confirmed successively by the Court of High Commission and the Star Chamber it was only reluctantly and imperfectly fulfilled. Bodley complained, too, in the early years, of the quality of such books as were delivered, and instructed his librarian, Thomas James, to exclude "suche bookes as almanackes, plaies, and an infinit number, that are daily printed, of very vnworthy maters and handling. . . ."[2]

This was, of course, a private agreement. The real beginnings of a copyright deposit system under state auspices came in the Restoration period, and were associated with Government

---

[1] Sir H. Gilbert, *Queene Elizabethes Achademy* (*c*. 1564, repr. Early English Text Society, Extra Series, No. VIII, 1869), p. 8. The Library Keeper was also to take his choice of all imported books, to be paid for out of an endowment of £40 per annum.

[2] G. W. Wheeler (ed.), *Letters of Sir Thomas Bodley* (1926), p. 221. Shakespeare's plays were amongst those excluded at this stage.

control of printing. The strict censorship which had been established in Elizabeth's reign by an alliance between the Crown, the Church, and the Stationers' Company collapsed during the Civil War, and efforts to restore it from 1643 onwards were only partly successful. In 1662, however, as part of a Licensing Act which once more placed the control of printing in the hands of the Stationers' Company, it was enacted that three copies of every book published, or reprint with additions, should be deposited before sale at Stationers' Hall, one copy being for the Royal Library, one for the Bodleian, and one for the University Library of Cambridge.

This Act was renewed, with modifications, until 1679, and again from 1685 to 1695, but in spite of all kinds of threats and penalties the printers were loth to give away their property and the number of books which reached the libraries in this way was very small. Richard Bentley, the distinguished Greek scholar who was appointed Keeper of the King's Library in 1694, succeeded in enforcing the delivery of arrears amounting to a thousand volumes, but since there was no requirement as to binding they were delivered in unbound sheets.[1]

With the lapse of the Licensing Act in 1695 the libraries lost their right to free copies. The printers soon found, however, that the abolition of control was a mixed blessing, for the old system had at least provided them with some legal protection for their works. They accordingly petitioned Parliament for redress, and the result was the Copyright Act of 1709, which for the first time fixed the period of copyright. This was vested in the author or his assigns, and extended to twenty-one years in the case of works already published. In the case of future publications the period was to be fourteen years, and if the author were still living at the end of that period, a further fourteen years. The number of libraries entitled to free copies, however, was increased now to nine, by the inclusion, first of Sion College, and secondly, as a result of the Act of Union of 1707, of the four Scottish universities and the Advocates' Library in Edinburgh.

[1] I am putting together here statements made in Bentley's *Proposal for Building a Royal Library* (1697) and his *Dissertation on the Epistles of Phalaris* (1699). Cf. E. Edwards, *Memoirs of Libraries* (1859), Vol. I, pp. 422–3, Vol. II, pp. 586–7.

The printers were furious. The copyright which they had been accustomed to regard as perpetual had been reduced, and the price they had to pay had been increased. In these circumstances they interpreted the Act to mean that the deposit of copies was required only when copyright was sought. They therefore declined to register expensive works which were unlikely to be pirated, and in the case of other works sought to evade their obligations in various ways, e.g. by registering the first volume only of works published in more than one volume. For the libraries, therefore, the results of the 1709 Act were exceedingly disappointing, most of the books deposited being cheap and ephemeral publications, usually in sheet form.

As we have seen, the Royal Library was transferred in 1757 to the newly founded British Museum, and its right to free copies of published works was afterwards adjudged to have been transferred at the same time. In 1801 the union with Ireland added Trinity College and the King's Inns, Dublin, to the list of privileged libraries, which now totalled eleven. Otherwise the position regarding the deposit of books remained substantially the same as in 1709, the publishers depositing whatever they thought fit. The British Museum Library, at this period, derived practically no benefit from the privilege it had acquired, and indeed took no steps to do so, partly because of lack of staff and partly because the books available were hardly worth collecting.

In 1812, however, the University of Cambridge sued a printer named Bryer for the non-delivery of a book, and to the dismay of the publishers secured a judgment that eleven copies of every new book must be deposited at Stationers' Hall whether the book was registered for copyright or not. This led to a furious agitation, and after two years to a new Copyright Act, under which, though author's copyright was extended to twenty-eight years, all published works must be registered. One copy was to be deposited immediately for the use of the British Museum, and ten more on demand. It was expected that the copyright libraries would make a selection of the works published, but in fact they decided to claim everything. The British Museum appointed an agent for the purpose at Stationers' Hall: he collected 500 works in 1814, over 1,000 in 1815.

The exaction of the eleven copies was bitterly resented as an unjustifiable tax on both authors and publishers, and every possible measure was taken to evade it and if possible to secure its abolition. It was not until 1836, however, that Parliament at last decided to reduce the number of copyright libraries to five: the British Museum, the Bodleian, the University Library of Cambridge, the Advocates' Library in Edinburgh, and the Library of Trinity College, Dublin. The remaining six libraries were compensated by an annual grant based on the number of works received during the years 1833–36: the sums agreed upon ranged from £320 per annum in the case of King's College, Aberdeen, to £707 per annum in the case of Glasgow University. With the addition of the National Library of Wales (founded in 1907), the list of copyright libraries has remained unchanged to this day,[1] and the annual payments to the libraries deprived of this privilege still continue.

The Copyright Act of 1836 was followed by the Imperial Copyright Act of 1842, which extended the period of copyright to forty-two years, or seven years after the death of the author, whichever period was the longer. This Act also defined some of the deposit rules more closely. The British Museum copy was now to be delivered to the Museum direct, and was to be bound and on "the best paper upon which the same should be printed"; the other four copies, on the paper used for the largest edition printed, were to be delivered on demand by the Stationers' Company or the libraries concerned. The Act also attempted to extend the provisions of copyright deposit to books published in other parts of the British Empire, but for various reasons these clauses were never effectively enforced.

Even in the home country publishers were still reluctant to comply with the Act, and it was not until Panizzi took the task in hand in 1850 that the law was fully enforced. Armed with powers to prosecute on behalf of the Museum, Panizzi began by bringing the London publishers to heel, and then set off on a tour of the rest of the country. He travelled throughout England, Wales, Scotland and Ireland, hunting down offending publishers and forcing them, if necessary by legal action, to yield up the copies to which the Museum was entitled. He made himself exceedingly unpopular – "Who is this d——d Italian?"

[1] The Advocates' Library became the National Library of Scotland in 1925.

asked an irate correspondent of *The Times* – but he got the books. In 1851 the number of items delivered to the Museum was less than 10,000; in 1856, when Panizzi gave up the Keepership of Printed Books to become Principal Librarian, the total exceeded 26,000.

The other copyright libraries did not take such drastic steps to enforce their rights, but they benefited indirectly by Panizzi's demonstration that the Act of 1842 was to be taken seriously. The publishers continued to grumble – they continue to grumble today – but they complied.

CLASSIFICATION AND CATALOGUING

This is a subject about which the layman does not think enough, and the librarian is apt to think too much. The layman commonly underestimates the complexity of the task; while on the other hand there have been librarians who have erected classification into a philosophy and cataloguing into an esoteric science.[1] The basic principles are, however, not difficult to understand and it is worth while to consider briefly how they developed.

The primary purpose of a library is to serve its readers, and the first task of the librarian is to arrange his books in such a way as to make them as readily available as possible both to himself and (if the readers are given access to the shelves) to the readers. For this purpose some sort of subject grouping has generally been thought best, but it has nearly always been necessary to take account also of the size of the books. Even the modern public library has its outsize books which have to be separately shelved, and in the older libraries, with folios, quartos, octavos, and duodecimos, the problem was so serious that within the subject grouping there was usually also a grouping according to size. The second task of the librarian is to provide a catalogue as a guide to the collection. This may follow the shelf-order, in which case the books will usually be listed under the subject divisions to which they belong. The advantage of this arrangement is that it assists the reader to

---

[1] A book by F. J. Wilson, published in 1866, is entitled *The Philosophy of Classification; being a base for thought, a measurement for morality, and a key to truth.*

discover what resources the library has in the field in which he is interested; its disadvantage is that it may be difficult to locate a particular book, especially if it does not fit easily into the subject classification adopted. This difficulty may be overcome by a supplementary index of authors, but many libraries have preferred to rely primarily on a catalogue arranged alphabetically under authors, with perhaps a supplementary index of subjects. Another solution, but a more complicated one, is to have what is called a dictionary catalogue, combining in a single alphabetical arrangement authors, titles and subjects.

Over many of these problems, and especially over the right kind of subject division and the best form of cataloguing, fierce conflicts have raged, and even today the waters of controversy are not entirely stilled. Some protagonists of particular systems seem to have overlooked the fact that libraries differ greatly in size and scope and in the needs of their students, so that a method of organization that suits one will not necessarily suit all.

We have seen in an earlier chapter that the first library to grapple seriously with the difficulties of classification and cataloguing in an expanding collection was the Bodleian at Oxford.[1] Throughout the two and a half centuries between the foundation of the Bodleian and the Public Libraries Act of 1850, librarians throughout the country had to face, usually on a smaller scale, the same kind of problems, and there can be no doubt that many of them were influenced by the Bodleian's pioneering work. The only other substantial library to issue a printed catalogue during the seventeenth century was Sion College in London, and it is significant that its catalogue of 1650 was closely modelled on James's alphabetical author catalogue of 1620. The only important difference was that Sion College also used some subject headings, e.g. Concordances, Discovery, Lexicon, London, Scotland, so that it was, in fact, a rudimentary dictionary catalogue.

The solutions found by other libraries were many and various, and since there was no training for librarianship, and no commonly accepted code of practice, the same mistakes were made over and over again. Many of the smaller endowed libraries were organized in the most haphazard fashion, and hardly

[1] See above, pp. 54–8.

catalogued at all, and though most cathedral libraries had at least a manuscript catalogue it was often half a century or more out of date. On the other hand some of these older libraries took considerable care over the arrangement and cataloguing of their books.

Sion College, already mentioned, was one. In 1724 it issued a second printed catalogue on a quite different plan. The books were now reclassified under twenty-nine subject headings, beginning in the mediaeval manner with Bibles, Concordances, and other branches of theology, but going on to more modern topics such as Biography and Political History. This library was arranged on the stall system, with folios on the lower shelves and smaller books on the upper shelves, and each book had a press-mark in the form C. 3. 25, where C represented the subject heading, 3 the shelf, and 25 the position of the book on the shelf. This was, in fact, a "fixed location" system, but it contained an element of flexibility in that the first symbol represented a subject group and not an actual bookcase or press.[1]

Chetham's Library, Manchester, published in 1791 a catalogue based on an entirely new classification devised by its librarian John Radcliffe. This was an elaborate affair with five main headings – Theology, Jurisprudence, History, Science and Arts, and Humane Letters – and thirty-nine sub-headings, of which some were further sub-divided; and in each section the books were also divided according to size. The books were numbered consecutively from the beginning to the end of the catalogue, which would not seem to the modern librarian a very sensible procedure.

The old City Library in Norwich, founded in 1608, had a particularly interesting set of catalogues: a manuscript subject catalogue (with author index) in 1658; printed author catalogues in 1707 and 1732; a manuscript catalogue according to languages in 1816;[2] and printed subject catalogues in 1825 and 1847. In the last two catalogues the books are incorporated with those of the Subscription Library of which at this period

---

[1] Cf. above, p. 54.

[2] An arrangement of books into subjects and then into languages was suggested by John Dury, Deputy Keeper of the Royal Library, in *The Reformed Librarie-Keeper* (1650, ed. J. C. Dana and H. W. Kent, Chicago 1906), p. 46. The relevant passage is also reprinted in J. L. Thornton, *Classics of Librarianship* (1957), pp. 14–18.

the City Library formed a part. Throughout all these cataloguing changes the library seems always to have been organized on a subject basis, with a division by size within each heading or sub-heading. Even when it was absorbed into the Subscription Library there are indications that it was separately shelved.[1]

A subject classification, both for books and catalogues, seems indeed to have been a common arrangement, in spite of the advice given by Thomas James in the Bodleian catalogue of 1620.[2]

In the cathedral and older endowed libraries this arrangement was often accompanied by a fixed location press-mark, or some adaptation of this, as at Sion College in 1724, but the subscription, circulating and institutional libraries of the late eighteenth and nineteenth centuries, which in the main were concerned with the provision of recent works, preferred less elaborate methods. The internal organization of these libraries has so far been little studied, and can only be guessed at from the character of their published catalogues, which were fairly frequent. It seems likely that in the smaller libraries, staffed by part-time and often honorary librarians, and even in the larger libraries in the earlier years, arrangements were pretty primitive. The historian of the Birmingham Library, for example, thus describes its second catalogue (1795):

"The catalogue is primarily an author catalogue of non-fiction combined in a single alphabetical sequence and including many entries under title. The main catalogue is divided into sections, each headed by an initial letter of the alphabet, and each section is divided into folios, quartos, octavos and duodecimos. Apart from grouping by initial letter there was no other alphabetization. The entries are brief. Surnames only are given, titles are abbreviated, no imprints are included and collations are limited to the number of volumes where more than one. Accession numbers are provided. At the end of the catalogue are to be found notes on its use. They include the following: 'In the foregoing catalogue the publications of different authors having the same surname, are to be found under that surname, without specifying the Christian name.' And 'The few remaining typographical errors the reader will be pleased to correct with his pen.' . . ."[3]

[1] After the transfer of the books to the Free Library they were rearranged and a new author catalogue was published in 1883.
[2] See above, p. 57.
[3] C. Parish, *An Eighteenth Century Proprietary Library* (F.L.A. thesis 1964; to be published by the L.A. 1966), p. 71.

The next catalogue (1798) listed the books under broad subject headings. As the entries were no more informative than
before and there was no author index, it must have been even
more difficult to use than the previous catalogue. It is significant,
however, that the President, Rev. Edward Burn, was thanked
for this "judicious arrangement" of the catalogue, which
suggests that the books themselves were not arranged according
to subjects but only alphabetically according to size as in the
1795 catalogue.

Many nineteenth-century catalogues show a subject division.
They have such headings as History, Biography, Travel,
Poetry, Fiction, Arts and Sciences, and under each heading the
books are listed in at least approximate alphabetical order of
authors, or sometimes of titles. Often the entries are numbered,
either consecutively under each heading, or consecutively from
the beginning to end of the catalogue, or in order of accession,
but many libraries relied on alphabetical arrangement without
numbering. This was clearly the easiest system where accessions
were frequent, and was probably used on the shelves as well as
in the catalogues.

Rough-and-ready arrangements of this kind sufficed for a
library of up to, say, 10,000 volumes, or even more if a large
proportion of the books were fiction. The larger the library,
however, and the more varied the collection, the greater was
the need for an adequate subject division either on the shelves
or in the catalogue. This was a matter that attracted more
attention on the Continent than in this country. Continental
scholars and librarians were prolific in schemes of library
classification from the sixteenth century onwards. Most of them
aimed at finding some "logical" order in which the subjects
could be arranged, and many of them based their proposals on
a philosophical classification of the field of knowledge. In Great
Britain, John Evelyn was interested enough to publish, in 1661,
a translation of Gabriel Naudé's *Avis pour dresser une biblio-
thèque;*[1] and at Cambridge, in 1723, Conyers Middleton compiled
a classification (never used) for the University Library. Otherwise the matter was little discussed, and librarians went on
using such subject groupings as the nature of the library and
their personal predilections suggested.

[1] Published under the title, *Instructions concerning Erecting of a Library.*

It might have been expected that the British Museum Library, at least, would be obliged to tackle this problem in a systematic way, but its first catalogue, printed in 1787, was an alphabetical author catalogue, and the first scheme for the arrangement of the books, compiled by Rev. Samuel Harper, Keeper of Printed Books, and Rev. Samuel Ayscough, Assistant Keeper, by 1790, was no more than a convenient division of groups of books among the fourteen rooms available. One room, for example, was allocated to literature, three to history, geography and allied subjects, and two and part of a third to divinity. Of the others, one had to contain medicine, surgery, trade and commerce, arts, mathematics, and astronomy; and another politics, philosophy (moral and natural), chemistry, and natural history. The arrangement was, of course, merely for the use of the Library staff.

A subject catalogue was ordered by the trustees in 1807, but was not started until 1824, when it was put into the hands of Rev. T. H. Horne, an experienced bibliographer whose *Outlines of Classification for a Library* was printed for the trustees in the following year.[1] Horne and a number of colleagues toiled on this project for ten years, when the plan was suspended because of the more urgent need for a new author catalogue to replace that published in 1813–19. The idea was never revived. Panizzi, who declared that no two men would ever agree on a scheme of classification, is generally supposed to have killed it; the new catalogue produced under his auspices was, as we have seen, an author catalogue.

Thus ended the British Museum's only attempt at a subject catalogue (apart from certain special collections). The project was revived in the 1880s, but what then emerged was not a classified subject catalogue but an alphabetical subject index. The first volume, published in 1886, covered accessions during 1880–85, and the series has been continued ever since. There were, indeed, peculiar difficulties about the publication of a subject catalogue for so large a library as that of the British Museum. Carlyle and other literary men who agitated for such a catalogue did not realise that a classification under fairly simple headings, such as they were accustomed to in the pub-

---

[1] The main headings were: theology and religion; philosophy; arts and trades; history; and literature; and there were 43 sub-headings.

17. ANTONIO PANIZZI

From the portrait by S. Gambardella.

18. THE BRITISH MUSEUM READING ROOM OF 1838

lished catalogues of subscription and institutional libraries, would produce lists of books so large as to be almost useless from the point of view of the reader; while a more detailed breakdown, though it would produce more manageable lists, would involve endless cross-reference.

The books themselves remained in this eighteenth-century classification (if classification it can be called) until 1838, when a move was made to the new buildings, and the opportunity was taken to reclassify. This time the arrangement was more systematic. It was devised by Thomas Watts, who super-intended the removal, and like Horne's scheme for the subject catalogue was much influenced by a system developed in France from the seventeenth century onwards, and elaborated in 1810 by J. C. Brunet. Watts's main divisions were ten: theology, jurisprudence, natural history and medicine, archaeology and the arts, philosophy, history, geography, biography, belles letters, and philology. Even with the 515 subdivisions which were allowed for, some of these divisions were rather awkward, resulting in such oddities as "games of chance" under "archae-ology and the arts", and "photography" under "philosophy".[1] Since, however, the British Museum Library has never been an open access library, the system has sufficed, and it remained in use, with certain modifications, until 1960.[2]

Watts's classification was accompanied by a press-marking system which at first sight closely resembles the old fixed loca-tion system. It was in the form 300.b., where 300 represents the press and b the shelf. Later (1875), a number was added to indicate the position of the book on the shelf, e.g. 300.b.12. In practice, however, the system allowed a great deal of flexibility. Each subject division had its press or group of presses, but spare numbers were left for additional presses, and in addition each "press" could be extended almost indefinitely by taking in extra shelves, and duplicating and triplicating existing shelves

---

[1] The sub-divisions are set out in J. Macfarlane, *Library Administration* (1898), pp. 153–61. An interesting attempt at a philosophical justifica-tion was made by Richard Garnett, afterwards Keeper of Printed Books, in a paper "On the System of Classifying Books . . . at the British Museum" in *Transactions and Proceedings of the Conference of Librarians, 1877* (1878).

[2] It is still in use for books acquired before that date. New accessions are being classified on a simpler plan.

(b, bb, bbb, etc.). There was, of course, no limit to the third figure, which was merely an accession number. The old system of marking was thus preserved, without the rigidity that had once accompanied it.[1]

Though it cannot be said that the British Museum made any revolutionary advance in the sphere of classification, it did establish, in Panizzi's time, the fundamental principles of alphabetical cataloguing. To those unaccustomed to library procedures the arrangement of a list of books in alphabetical order seems at first sight a simple matter, but there are in fact all kinds of difficulties. Apart from the problem of anonymous works which has already been referred to, and which became increasingly important as Government and other official reports multiplied, there are many questions arising even when the author's name is known. Do we catalogue Walter de la Mare under D or M? Benjamin Disraeli, Lord Beaconsfield, under D or B? S. L. Clemens ("Mark Twain") under C or T? Iris Murdoch (Mrs. J. Bayley) under M or B? Quiller-Couch under Q or C? and so on. Then again there are questions as to whether Christian names should be given in full or by initials, whether titles should be abbreviated (some older books have titles extending over half a page), whether it is desirable to state the names of editors and translators, the date of publication, the size, and the number of pages. On all these problems, and others of a similar kind, a decision has to be taken, and a uniform practice established: otherwise, in a large library, the waste of time to readers and library staff may be considerable.

At the British Museum these matters were much debated in the 1830s. Panizzi's predecessor Baber drew up in 1834 fairly simple rules, which were elaborated by Panizzi and his staff and after discussion and amendment by the trustees were officially adopted in 1839. These were the famous Ninety-One Rules, which provided a systematic cataloguing code for the Museum Library for the next half-century, and in essentials still operate today.[2]

The 1839 Rules extend over five closely printed folio pages,

---

[1] Cf. above, p. 54, on James's use of this sytem.

[2] Under the latest revision (*Rules for Compiling the Catalogues of Printed Books, Maps and Music in the British Museum*, 1936), the rules number 41.

and are exceedingly detailed. They provide for the inclusion of the author's surname and full Christian names, the names of editors and translators, the title of the book ("expressed in as few words, and those only of the author, as may be necessary to exhibit to the reader all that the author meant to convey"), the number of parts or volumes, the place of publication, date and edition, the size, and any features of special interest, e.g. in paper or printing. There are rules for cataloguing works by joint authors, noblemen, bishops, foreign authors, authors who change their name, anonymous authors, pseudonymous authors, and so forth; and for dealing with encyclopaedias, catalogues, periodicals, Bibles, service books, and the publications of universities, learned societies, and official and unofficial bodies of all kinds. There is also provision for systematic cross-referencing wherever necessary. Some of the decisions taken have mystified and infuriated subsequent users of the reading room, but by and large the Rules represent a logical and well-considered system, which has had an influence far beyond the walls of the British Museum.

THE ADVOCATES' LIBRARY

The National Library of Scotland, though officially inaugurated only in 1925, had its origins in a much older institution, the Library of the Faculty of Advocates, which traced its foundation to the seventeenth century. Its historian, W. K. Dickson, has drawn attention to the importance of the part played by the Scottish Bar in the national life of Scotland. "Its members", he remarks, "have always taken a large share in Scottish public affairs, and it has comprised not a few of the most famous Scottish men of letters, including James Boswell and Walter Scott, Lockhart, Aytoun, and Robert Louis Stevenson." He quotes, in illustration of its liberal attitude to learning, the remark of Counsellor Pleydell in *Guy Mannering*: "A lawyer without history or literature is a mechanic, a mere working mason; if he possesses some knowledge of these, he may venture to call himself an architect."[1]

It was in 1680, just a hundred years after Clement Little,

---

[1] "The Advocates' Library", in *Library Association Record*, N.S., Vol. V (1927), pp. 169–70.

advocate, had founded the town library of Edinburgh, that a committee of the Faculty recommended the establishment of "a Fonde for ane Bibliothecq whereto many Lawers and others may leave ther Books".[1] One of those who took a leading part in promoting the project, though he was not one of the original committee, was the Lord Advocate, Sir George Mackenzie of Rosehaugh, an accomplished jurist and scholar whose activity in the persecution of the Covenanters had earned from his enemies the name of "Bluidy Mackingie". The first problem was to find a room, and it was not until 1682 that the library was actually established, in a rented house in the corner of the Parliament Close of Edinburgh. Two curators (*curatores biblio-thecae*) were elected annually to supervise the arrangements, and the first librarian, James Naismith, advocate, took office in 1684. Funds for the support of the library were derived mainly from the fees of new entrants to the Faculty.

From the beginning the curators seem to have had in mind the formation of a general rather than an exclusively legal library. The first catalogue, printed in 1692, was already able to list over 3,000 volumes, and although rather more than half the catalogue was taken up with law books there were also sections for historical, theological, and miscellaneous books, the last section including fine editions of the classics and ancient and modern philosophers. This catalogue, in the seventeenth-century fashion, sub-divided the books in each class according to size, and though no press-marks are given, this probably indicates the system on which the books were arranged.

In 1700 a disastrous fire in Parliament Close destroyed the library building, and would have destroyed the library too had it not been for the devotion of the librarian of that time, James Stevenson, who rescued the books while his own goods and chattels burnt. It is satisfactory to note that he was rewarded by the Faculty with the then substantial sum of £50 sterling. In the following year new accommodation was found in the Laigh Parliament House, underneath the great hall where the Estates of Parliament met. Until quite recently this room still formed part of the library premises. At first the Advocates' Library occupied only the south end, but in 1790 it was able to

[1] W. K. Dickson, "The Advocates' Library", in *Juridical Review*, Vol. XIV (1902), p. 2.

take over the rest of the room. In the early nineteenth century it also spread to adjoining buildings, including for a time (1815–33) the splendid hall on the south side of Parliament Square which was afterwards occupied by the library of the Writers to the Signet.[1]

These successive expansions bear witness to the library's growth. The inclusion of the Advocates' Library in the list of libraries privileged under the Copyright Act of 1709 did not immediately produce any large accession of books, but it was a recognition of the Library's outstanding position. By 1742, the second catalogue was able to record 25,000 works; in 1849 the number of printed works was returned as 148,000, and there were, in addition, 2,000 MSS.

The 1742 catalogue was admirably compiled by Thomas Ruddiman, printer and scholar, who was one of a number of notable librarians during the eighteenth century. Another was David Hume the philosopher, who succeeded Ruddiman in 1752 and held office till 1757. In a letter to a friend Hume describes the great excitement and keen partisanship which his election caused. The cry of "Deism, atheism, and scepticism" was raised against him. Wives took part against their husbands, and sweethearts were divided from their lovers. When the result was finally announced:

"The whole body of cadies [the society of porters] brought flambeaux and made illuminations to mark their pleasure at my success; and next morning I had the drums and town music at my door, to express their joy, as they said, of my being made a great man."[2]

Hume was indignant when, two years later, the curators of the Library ordered three French classics which he had acquired (one of them the *Fables* of La Fontaine) to be "struck out of the Catalogue of the Library, and removed from the shelves, as indecent books, unworthy of a place in a learned Library".[3] Attempts at censorship in libraries have a way of looking ridiculous in the eyes of posterity.

[1] The Scottish term for solicitors.
[2] J. Y. T. Greig (ed.), *The Letters of David Hume* (Oxford 1932), pp. 166–70.
[3] E. Edwards, *Memoirs of Libraries*, (1859) Vol. II, p. 7, citing Minutes of the Faculty.

As time went on the Library increasingly assumed a national character, and became a place of deposit for material relating to the history and literature of Scotland. Amongst treasures of this kind acquired before 1850 were the Balfour Papers, purchased in 1698, and the Balcarres Papers, presented in 1712, both including important correspondence and state papers relating to the sixteenth and seventeenth centuries; the Wodrow Collection, acquired in 1734, relating to the history of the Church of Scotland; the genealogical and geographical collections of Walter Macfarlane, purchased in 1785; the Bannatyne MS., a collection of sixteenth-century Scottish poetry presented by James Boswell's father in 1744; and the unique copy of a volume printed by Chepman and Myllar in Edinburgh in 1508 – the earliest known production of the Scottish press. The MS. of Scott's *Waverley* was presented to the Library in 1850.

During the latter part of the nineteenth century, when copyright books at last began to arrive in quantity, it became increasingly difficult for the Library to provide an adequate service, for it was still a private library, and its resources were inadequate to cope with the flood of new works. In the early part of the century, however, it was a haven of peaceful scholarship. Only members of the Faculty of Advocates were permitted to borrow books, but it was from the beginning the policy to give free access for purposes of reference to all genuine students. Thomas Maitland, Solicitor General for Scotland, told the 1849 Committee on Public Libraries that "there is no library in Great Britain where the access given to the public generally is more liberal than in the Advocates' Library". Nominally an order was required to secure admission, but in practice this was dispensed with: "Every person of respectable appearance applying for access to books or manuscripts is supplied with them."[1]

Dr. Hill Burton, the biographer of Hume, has left an impression of the Library as it was about this period:

"When I first made use of the Library in 1831, and for many years afterwards, there was a quiet seclusion about its apartments that adapted them with much felicity to the purpose of study and research. Instances are known of men who have come to Edinburgh for the accomplishment of literary projects, on account of the facilities afforded

[1] *Report from the Select Committee on Public Libraries* (1849), p. 93.

by the Advocates' Library for quiet, uninterrupted study and ready access to authorities. Several authors and scholars have testified to these attractions. For instance, when, about twenty years ago, the Commission on the Library of the British Museum was taking evidence Thomas Carlyle said, speaking of his experience of the Advocates' Library, that there was 'a room larger than the one we sit in at the British Museum, and there were not more than twenty people in it, each sitting in an alcove with a window as large as the window here; all in profound silence; a large thick Turkey carpet on the floor'. This little sketch of a library interior attracted much attention, and I believe it had considerable influence in the creation of the reading-room of the British Museum, where the quiet and order are not less remarkable than the costly facilities put at the command of those who are privileged to pursue their researches there."[1]

We may conclude with a tribute paid by Carlyle in later life:

"I found it my one resource for serious reading whilst first attempting literature in Scotland; and still remember with thankful pleasure the free access and useful help afforded me there, while my claims on it, if any, were all in a prospective or incipient state. I was at once courteously admitted. . . . I had free admittance at all times afterwards, and the best accommodation for silent study; and such helps, bibliographical and others, as I have never met with elsewhere, and found the Library by very far the best I had ever been in, and indeed, putting all qualities together, one of the best I have ever since become acquainted with."[2]

[1] Quoted by W. K. Dickson, "The Advocates' Library", in *Juridical Review*, Vol. XIV (1902), p. 123.
[2] *Report from the Select Committee on Public Libraries* (1849), p. 93.

Bibliographical Note

A. Esdaile, *The British Museum Library* (1946), is the standard modern authority. Much interesting material is also to be found in G. F. Barwick, *The British Museum Reading Room* (1929). On the movement towards a national library see R. Irwin, *The Heritage of the English Library* (1964), Ch. xii. Of older works the most notable are those by E. Edwards: *Memoirs of Libraries* (2v. 1859), Vol. I, Bk. III, Chs. i–v; *Libraries and Founders of Libraries* (1864), Ch. vii; and *Lives of the Founders of the British Museum* (1870). R. Cowtan, *Memories of the British Museum* (1872), is also of interest.

On the foundation collections see the Prefaces to *A Catalogue of the Manuscripts in the Cottonian Library*, ed. J. Planta (1802); *A*

Catalogue of the Harleian Manuscripts in the British Museum (4v. 1808–12); and *Catalogue of Western Manuscripts in the Old Royal and King's Collections*, ed. Sir G. F. Warner and J. P. Gibson (4v. 1921), all published by the Museum; articles on Sloane and his collections in the *British Museum Quarterly*, Vol. XVIII (1953); S. Jayne and F. R. Johnson (eds.), *The Lumley Library: the Catalogue of 1609* (1956); and F. Wormald and C. E. Wright (eds.), *The English Library before 1700* (1958), Ch. ix (on the Cottonian Library).

The fullest study of Panizzi is still L. Fagan, *Life of Sir Anthony Panizzi* (2v. 1880), but there is a valuable paper by C. B. Oldman, "Sir Anthony Panizzi and the British Museum Library", in *English Libraries, 1800–1850* (University College, London, 1958). "Anthony Panizzi", in *The Library*, N.S. Vol. II (1901), is a useful short survey, and there are three articles by A. Predeek (transl. E. Isaacs), on "Panizzi and the British Museum Catalogue", in *Library Association Record*, 4th Ser., Vol. IV (1937). C. Brooks, *Antonio Panizzi* (Manchester 1931), is mainly concerned with his political and literary career. On Edwards see W. Munford, *Edward Edwards, 1812–1886* (1963), Ch. ii.

The history of copyright deposit is fully described in R. C. B. Partridge, *The History of the Legal Deposit of Books* (1938). D. M. Norris, *A History of Cataloguing and Cataloguing Methods* (1939), gives brief examples from a large number of catalogues, and deals also with classification, but only incidentally with shelf arrangements. On the British Museum there is a valuable unpublished F.L.A. thesis by F. J. Hill, *The Shelving and Classification of Printed Books in the British Museum, 1753–1953* (1953). Theories of classification are dealt with in many works for library students, e.g. W. C. B. Sayers, *A Manual of Classification* (1926, 3rd edn. rev. 1959), Chs. x–xi; but the fullest account is still that in Edwards, *Memoirs*, Vol. II, Pt. II, which also includes a chapter on copyright deposit.

W. K. Dickson, "The Advocates' Library", in *Juridical Review*, Vol. XIV (1902), is a detailed record, supplemented in some particulars by the same author's briefer account, under the same title, in *Library Association Record*, N.S. Vol. V (1927). See also A. Esdaile, *National Libraries of the World* (1934, 2nd edn. 1957), Ch. i, App. A; D. Duncan, *Thomas Ruddiman* (Edinburgh 1965), Ch. iii.

CHAPTER VIII

Prelude to the Public Libraries Act

THE first Public Libraries Act was passed in 1850. It was preceded by the appointment of a Select Committee on Public Libraries, which reported in 1849. This Committee, of which William Ewart, M.P., was the chairman, was concerned from the outset to establish three propositions: first, that the existing public library service was totally inadequate; second, that much better arrangements were made in continental countries, and in the United States; and third, that an extensive provision of public libraries was essential for the welfare of the country. Its witnesses, clearly, were selected with these ends in view, and although the resulting report is full of useful information, and makes fascinating reading even today, it cannot be regarded as presenting a complete picture of the facilities for reading and borrowing books as they existed at that time.

The Committee reported, in fact, that only one important library in Great Britain, namely Chetham's Library in Manchester, was fully and freely accessible to the public. This was quite true. There were virtually no public libraries in the sense in which we now understand the term, i.e. libraries provided from public funds and freely accessible to all. What the report does not reveal, however, is that in default of such a service there had come into being a whole network of library provision on a private or institutional basis. We have seen the beginnings of this network in the years before 1800, and in the half-century that preceded the first Public Libraries Act it developed with great rapidity. Rate-aided public libraries might still be lacking in 1849, but libraries open to the public by payment of a subscription, or through membership of an institution, were more numerous than ever before.

THE GROWTH OF WORKING-CLASS LITERACY

Most of the libraries which grew up before 1800 were directed to the needs of the middle classes – clergy, gentry, school-

masters, professional men, well-to-do tradesmen. The characteristic feature of the fifty years now under review, and especially
of the period after 1820, is the increase in provision for humbler
people – for the clerk, the craftsman, the operative, the small
shopkeeper. This change is directly linked with the general
increase in literacy, which in turn is linked with the advance of
popular education, with political and economic change, and with
the availability of cheap literature.

With increasing educational facilities, the spread of literacy
seems to have continued without serious interruption until at
least the middle of the eighteenth century.[1] In the closing
decades of that century, however, there was almost certainly
a sharp deterioration in the position. The influx into the great
commercial and manufacturing centres of large numbers of immi-
grants from Ireland, and the backward rural areas of England
and Wales, quickly gave rise to slum conditions which persisted
for the best part of a century, and created problems with which
the old grammar schools, charity schools, dame schools, and
the like, were quite unable to cope.

It was just at this time, paradoxically, that the idea of universal education, which in the previous century had been a
utopian dream, began to be seriously advocated. Both the con-
servative Adam Smith and the radical Tom Paine pronounced
it to be an essential duty of government. "Though the state was
to derive no advantage from the instruction of the inferior ranks
of people", wrote Smith cautiously, "it would still deserve its
attention that they should not be altogether uninstructed."[2]
"A nation under a well-regulated government", declared Paine
more incisively, "should permit none to remain uninstructed."[3]
By the early nineteenth century some measure at least of
universal education was widely accepted as an objective of
social reform.

Charitable enterprise was not slow in finding new methods
to tackle the new situation. The Sunday school movement,
which was launched by Robert Raikes from Gloucester in 1783,

---

[1] R. D. Altick, *The English Common Reader* (Chicago 1957), pp. 35–6,
detects some falling off in the late seventeenth century, but I have still
to be convinced of this.
[2] *Wealth of Nations* (1776), Bk. V, Ch. i, Pt. III, Art. ii.
[3] *Rights of Man*, Vol. II (1792), Ch. v.

and spread rapidly throughout the country, gathered not only children but many adults into its net, and provided schooling of a sort for many who would otherwise have been neglected, especially in Wales and in industrial Lancashire and Yorkshire. A few years later Hannah More and her sister Martha set to work, with all the courage of missionaries in darkest Africa, amid the illiterate farm labourers, miners, and glassworkers of the Mendips. The adult school movement, a religious movement designed to provide teaching in reading, and sometimes also in writing and arithmetic, for the adult poor, had its effective beginning in Nottingham in 1798, but became widespread only in the second and third decades of the nineteenth century.

In the meantime Robert Owen, at New Lanark, was seeking to demonstrate his principle that man's character is formed for him, not by him, and that consequently education is the foundation of all the virtues. More important, from the point of view of its immediate effects, was the discovery by Joseph Lancaster and Andrew Bell of a way of applying mass production methods to primary education. The secret lay in the monitorial system: the teacher taught the monitors and the monitors taught the pupils. This idea was at once enthusiastically taken up, though unfortunately on sectarian lines. The Nonconformists espoused the cause of Lancaster, who was a Quaker, the Church of England that of Bell, who was an Anglican, and before long hundreds of schools were being founded, or re-founded, on the monitorial plan. The teaching methods were crude and the instruction given was brief and inadequate, but for the children of the poor it was vastly better than nothing.

From the 1820s the mechanics' institutes and similar bodies brought a powerful reinforcement to the cause of education. From Edinburgh, Glasgow and London as centres they spread first to the great ports and manufacturing towns, then to the smaller industrial and market towns. By the middle of the century there were about 700 of them, including about 50 in Scotland – mostly in the Forth-Clyde area. The first to be founded, the Edinburgh School of Arts in 1821, defined its objective as to provide instruction for working men "in such branches of physical science as are of practical advantage in their several trades", and some such formula was commonly

adopted in the early years. It is a formula which shows clearly
the influence of the Industrial Revolution. More and more, by
this date, the processes of industry and commerce needed the
services of literate workpeople. Alexander Galloway, an
engineering employer, put the matter very clearly in evidence
before the Select Committee on Artizans and Machinery: "From
the mode of managing my business", he declared, "by drawings
and written descriptions, a man is not of much use to me unless
he can read and write."[1]

There was, therefore, an incentive to working men to acquire
education, and an incentive to employers to assist them in doing
so. The early institutes were founded sometimes on the initiative
of the workers and sometimes on the initiative of the employers,
but nearly always they came to depend in greater or lesser
degree on the financial support of the merchant and manufacturing classes. Few of them, however, kept to their original
objective of systematic technical education: instead they became
agents for general cultural education, and in many instances for
basic education in the three Rs.

Another great stimulus to adult education was the growing
demand among the working classes for political and social
reform. This demand, driven underground during the period
of the French wars, sprang up again with renewed vigour in the
1820s. Many of those who were active in promoting the first
mechanics' institutes, e.g. Francis Place and William Lovett in
London, and G. J. Holyoake in Birmingham, did so partly in
the hope that they would prove instruments of emancipation.
In this they were disappointed: most of the mechanics' institutes
were so nervous about alienating public opinion that all controversial issues of politics, economics, and religion were barred.
The working-class Radicals, therefore, and their middle-class
supporters, were obliged to turn to other means of action –
co-operation, trade unionism, Chartism, Owenism. All these
movements attached a high importance to education, both for
children and for adults. "Knowledge is power", they constantly
quoted, and each of them in its own way contributed to the
spread of knowledge.

The cheap literature movement, which began in the 1820s
and was specially characteristic of the 1830s and 1840s, has

[1] 1st *Report* (1834), p. 25.

naturally been associated with the advance of literacy, though it was at least as much a consequence of that advance as a cause. The idea of cheap literature was not at this time new. The S.P.C.K. had been producing cheap religious literature for more than a century, the Religious Tract Society since 1799. Hannah More had scored a great success with her *Cheap Repository Tracts*. John Wesley had published not only religious books but cheap abridged editions of the classics and other miscellaneous works. And of course there was no shortage of cheap pamphlets and novels of a more or less sensational or scurrilous character. The feature of the new movement was a conscious attempt to provide sound and wholesome literature, free from religious or other propaganda, at a price within the reach of the working masses.

The pioneers in this task were the Society for the Diffusion of Useful Knowledge, formed in 1826 under the leadership of the brilliant but erratic Henry Brougham; Charles Knight, who was closely associated with the Society and also published on his own account; and the brothers William and Robert Chambers. John Cassell, another great popular educator, came a little later: when the Select Committee on Public Libraries reported in 1849 his publishing career was only just beginning. The *Library of Useful Knowledge*, the first venture of the Society for the Diffusion of Useful Knowledge, illustrates the new approach: it was a series of fortnightly pamphlets, each an original and authoritative work of 32 closely printed pages, at 6d. a copy. The *Library of Entertaining Knowledge* and other series followed. The Chambers brothers, likewise, produced from 1833 *Chambers's Information for the People* and similar works, the keynote being regular publication in cheap and easily manageable instalments.

The year 1832, the year of the great Reform Bill, was also a landmark in cheap publishing. *Chambers's Edinburgh Journal*, a weekly popular miscellany at 1½d. a copy, was followed by the *Penny Magazine* of the S.D.U.K. and a rival penny magazine, the *Saturday Magazine*, published by the S.P.C.K. To realize the significance of these prices we must remember that at this time an ordinary newspaper, owing to stamp duty and other taxes, cost 7d.; even after 1836, when the stamp duty was reduced to 1d., the price was still 5d. The year 1832 saw also the launching of the S.D.U.K.'s most ambitious enterprise, the

Penny Cyclopaedia, which took twelve years to publish and extended in the end to twenty-seven volumes.[1]

Some of these cheap publications, especially those of the S.D.U.K., were above the heads of those whom by the 1840s it was usual to call "the operative classes", but they found a market in the group accurately defined by William Ewart as the users of the mechanics' institutes, i.e. "the higher class of mechanics, and the lower order of the middle classes".[2] It was an ill-advised attempt to produce a *Biographical Dictionary* which brought the Society to an end in 1846. Charles Knight, as an independent publisher, was more successful, and so were the Chambers brothers, perhaps because they relied to a considerable extent on the Scottish market. All in all, the cheap literature movement must have done a great deal to stimulate and foster popular education.

Estimates of literacy, even at this period, are extremely hazardous, but it is safe to say that by about 1840, though pockets of ignorance remained in rural areas and the slums of great cities, the majority even of the working class were literate at least in the sense of being able to read, and some acquired, by one means or another, a very good education indeed. Outstanding examples are Francis Place, the veteran organizer of working-class movements; William Lovett, the pioneer of Chartism; and Thomas Cooper, leader of the Leicester Chartists. Much interesting evidence regarding the quality, as distinct from the quantity, of literacy is to be found in the Select Committee's Report. At the lowest level J. Imray, a civil engineer, testified of the young men who attended his Ragged School in Marylebone, who were street vendors and the like:

" . . . a great number of those same persons had been in the habit of reading before, but they had read the bad cheap publications which are circulated in thousands among those classes. I may say, that among those classes there is perhaps a greater amount of reading than among the better classes in London, but it is reading of the worst description."[3]

---

[1] We might mention also, in this year, the publication of the first of Harriet Martineau's famous stories, the *Illustrations of Political Economy*, but this was just Hannah More over again, with economics instead of religion as the dominant theme.

[2] *Report from the Select Committee on Public Libraries* (1849), p. 125 (cited henceforward as *1849 Report*).

[3] *1849 Report*, p. 207.

The agricultural labourers of Buckinghamshire were probably at about the same level of literacy. Of them W. R. Fremantle, a Church of England clergyman, remarked:

"I might observe that people are very little acquainted with the extraordinary ignorance of the poor people in rural districts, such as Buckinghamshire, and many of the books which we select for those [village] libraries I find lie upon the shelves unread, and the consequence is we require duplicates over and over again of such works as Bunyan's Pilgrim's Progress, Robinson Crusoe, Cook's Voyages, and works of that description. . . . Shakespeare would be lost upon them, I think."[1]

On the other hand George Dawson, a Nonconformist minister who lectured extensively in mechanics' institutes, testified that many working men were keenly interested in history, politics, travels, and poetry. Poetry, he said, was very much read, and many even tried their hand at writing it. "Shakespeare is known by heart, almost. I could produce men who could be cross-examined upon any play."[2] Dawson also stated that he had observed "among the working men a great spread of knowledge of French and German".[3] This statement was supported by a later witness, J. B. Langley of Stockport, who reported that as a result of Dawson's lectures on Carlyle a great interest had been aroused in German philosophy, and at the Manchester Mechanics' Institute the demand for the works of Kant, Fichte and Hegel far exceeded the supply.[4]

The first half of the nineteenth century, therefore, was a time of increasing popular education, and increasing interest in books. Let us now consider how these influences were reflected in library developments.

THE CATHEDRAL LIBRARIES

We may begin with religious libraries – the cathedral libraries, the old town and parochial libraries, and the various new experiments in this field which emerged after 1800.

As indicated in an earlier chapter, the public usefulness of the

[1] *Op. cit.*, p. 90.
[2] *Op. cit.*, p. 89.
[3] *Op. cit.*, p. 81.
[4] *Op. cit.*, pp. 153–4.

English and Welsh cathedral libraries at this period was exceedingly limited.[1] Most of them were quite small, and few had any regular income for the maintenance and renewal of books. In a number of cases the public were still excluded, in others access was very troublesome, but even where there was moderate freedom of access, as at Durham, Peterborough and York,[2] the libraries were so formidably theological that the ordinary reader was not encouraged to use them. The situation at Carlisle, as reported in 1849, was typical of many cathedrals: "Others besides the clergy are allowed to use the books freely, but as they are principally on theology, their use is almost confined to the clergy."[3] It is indeed probable that the cathedral libraries were less used by the public in the mid-nineteenth century than in the eighteenth century, when the books were less out of date and theology was more to the popular taste.

In Scotland the old diocesan library founded by Bishop Leighton at Dunblane[4] was still maintained, but was apparently little used, for in 1840 the building was adapted to serve as a subscription reading room. Further north, however, what seems to have been a very useful library was established in the diocese of Brechin. Though planned in 1792, it was not until 1819 that it was actually fitted up in the episcopal chapel at Laurencekirk. It was made available, at a small annual subscription, to the diocesan clergy of Brechin and Dunkeld, and also, by special request, to the congregation of Laurencekirk. A subsidiary collection was formed in 1827 at Brechin, which in 1854 became the home of the entire library. This library received many gifts and seems to have been much appreciated. In 1845 the Laurencekirk collection already numbered over 1,000 volumes, and was said to be accessible to "persons of literary education or pursuits".[5]

---

[1] See above, pp. 63–5.
[2] Edward Edwards in 1849 mentions also Canterbury, Chester, Norwich and Rochester as open to "all persons bringing some guarantee of their respectability"; and Salisbury had recently made its books available on loan to citizens of the town – *1849 Report*, pp. 23, 147.
[3] *Op. cit.*, p. 228.
[4] See above, p. 65.
[5] *New Statistical Account of Scotland* (1845), Vol. XI, Kincardineshire, p. 150. The Brechin Diocesan Library was transferred to University College, Dundee, in 1961.

19. INNERPEFFRAY LIBRARY

View of the Library (left) and Chapel from the River Earn.

20. LYCEUM LIBRARY, LIVERPOOL

THE OLD ENDOWED LIBRARIES

Of the old town libraries, the 1849 Report, as already noticed, singled out Chetham's Library in Manchester on the grounds of its unusual accessibility to the public. This is confirmed by another contemporary witness, who writes:

"This Collection is remarkable as the most easily accessible in the United Kingdom. Any person, however humble in station, or homely in appearance, whencesoever he may come, has a right to demand a sight of any book in the Library. This rare facility of access has not been without its abuses, since some volumes have been mutilated, and in severe weather, as in the National Gallery of London, many persons come and ask for a book of light reading for the sake of a warm and comfortable apartment."[1]

Chetham's Library was, in fact, the nearest approach then existing to the modern conception of a public library. George Dawson declared that it consisted "very much of old dry books that nobody reads nowadays, not even a professional man",[2] but the evidence of other witnesses shows that he exaggerated. The basis of the library was indeed still mainly theological, but its collection of nearly 20,000 volumes included a substantial number of works in other fields, and it also received the major current periodicals. The librarian testified that about twenty-five readers a day used the library, amongst them many working people. He regarded it as primarily a scholar's library, and lamented that too many people came "merely to amuse themselves; they ask for the Edinburgh Review, the Quarterly Review, or the Gentleman's Magazine".[3] He admitted, however, that members of the artisan class frequently asked for works in foreign languages.

Two other town libraries which might, in more favourable circumstances, have rivalled the Chetham's Library were the Shepherd Library at Preston (1761) and the Stirling Library at Glasgow (1791). Unlike most such libraries, these were general collections, not primarily theological in character, but unfortunately neither library possessed endowments equal to its needs. Of the Stirling Library, the 1849 Report has little to say except that it was not used by the public – it had, as we

---

[1] B. Botfield, *Notes on the Cathedral Libraries of England* (1849), pp. 328–9.   [2] *1849 Report*, p. 85.   [3] *Op. cit.*, p. 77.

have seen, been converted into a subscription library.[1] Actually at this time it was at the beginning of an era of relative prosperity: in 1844 it had been moved to new premises; in 1848 it was made available to annual subscribers in addition to the life members who had monopolized it hitherto; and in 1849, as a result of the introduction of gas lighting, it was opened in the evenings.

The Shepherd Library is barely mentioned in the Report, though the Mayor and Aldermen, as trustees, did their best to make it available to the public, especially after the Municipal Reform Act of 1835. It was provided with its own building and librarian, and from 1836 was open not only in the daytime, from 10 to 4 daily, but also – and this was quite exceptional at this period – in the evenings from 6 to 9.45. The library was accessible to anyone on application to one of the trustees and (from 1839), on payment of 3s. for a copy of the printed catalogue, but it is not clear how extensively it was used.

The Select Committee directed considerable attention to the libraries of London, including the British Museum Library, of which an account has already been given. Sion College Library, with 35,000 volumes or more, and Dr. Williams's Library with 20,000 volumes and half that number of tracts, remained primarily theological, and though fairly readily accessible to the public were used in fact mainly by the clergy. Sion College, with over 300 readers a year and over 5,000 loans, was the more active of the two, and served readers from all over London. Archbishop Tenison's Library at St. Martin's was in a poor way: the books were still there, but they were locked up and in bad condition, the premises having been taken over in 1839 (as at Dunblane), for the use of a subscription reading-room.[2]

Regarding other early town and parochial libraries the Report has little to tell us, and it is clear that the existence of most of them was unknown to the Committee. Of all the libraries known to have been founded before 1800 (excluding the Bray libraries) only about thirty are even mentioned, though probably at least four times that number still survived.[3] This ignorance on the

---

[1] See above, pp. 102-3.   [2] The library was sold in 1861.
[3] Substantial remains of about one hundred endowed libraries of this period have survived to the present day, two-thirds of them in the institutions to which they were originally granted.

part of the Committee is not difficult to understand, for by this time the great majority of these older libraries, through lack of adequate funds for their maintenance, had long since ceased to be of practical value. A few only showed signs of life. One of the most flourishing, in spite of its isolated position, was that at Innerpeffray in Perthshire, where during the years 1801–50 loans were three times as numerous as during the previous half-century. The Select Committee Report described it as "the most valuable library in this part of Perthshire",[1] and it is significant that, although the collection was predominantly religious in character, loans of secular works showed a marked increase.

At Holy Trinity, Hull, an endowment of £2 a year enabled small annual additions to be made to the library until at least 1860. The Maldon Library, which also had an endowment for maintenance and the purchase of books, had grown by 1843 to a total of 5,330 books and manuscripts, lodged in the National School.[2] The regulations drawn up for the Bamburgh Castle library in 1810[3] suggest that it was still in active use at that date. In the same year the Maidstone library was restored after having been seriously damaged by damp and worm. There were short-lived attempts to revive the town library at Newcastle in 1829, and that at Wisbech in 1838. The Reigate library was still "in partial use" in 1849.[4]

As to the rest, some had actually been disposed of: the library at Lewes was sold in 1823; that at Bedford was transferred in 1831 to the local Literary and Scientific Institution; the Bolton parish library was transferred in 1836 to the Grammar School; cartloads of books from the Boston parish library are said to have been sold as waste paper.[5] Others, such as Bristol, Norwich, Gainsborough, Spalding, Nottingham, Doncaster, Beccles, and Bury St. Edmunds, had been taken over by subscription libraries or converted to a subscription basis.[6]

---

[1] *1849 Report*, p. 305.
[2] *Parliamentary Gazetteer* (1842–43), Vol. III, *s.v.*
[3] See above, p. 97.
[4] *1849 Report*, p. 148.
[5] *Notes and Queries*, Ser I, Vol. VII (1853), p. 507.
[6] The Committee commended the example of Beccles, which in 1840 had removed its parish library from the church to provide the nucleus of a town library, but the evidence shows that it was in fact on a subscription basis – see *Report*, pp. vi–vii, 25.

Others again were just mouldering away in oblivion. The library at Whitchurch, Hampshire, we are told, consisted of "several hundred volumes of books, some of them curious and valuable", but had "fallen into almost total neglect and misuse".[1] In the old town library at Leicester, "unless it may be that some clergyman comes and looks in occasionally, the greater part of the books are scarcely ever touched".[2] At Halton in Cheshire the existence of a valuable library of over 400 volumes, mainly folios, was "almost unknown".[3] At Langley Marish a similar library was "well preserved", but "applications for admission to it excepting from curiosity, are very rare".[4] We can have little doubt that even if the witnesses had been familiar with a much greater number of libraries, their comments on them would not have been very different.[5]

We cannot, however, omit the picture of the old town library of Gainsborough as given in the autobiography of Thomas Cooper, the Chartist. It illustrates alike the condition of these libraries and the heroic zeal for learning which characterized many of the working-class leaders of this period. It was in the early 1820s, when Cooper was a lad of about eighteen, an apprentice shoemaker, that he discovered the library left to the town by Nathaniel Robinson, mercer, ninety years before:[6] "it had been thrust into a corner", he tells us, "and almost forgotten".

"I was in ecstasies to find the dusty, cobwebbed shelves loaded with Hooker, and Bacon, and Cudworth, and Stillingfleet, and Locke, and Jeremy Taylor, and Tillotson, and Bates, and Bishop Hall, and Samuel Clarke, and Warburton, and Bull, and Waterland, and Bentley, and Boyle, and Ray, and Derham, and a score of other philosophers and divines – mingled with Stanley's "History of Philosophers", and its large full-length portraits – Ogilvy's "Embassies to Japan and China", with their large curious engravings – Speed's and Rapin's folio

---

[1] *1849 Report*, p. 25.   [2] *Op. cit.*, p. 80.
[3] *Op. cit.*, p. 109.   [4] *Op. cit.*, p. 223.
[5] The splendid library of more than a thousand seventeenth- and eighteenth-century works presented to the town of Southampton by George Frederick Pitt in 1831 was at this period still hidden away in the Corporation Audit House. Not until 1857 was it made accessible to the public, and then only to a limited extent and for a brief period. See the *Catalogue of the Pitt Collection* published by Southampton Public Libraries (1964), Introd.
[6] See above, p. 91, note 2.

histories of England – Collier's "Church History" – Fuller's "Holy War" – Foxe's "Book of Martyrs", the first edition, in black letter, and with its odd, rude plates – and countless other curiosities and valuables."[1]

NINETEENTH-CENTURY RELIGIOUS LIBRARIES

There were, however, a few parochial libraries of more recent foundation which were accessible to the public. The library at Elham in Kent was bequeathed to the vicar and churchwardens in 1809 on behalf of the parishioners; that at Bewdley in Worcestershire was bequeathed ten years later for the use of the clergy and other respectable inhabitants "as a public library",[2] with the provision that the books might be lent. At Castleton in Derbyshire the vicar Frederick Farran, who had been in the habit of lending books to the villagers, and had even bought books for their use, left his books on his death in 1817 to be lent "at the Discretion of the Vicar". In one volume he had written:

"To my parishioners – Read good solid practical books tending to promote *holiness of life*, many of the *Methodist* books . . . tend to nourish delusions, conceit, raptures, and I know not what of sinful presumption, and false confidence. . . ."[3]

The collection was supplemented after Farran's death, and was in fairly active use in mid-century. As the quotation suggests, it was mainly theological, and although it contained a certain amount of general literature it included no fiction and almost no poetry. It amounted in all to some 1,100–1,200 volumes.

Many Scottish parochial libraries founded at this period seem to have been very well used. That at Kinnell in Angus (1827) was "eagerly sought after by the parishioners".[4] At Fordoun in Kincardineshire, where a library was founded in the same year, it was reported in 1845 that "the number of readers

[1] T. Cooper, *Life*, (1872, 4th edn. 1873), p. 51.
[2] P. Morgan, "Wigan's Library, Bewdley", in *Trans. Worcs. Archaeol. Soc.*, N.S. Vol. XXXV (1958), p. 61. The library was originally kept in the Grammar School. It is now in the Birmingham University Library, and comprises over 3,000 books and pamphlets.
[3] E. D. Mackerness, "The Castleton Parish Library", in *Journ. of the Derbyshire Archaeol. and Nat. Hist. Soc.*, Vol. LXXVII (1957), p. 39.
[4] *New Statistical Account of Scotland* (1845), Vol. XI, Forfarshire, p. 410.

is considerable, and yearly increasing",[1] while at Benholme in the same county "the library is highly valued by the people; and at present upwards of 300 individuals read from it" (out of a total population of 1,484).[2] Yet another Kincardineshire library, at St. Cyrus, was founded some time before 1845 "by a collection at the church doors, and by small subscriptions among the parishioners".[3] This library was free to all inhabitants. At Collace in Perthshire (1830), the library was "most acceptable to the people, and . . . rapidly diffusing a taste for reading among them".[4]

We have seen that a number of the older parochial libraries were converted in the eighteenth or nineteenth century to a subscription basis, but new parochial libraries on this plan were surprisingly few. Indeed, only two examples seem to be recorded before the mid-nineteenth century. The first was at Stockton-on-Tees, where in 1800 the vicar created a subscription library alongside the old Latin library founded in 1719. The second was in the newly formed parish of St. John's, Keswick, where a "parochial library of general literature" was founded by the vicar in 1849 "to encourage the spirit of self-culture, and to promote the combination of secular and spiritual instruction in this district".[5] It had a long and successful life, and was eventually taken over by the Cumberland County Library in 1958.

Alongside the Church of England libraries there were now numerous libraries attached to Dissenting churches. Records of these are scanty before 1800, though in London the Quakers had a library at the old Devonshire House by Bishopsgate as early as 1673, and the Baptists had a library at the Barbican by 1708. The growth in the early nineteenth century, however, must have been very rapid. The historian of Newcastle, for example, records no fewer than six Nonconformist libraries there in 1827, besides other smaller collections.

The Unitarian library at Hanover Square Chapel is mentioned as one of the best. Its collection of several hundred volumes was

---

[1] *Op. cit.*, Vol. XI, Kincardineshire, p. 106.
[2] *Ibid.*, p. 63.
[3] *Ibid.*, pp. 294–5.
[4] *Op. cit.*, Vol. X, p. 218.
[5] W. E. Alder-Barrett, "St. John's Library, Keswick", in *Library Association Record*, Vol. LXI (1959), p. 35.

mainly religious in character, and was open not only to members
of the congregation, but to "any other person for whom a
member will be answerable". The Methodist library at Bruns-
wick Chapel, founded in 1808, was wider in scope, including
"Biography, Travels, Voyages, the Sciences", etc. It was open
on Monday and Thursday evenings and on Saturday from 12 to
1, and had over 1,000 volumes. The small Friends' Library
(some 280 volumes), had the unusual distinction of a printed
catalogue, published in 1826, with an index showing "the
volume and page where every particular subject is noticed".
Some of these libraries had a small annual subscription: in the
case of the Methodists it was 6s. a year, but the Unitarians were
content with a voluntary subscription of 2s. 6d.[1]

There is plenty of evidence, in local histories and directories,
that the situation at Newcastle was paralleled in other large
towns. At Aberdeen, to choose a Scottish example, there were
in 1822 five church libraries belonging to different denomina-
tions, including the Roman Catholics.[2] The 1849 Committee,
curiously, paid little attention to libraries of this kind, though
Samuel Smiles testified that in Leeds there was "a library
connected with almost every chapel, both dissenting and otherwise".[3] Ten years earlier the energetic Vicar of Leeds, W. F.
Hook (afterwards Dean of Chichester and a well-known
ecclesiastical historian), had established a central Church of
England library and three branch libraries, "with Saturday and
Penny Magazines, and various good works . . . to counteract
the Socialists".[4]

In some rural areas, such as the West of England, Buckinghamshire, Derbyshire, the Scottish Lowlands and Aberdeen-
shire, the clergy were active in promoting village lending
libraries, sometimes with a nominal subscription, e.g. 1d. per
month. These might be parish libraries, in the sense that they
were available to all inhabitants of the parish, but they were
not necessarily under the control of the parochial authorities.
Their aim, according to the Buckinghamshire clergyman already
quoted, was to "intermingle books of instruction and amusement

[1] E. Mackenzie, *A Descriptive and Historical Account of . . . Newcastle
upon Tyne* (Newcastle 1827), Vol. II, pp. 457–8.
[2] R. Wilson, *An Historical Account and Delineation of Aberdeen* (Aberdeen
1822), p. 170.   [3] *1849 Report*, p. 128.
[4] J. F. C. Harrison, *Learning and Living, 1790–1960* (1961), pp. 181–2.

with religious books",[1] but even so they were often, in the opinion of George Dawson, "too theological for the people".[2] They were usually small, and public interest tended to fade when the most popular books had been read.

An early example of this type of library is described by Rev. Francis Wrangham, Vicar of Hunmanby, near Scarborough, in a report to the Society for Bettering the Condition and Increasing the Comforts of the Poor in 1807:

"I have lately founded a small parish library, which I keep in my vestry, consisting of the twelve volumes of the Christian Society's Tracts, the Cheap Repository Tracts, the Cottage Library, two volumes, the Pilgrim's Progress, Gilpin's Lives of Truman and Atkins, Doddridge's Gardiner, Susan Gray, Lucy Franklin, etc. etc., under an idea that the lower classes delight more in *concretes* than in *abstracts;* or (in other words) that sermons are less read than tales. It would be important to ascertain what other volumes may have been found useful and popular in similar institutions. My present collection is already nearly all in circulation. The schoolmaster attends on Sundays for half an hour prior to the beginning of the morning service, to receive and give out such books as are returned, or required; and fifteen or twenty volumes are usually exchanged or issued upon these occasions. The masters of families read them to their children, etc. in the evenings; and thus a few visitors are perhaps detained from the ale-house."[3]

Libraries such as this, even when a subscription was involved, were not in the strict sense subscription libraries, since the subscription covered only part of the cost. They were in effect a combination of the endowed and the subscription library, and can perhaps best be classed, along with certain secular libraries for the working classes to be described shortly, as "philanthropic libraries".[4]

A novel type of religious library, in which the 1849 Committee was particularly interested, was introduced into East Lothian in

[1] *1849 Report*, p. 128. Cf. above, p. 191.   [2] *Op. cit.*, p. 86.
[3] *Reports of the Society* . . . , Vol. V (1808), pp. 223–4. On Wrangham see M. Sadleir, *Archdeacon Francis Wrangham* (*Bibliog. Soc. Trans.*, Suppl. No. 12, Oxford 1937). Another advocate of popular libraries was Rev. E. W. Grinfield of Bath, who in an appendix to his *Reflections on the Influence of Infidelity and Profaneness upon Public Liberty* (Bath 1817), suggested the establishment of lending libraries at 2d. per month in connection with Church of England schools.
[4] See below, App. I.

1817 by Samuel Brown, a merchant of Haddington (great-uncle of John Brown of the *Horae Subsecivae*). This was the "itinerating library". Brown's son, Rev. John Croumbie Brown, explained to the Committee that his father's object had been "to have a library within a mile-and-a-half of every inhabitant of the county, if possible. The plan was to station a division of fifty volumes in every village and hamlet where a librarian could be found; those were removed at the end of two years, and a general exchange took place."[1] One half to two-thirds of the books were religious, the remainder popular works of general interest. The cost was borne by Brown himself and by the contributions of his friends.

The scheme was at first very successful, and by 1830 there were about fifty libraries in circulation, but thereafter a decline set in, partly because of the introduction in 1832 of a charge of 1d. per volume during the first year in which the books were available in each place. The scheme was copied in Berwickshire about 1822, in Roxburghshire and in the Scottish Highlands in 1829, in Edinburgh and Leith in 1834, and at Dunfermline in Fifeshire in 1837, but nowhere with enduring success. In the Highlands the libraries were attached to schools, and were under the auspices of the Church Assembly. In Peeblesshire, in 1849, an experiment had just been decided upon under the auspices of the Free Church.[2]

The Committee was also impressed by the story of the successful but unfortunately brief experiment by the curate of St. Martin in the Fields in the organization of a working men's library, at a subscription of 1d. per week, in one of the poorest quarters of the parish; and by the record of the small free library attached to the Ragged School at Marylebone.

Finally we must mention Sunday school libraries, which by this time had become almost universal. The invaluable series of reports on the state of education in various northern towns prepared by the Manchester Statistical Society during the years 1834–40 reveals that at this time three-quarters of the Sunday schools in these towns had libraries: Manchester had 74, Salford 22, Liverpool 30, York 15, and Hull 28. Even in the county of

[1] *1849 Report*, p. 111.
[2] For English and Welsh examples of itinerating libraries, see below, pp. 217, 234.

Rutland 8 out of 69 Sunday schools had libraries.[1] Though small, and intended primarily for children, these libraries did also to some extent serve the needs of adults, especially in Wales and the north of England, where there was a tradition of adult attendance at such schools. In Spitalfields, where in 1849 nearly every church and chapel had a Sunday school library, it was reported that "children take those books home, and very often they are read by the parents when they are not read by the children".[2] The reference here is to works of general interest such as it was customary to mix with religious books ("we of course allow nothing immoral").

For the Associates of Dr. Bray the 'forties were a period of particular activity, old libraries being refurbished and nearly forty new libraries founded, including the only Bray library in Scotland, at Ballachulish in 1840. From 1841 onwards nearly all the new foundations were lending libraries, and though they continued to be restricted to the use of the clergy, the old requirement that a borrower must deposit the value of the book was dropped.

In the provision of lay libraries the work of the Religious Tract Society and the S.P.C.K. was much more helpful. The former was particularly helpful in the foundation of church and chapel libraries: in 1849 it was reported that it had, since 1832, distributed more than 4,000 libraries in England, Scotland and Wales. Two-fifths of these went to churches and chapels or to "destitute districts . . . in which the people are far from a church or chapel".[3] The rest went mainly to Sunday schools and day schools. The libraries were placed, according to the secretary, "wherever persons are found disposed to superintend them and pay a portion of their value".[4] They comprised, on the average, about a hundred books, and were limited to the Society's own publications, but no objection was raised to the introduction of "other moral, religious or scientific books which the local friends may wish to place in them".[5]

In England the work of the S.P.C.K., though only briefly referred to in the 1849 Report, was on a similar scale. It began

---

[1] Manchester Statistical Society, *Report of a Committee on the State of Education in the Borough of Manchester* (1834); *Salford* (1836); *Liverpool* (1836); *York* (1837); *Rutland* (1839); *Hull* (1840).
[2] *1849 Report*, p. 173.
[3] *Op. cit.*, p. 168.   [4] *Ibid.*   [5] *Op. cit.*, p. 169.

under the auspices of the diocesan and district committees which were established by the Society in 1810 and the years immediately following, and was taken up in earnest from 1820 onwards at the instance of a special committee for combating blasphemous and infidel publications.[1] The Society now offered assistance in the formation of parochial lending libraries for the use of parishioners. It laid down the condition that each library should be under the control of the minister, and that the books should be selected either from the Society's own publications or from a supplementary list of approved (and improving) books by other publishers which the Society was prepared to supply at reduced rates.[2] In spite of this restriction the Society was able to report that about 800 libraries had already been established, more than one-third of them during the past year.[3] How many existed in 1849 is not clear, but the Annual Report for that year listed 150 libraries "established or augmented" during the year. For 1850 the figure was over 200. In that year the rule that the S.P.C.K. grant would be forfeited on the introduction into the library of any volume not on the Society's lists was quietly dropped. This made it possible for the S.P.C.K. books to be used to supplement more general libraries, on condition only "that in the arrangement of volumes the Society should not appear to give its sanction to publications which are not on its own Catalogues".[4]

It is evident, therefore, that the number of church, chapel and Sunday school libraries must by mid-century have run into several thousands; and it is equally clear that most of them relied either on the R.T.S. or on the S.P.C.K. for their supplies.[5]

---

[1] S.P.C.K., *Annual Report*, 1820, pp. 118, 124. In this year R. G. Bouyer, Archdeacon of Northumberland, began to form a small library of S.P.C.K. publications in each of his ninety-two parishes. Before his death in 1826 he had provided at his own expense a total of some 30,000 volumes. – *D.N.B.*

[2] *Annual Report*, 1820, pp. 184–5.   [3] *Annual Report*, 1825, p. 43.

[4] See *Annual Reports* for 1849, 1850. The revised rules are given in the *Report* for 1850, p. 127.

[5] In 1922 the Bray Associates revised their rules so as to admit lay users, and thus bring the libraries within the scope of S.P.C.K. grants. The 1963 *Report of the Associates* lists fifty-five libraries in England and one in Wales, and I understand that only one of these, at Hull, fails to qualify for S.P.C.K. support, by continuing to confine its membership to the clergy. S.P.C.K. grants in aid of parish lending libraries continued until 1950.

MIDDLE-CLASS SUBSCRIPTION LIBRARIES

The type of library which in the previous chapter we have
called the gentlemen's subscription library became very common
at this period, not only in the great provincial cities, which
usually boasted more than one, but even in quite small market
towns. Such libraries often had their own buildings, and many
of the older city libraries had now accumulated very substantial
and valuable collections. The original Liverpool Subscription
Library, known since 1803 as the Lyceum, was probably the
largest, with 21,400 volumes in 1830 and 36,760 in 1850. Hull
is credited with 21,000 volumes in 1849, the first Manchester
Subscription Library with 20,000, and Norwich with 14,000.[1]
In Scotland the Glasgow "Public Library", established in 1804,
had at mid-century 16,000 volumes, and Greenock Library had
about 10,000 volumes.[2] The average subscription library, however, was smaller than these: Lewes, Kendal and Dundee, with
5–6,000 volumes apiece, may be regarded as fairly typical.

These libraries catered for a clientèle which included, in
varying proportions, gentry, clergy, professional men, manufacturers and well-to-do tradespeople. Their aim was, in general,
to provide for their members a collection of standard works of
permanent value. The more ephemeral kind of current fiction
was eschewed, and the demand for it, where it arose, was
frequently met by a subscription to a good commercial circulating library. In some towns there were special libraries for
foreign works.[3]

The larger subscription libraries were generally recognized
to be of value not only to the ordinary reader but to the scholar:
the Government, for example, included them along with the
cathedrals, universities, and learned societies, in the free distri-

---

[1] I take these figures from G. Lewis, *Topographical Dictionary of England*
(7th edn. 1849). Higher figures are sometimes given.

[2] This library, founded in 1783, was now handsomely accommodated in
the Watt Monument Buildings, which also housed a Scientific Library
founded by James Watt in 1816. See R. M. Smith, *The History of
Greenock* (Greenock 1921), pp. 331–9.

[3] The most notable example was the Foreign Library at Manchester,
founded in 1830. It is described in W. E. A. Axon, *Handbook of the
Public Libraries of Manchester and Salford* (Manchester 1877), pp. 132–3.
For the foreign library at Leeds see above, p. 131, note 2.

bution of Record Commission publications.[1] John Lingard, the great Catholic historian, whose *History of England* was published in 1819–30, declared: "I owe a debt of gratitude to the Liverpool Library (i.e. the Lyceum), for affording me many facilities when writing my History of England, and without those it would have cost me many journeys to London."[2] Lingard was living at Hornby, near Lancaster, at the time, so was presumably a member, but the proprietors of the library boasted that they had "always shown the greatest readiness in giving access to all their books, to authors and others, not proprietors, who might wish to consult them".[3] At the Manchester Portico, a subscription library and newsroom opened in 1806, there were special arrangements for the temporary admission of strangers, and a similar rule operated at Birmingham.

The scholarly character of the Birmingham Library in the early 'fifties is revealed in a rather satirical description given twenty-five years later by the then editor of the *Birmingham Post*, J. Thackray Bunce:

"There were few readers then, there was little money to spend, the Committee was often hard set to make both ends meet, there were empty rooms, a good deal of learned leisure and space to enjoy it in, and a very restricted range in the selection of books. Folios there were enough, for our predecessors bought every folio they could lay their hands on, and I dare say my friend Mr. Woodhill and many others remember seeing Mr. Fenwick, the old vicar of Aston, carrying off a folio in each of his enormously capacious coat-pockets, and another folio under his arm. Quartos there were in plenty; they were looked upon with a moderate degree of respect by the Committee of that day. Octavos were regarded as nearly if not all absolutely wanting in character, and as coming somewhat within the range of light literature; but of light literature itself, properly so-called, there was either nothing or next to nothing, excepting a limited selection of magazines. Novels were looked upon with horror, unless they were recognized as standard ones."[4]

[1] This was especially so after 1831: see the list of receiving libraries in *Report from the Select Committee on Record Commission* (1836), pp. 784–7. The practice continued, though on a reduced scale, into the second half of the nineteenth century and even into the early years of the present century.
[2] P. MacIntyre, "Historical Sketch of the Liverpool Library", in *Trans. Hist. Soc. of Lancs. and Ches.*, Vol. IX (Liverpool 1856–57), pp. 242–3.
[3] *Ibid.*
[4] S. Timmins, *Centenary of the Birmingham Library* (Birmingham 1879), p. 90.

The best comment, quoted in a presidential address of 1879, came from one who was probably a member of the library at the time to which Bunce referred: "Some people complain that there are so many books in the Library that no one reads. The fools do not know that is the very thing which makes the Library valuable."[1]

Like all voluntary organizations, the subscription libraries occasionally ran into difficulties. Finance was almost always a problem, and underpaid librarians were apt to be inefficient. An entertaining example comes from Sheffield. Joseph Hunter, in his *History of Hallamshire* (1819), complained that the old subscription library there "seemed to resist every attempt made for its improvement". In 1825 the President, T. A. Ward, defended the library against these strictures in the following terms:

"At the time he wrote, it contained upwards of 4,000 volumes, many of them well selected and of considerable value; and if it was ill-managed, yet its existence must have been of great advantage to the town. . . . The books were in a very dirty and tattered condition in consequence of the librarian's attendance not being constant. The subscribers frequently supplied themselves with books, which were not properly and duly entered in a register, and were consequently lost in considerable numbers. More were taken out by some members than their legal share, and favourite books were reserved for favourite subscribers. The publications most eagerly sought after were concealed in cupboards, drawers, and even in the warming-pan, for the more zealous, eager, and vigilant readers, while many unsuspicious members wondered that no new books could be had. Still, there was a mine of intellectual treasure. True the approach was bad; the staircase was winding, the room was dark and inconvenient but still there was no small number of good books."[2]

This was not, of course, typical. The trouble here lay in the employment as librarian, at a salary of £30 a year, of an elderly lady who lived on the premises and neglected the library to attend to her household duties. T. A. Ward could afford to be ironical on the subject, for in 1818, on the death of this good lady, the library had been moved to new premises and placed

[1] *Op. cit.*, p. 82.
[2] T. A. Ward, *A Short Account of the Sheffield Library* (Sheffield 1825), p. 4.

in the charge of an efficient librarian, though the salary (£45 a year in 1821) was still small. At Birmingham and Hull, by this time, the librarian's salary had risen to £100.

Some of the larger libraries had now become so exclusive that their claim to be included in an account of public libraries is very doubtful. Entrance fees continued to rise in the years following the Napoleonic Wars, and in some places reached almost prohibitive levels. At Hull, for example, the fee was raised in 1817 to £20; at Leeds, five years later, it was fixed at £21. The scholar and the distinguished stranger might be welcomed to such establishments as these, but woe betide any ordinary mortal who dared to cross their thresholds. Herman Melville, visiting Liverpool as a young sailor-boy in 1837, describes how he made the attempt at the Liverpool Lyceum:

"But I had not got far into that large and lofty room, filled with many agreeable sights, when a crabbed old gentleman lifted up his eye from the *London Times*, which words I saw boldly printed on the back of the large sheet in his hand, and looking at me as if I were a strange dog with a muddy hide, that had stolen out of the gutter into this fine apartment, he shook his silver-headed cane at me fiercely, till the spectacles fell off his nose. Almost at the same moment, up stepped a terribly cross man, who looked as if he had a mustard plaster on his back, that was continually exasperating him; who throwing down some papers which he had been filing, took me by my innocent shoulders, and then, putting his foot against the broad part of my pantaloons, wheeled me right out into the street, and dropped me on the walk, without so much as offering an apology for the affront. I sprang after him, but in vain; the door was closed upon me."[1]

The greatest of all the English subscription libraries, the London Library, was born belatedly in 1841. Founded on the initiative of Thomas Carlyle, it has always been essentially a scholar's library: as the original prospectus put it, "a collection of standard books in various languages, calculated for the use of literary men and of all who prosecute self-instruction and rational entertainment by reading".[2] From the first it enjoyed the patronage and assistance of a galaxy of distinguished men. W. E. Gladstone prepared a list of recommended works on

---

[1] *Redburn* (1924 edn.), p. 209.
[2] S. Nowell-Smith, "Carlyle and the London Library", in *English Libraries, 1800–1850* (University Coll. London 1958), p. 67.

A catalouge of those who have beene Benefact[ors]

towards the fittinge this place and furnishinge

it with bookes. and God send us a Better
Librarian 1774 Usuin Revd My

21. WISBECH TOWN LIBRARY

Title-page of the seventeenth-century Catalogue of Benefactors, with a disgruntled comment by an eighteenth-century reader.

Concordia Difcors.——HOR.

22. THE COUNTRY BOOK-CLUB

A satirical sketch by Rowlandson, from *The Country Book-Club: A Poem* (1788)

ecclesiastical history; Grote and Hallam did the same for classical and mediaeval history and literature, John Stuart Mill for philosophy and political economy, and Mazzini for Italian literature and history.[1] At the opening date there were already 500 subscribers and 3,000 books, including contributions from the Prince Consort and the Emperor Napoleon III; and by 1852 the collection had increased to over 60,000 volumes. It was at this time the only substantial library in London (apart from the commercial circulating libraries) from which books might be borrowed. At the present day it has some 5,000 subscribers and about three-quarters of a million books.

WORKING-CLASS SUBSCRIPTION LIBRARIES

Though much research is still needed into the provision of libraries for working people during this period, it does not appear that working-class subscription libraries ever became very numerous. We have noted that such libraries first made their appearance in the eighteenth century, but they were a mere handful in comparison with their middle-class counterparts. The reason, of course, was financial: the working man could not as a rule afford to pay an entrance fee and subscription sufficient to support an adequate library. It is significant, in this connection, that the first three working-class libraries in Scotland, at Leadhills, Wanlochhead, and Westerkirk, were in highly paid mining communities, and Leadhills, at least, received some help from the local gentry; while of the two late eighteenth-century English examples one, the Artizans' Library at Birmingham, began as a company library, and the other, at Kendal, was crippled from the outset by lack of funds.[2] To be successful, in fact, a working-class subscription library required either specially favourable circumstances or financial assistance from outside. Without such conditions, the library was bound to be small and was apt to be short-lived.

The three earliest Scottish libraries, as we have seen, maintained their existence throughout the nineteenth century, and

---

[1] *Ibid.*
[2] See above, pp. 122–4, 127–8. It is possible that Westerkirk also began as a company library.

still exist today.[1] The Leadhills library seems to have been particularly prosperous in the early years of the nineteenth century: when Dorothy Wordsworth visited the village in 1803 one of the miners recounted with pride that the library had just acquired a book which had cost £30.[2] At Westerkirk, in Dumfriesshire, when the antimony mining operations ceased in 1800, the miners' library became a general village library, which in 1834 had the good fortune to receive a legacy of £1,000 from the engineer Thomas Telford, who was a native of the place. A few years later a generous benefactor provided "a suitable and commodious library-room" in the new schoolhouse. Thus provided with accommodation, and with an income sufficient for the purchase of new books, the library was able to manage with an entrance fee of 5s. and a modest annual subscription.[3]

Of this library Samuel Smiles wrote rather romantically, a little later than the period now under review:

"The books are exchanged once a month, on the day of the full moon; on which occasion readers of all ages and conditions – farmers, shepherds, ploughmen, labourers, and their children – resort to it from far and near, taking away with them as many volumes as they desire for the month's reading.

"Thus there is scarcely a cottage in the valley in which good books are not to be found under perusal; and we are told that it is a common thing for the Eskdale shepherd to take a book under his plaid to the hillside – a volume of Shakespeare, Prescott, or Macaulay – and read it there, under the blue sky, with his sheep and the green hills before him."[4]

Telford also bequeathed £1,000 to the neighbouring library of Langholm – a middle-class subscription library founded in 1800 – but in this case the money was not paid over until 1850, the legacy being disputed by another Langholm library, the New Library or Trades Library, founded in 1813. This was

---

[1] The only other working-class subscription library founded in Scotland during the eighteenth century, at Langloan in Lanarkshire, also seems to have survived until mid-century, though not on a very large scale. A library of 500 volumes is recorded there as late as 1851 (S. Lewis, *Topographical Dictionary of Scotland*, 2nd edn. 1851, *s.v.*).

[2] *Journals of Dorothy Wordsworth*, ed. E. de Selincourt, Vol. I (1941), p. 209.

[3] Westerkirk Library, *Catalogue* (Langholm 1925), p. 3.

[4] S. Smiles, *Lives of the Engineers: Metcalfe and Telford* (1861–62, new edn. 1874), p. 324.

evidently a working-class library: the members were chiefly "tradesmen, mechanics and artizans", the entrance fee was 3s. 6d., and the annual subscription 2s. After the receipt of the Telford legacy the original library was able to improve its stock and reduce its subscription, and the Trades Library was virtually absorbed.[1]

Fifeshire also had its working men's libraries. At Dunfermline a Tradesmen's Library was established in 1808, with 107 volumes in its first catalogue. In 1832 it joined forces with the Mechanics' Institute (founded in 1825) to form the United Tradesmen's and Mechanics' Library, and by 1845 the joint library possessed 1,500 volumes. The entrance fee at this time was 2s. 6d., and the subscription 1s. per quarter. Dysart, in the same county, had a Trades Library founded in 1824. The historian of these libraries has pointed out that the standard of book selection was very high, and "while numerically the book-stocks were at first very small, their excellence and comprehensiveness must have compensated to a great extent for the small number of volumes".[2] One diligent early reader is credited with having read, one after another, "the greater portion of the twenty-eight volumes of the *Encyclopaedia Britannica*".[3]

The outstanding working men's library in Scotland, however, was the Edinburgh Mechanics' Subscription Library, founded in 1825 by three members of the School of Arts who wished to pursue their studies in the summer when the School was closed.[4]

[1] See the historical account by R. McGeorge in *Supplementary Catalogue of Langholm Library* (Langholm 1900), pp. 1–12. The Langholm Library, in the early years of this century, provided a happy hunting-ground for the young C. M. Grieve (now better known as "Hugh McDiarmid"), who lived in the same building and used to borrow the books in basketfuls. See his *Lucky Poet* (1943), pp. 8–13.

It should perhaps be explained here that the terms "tradesman" (in the northern sense of one who had been apprenticed to a trade) and "mechanic" (a skilled craftsman) were practically synonymous at this period. On the later shift in meaning, by which a tradesman became a shopkeeper and a mechanic a machine operative, see T. Kelly, *George Birkbeck* (Liverpool 1957), pp. 243–5.

[2] A. Anderson, *The Old Libraries of Fife* (Fife County Library 1953), p. 10.

[3] A. Stewart, *Reminiscences of Dunfermline* (Edinburgh 1866), p. 263.

[4] The Edinburgh School of Arts (1821) was in effect the first mechanics' institute, and this name is also found elsewhere in Scotland. The name Mechanics' Institute was first adopted at Glasgow in 1823 and London later in the year, and became the general one.

It began with 124 members and 428 volumes, and was at first open only in the evenings, but later it was open during the day as well. In 1851 J. W. Hudson, the first historian of adult education, gave the following account of it:

"In the first five years the members rose to an average of three hundred and fifty two, and increased annually until it attained twelve hundred members, paying five shillings as an entrance fee and one shilling and sixpence per quarter subscription. The subscribers to the library are chiefly working men and are all readers. The library contains nearly eighteen thousand volumes, and the issues nearly amount to two hundred thousand per annum, as each member is allowed to take out two entire works. This establishment so extensive in its workings, and so moderate in its fees, one shilling and sixpence per quarter, is located in the basement of a large house, in a back street, in the centre of Edinburgh. The library which is attained by a back stair dimly lighted, and ever thronged, owes much of its success to its economical management, if not to its unobtrusive and silent operations. Its chief defect is the want of a reading-room, or convenience for examining the works known only by the titles, before they are con- veyed from the premises; but as novels and light literature form two-thirds of the issues, this desideratum has not been obtained, although frequently demanded by many of the subscribers."[1]

This library maintained an independent existence until 1893, by which time it was suffering from the competition of the free public library. A merger with the Edinburgh Literary Institute enabled it to survive for a further seven years.

A few other working-class libraries are recorded in Scotland before mid-century. At Greenock a Mechanics' Library was formed by a group of working men in 1830, and at Lochwinnoch, not far to the south, a Working Man's Library was formed in 1834 as a protest against the exclusively religious character of the two parochial libraries there. The new library admitted "all kinds of books upon every subject . . . though containing the most conflicting opinions, except such as are hostile to evangelical religion."[2]

In England, in the early years of the century, there were small libraries associated with mutual improvement societies in the

---

[1] J. W. Hudson, *History of Adult Education* (1851), p. 201.
[2] *New Statistical Account of Scotland* (1845), Vol. VII, Renfrewshire, p. 108.

capital, but apart from the libraries previously mentioned at Birmingham and Kendal we do not hear of any independent working-class libraries until the 1820s, just about the time the mechanics' institute movement was getting under way. The two outstanding examples were both founded in the North of England, one at Liverpool and one at Sheffield, in the year 1823.

The Liverpool venture was started in July of that year on the initiative of Egerton Smith, editor of the *Liverpool Mercury*, who, hearing from a friend of the success attending the formation of mechanics' and apprentices' libraries in the United States,[1] decided to try an experiment of the same kind in Liverpool. The response was so enthusiastic that in January, 1824, the Liverpool Mechanics' and Apprentices' Library was formally launched on a subscription basis and placed under the management of a committee of well-to-do donors and supporters. The subscription was 4s. per annum. At the inaugural meeting the librarian unfurled, amid enthusiastic applause, a white silken banner sent by the apprentices of New York and bearing a painted design embodying a lion and an eagle with the inscription: NEW YORK SENDS HER GOOD WISHES TO LIVERPOOL; he also reported the gift, from New York and four other American cities, of "thirty volumes, elegantly bound" for the new library.[2]

The controlling interest given to the well-to-do was a feature which the library shared with many of the early mechanics' institutes, and was a means of ensuring financial support. Lord Brougham, a fervent advocate of popular adult education, strongly disapproved of this arrangement, contending that "the people themselves must be the great agents in accomplishing the work of their own instruction".[3] He recommended that at least two-thirds of the management of such institutions should be drawn from the working class. In spite of its undemocratic management, however, the Library flourished: by 1832 it had

---

[1] There were libraries of this kind in Bristol, Connecticut, as early as 1818, and in New York and Boston by 1820 – C. A. Bennett, *History of Manual and Industrial Instruction up to 1870* (Peoria, Ill., 1926), p. 317; J. H. Shera, *Foundations of the Public Library* (Chicago 1949), pp. 230–1.
[2] The description is preserved by Francis Place (Brit. Mus. Add. MSS. 27,284, f. 28), and is quoted in M. Tylecote, *The Mechanics' Institutes of Lancashire and Yorkshire before 1851* (Manchester 1957), pp. 55–6.
[3] H. Brougham, *Practical Observations upon the Education of the People* (1825), p. 1.

3,500 books, 1,200 readers, and an annual circulation of 25,000 volumes. After this there was a rather sharp falling away, but within a few years the Library became linked with the Brougham Institute, founded in 1836, which provided a newsroom, lectures, concerts, a discussion class, and other activities. The two bodies jointly were thus able to offer practically all the facilities of a mechanics' institute, and a popular feature was that non-subscribers might make use of any of the facilities of the combined institutions at 1d. for each admission.

J. W. Hudson waxed lyrical in his enthusiasm for this institution:

"The Liverpool philanthropists, and the zealous Lancashire advocates of universal instruction, dazzled by those noble edifices the Collegiate and the Mechanics' Institution . . . are ignorant of the silent yet extensive operations of the Institution which supplies the working-men of Liverpool with a large assortment of newspapers, of magazines, and an extensive library of books for the sum of one penny. The society which has attracted twenty-five thousand casual visitors in a single year has no chronicler – no monster soirée – for the recipients of its treasures are all labouring men. . . . Their Parnassium is reached from a back street by a narrow intricate stair, dimly lighted on winter evenings. The upper floor of a large warehouse is the great news-room. . . .

"In this humble seminary the mind of the working-man, the journeyman baker, and the dock labourer, receive cultivation, not in reading the latest accounts of misdemeanours and local calamities, but in imbibing instruction and high gratification from the perusal of select and valuable works, whether they lead him with the traveller across the pathless tracts of ocean, or cheer and console him with moral sketches of human nature."[1]

Within two years of the publication of Hudson's account, however, the Mechanics' and Apprentices' Library disappears from our ken – a victim, no doubt, to the competition of the Free Public Library established in 1852.

The Sheffield Mechanics' and Apprentices' Library, founded in December, 1823, also owed its origins to a newspaper editor – T. A. Ward, editor of the *Sheffield Independent*, whom we have already met as President of the Subscription Library. A Whig and a Unitarian, Ward was also at one time President of the

[1] J. W. Hudson, *The History of Adult Education* (1851), pp. 44–45, 48.

Literary and Philosophical Society, and in general a leading figure in the social and political life of the town. It was probably under his influence that the library was given a constitution much more democratic than that of Liverpool. It was, in fact, made into a proprietary library. The working-class members purchased a 5s. share, paid a quarterly subscription of 1s. 6d., and elected two-thirds of the committee. Apprentices paid 1s. a quarter. Provision was also made for honorary members – donors of £3. 3s. or books of that value, or subscribers of 7s. per annum.

Unlike the Liverpool Library, which early decided to admit all works except those of an immoral tendency, the Sheffield Library from the beginning excluded "novels, plays, and works subversive of the Christian religion".[1] This rule was not consistently carried out, but it led to such absurdities as the banning of Scott's novels in 1832, and the sale by auction of a set of Shakespeare acquired by way of bequest. None the less the Library prospered, with a steady six or seven hundred members throughout the thirties and 'forties. By 1850 it had over 6,000 volumes, with an annual issue of about 30,000. It survived until absorbed into the Free Public Library about 1860.

Kendal also had a Mechanics' and Apprentices' Library, which was established in 1824 and quickly developed into a Mechanics' Institute; and another library of this name is recorded at Bishopwearmouth in Durham, though not until 1851. Nottingham had an Operatives' and Artizans' Library, founded in 1824. From various sources one can trace a dozen or so other libraries, nearly all in the north or midlands, which were or seem to have been designed for working people, and there were probably others. Most of them are first recorded in mid-century and seem to have come into existence in the 'thirties and 'forties. Ackworth in Yorkshire and Penrith in Cumberland had Mechanics' Libraries, and in Derbyshire we find a group of four Artizans' and Mechanics' Libraries;[2] elsewhere working men's libraries often have no special distinguishing title, and are identifiable

---

[1] *Op. cit.*, p. 159. Hudson's account of the later years (pp. 158–61) supplements that given by J. Taylor in *Adult Education*, Vol. XI, (1938–39), pp. 151–60.

[2] Ilkeston (1834), Codnor Park and Heanor (1842), and Ironville (1843), all small industrial towns.

only by the low rate of subscription, usually from 6d. to 1s. 6d. a quarter.[1] Many of these libraries, like their middle-class counterparts, had reading rooms or newsrooms attached to them, and some, which also arranged a few lectures and classes, were barely distinguishable from mechanics' institutes.

Working men's libraries which hoped for widespread support, and especially those which looked for financial assistance from the middle classes, were apt, as at Sheffield, to be cautious in their book selection. This timidity often gave rise to criticism from the more radically minded workers, and in England as in Scotland sometimes led to the foundation of rival libraries. George Dawson, for example, told the 1849 Committee that at Nottingham, because the Operatives' and Artizans' Library refused to admit theological or political works, "many working men have withdrawn from it, and formed a new library, and the books are kept in public houses, and there they go, and pay a small subscription, and perhaps take a glass of ale, and read".[2] These public-house libraries were sometimes lending libraries, but not always: "sometimes they go there and read; of course it is to the interest of the publican that they should read there."[3] Similar evidence was given by J. B. Langley, who testified that in the colliery districts of the north and midlands the miners refused to participate in mechanics' institutes because of the exclusion of politics and theology, but that in many villages they had small libraries of their own.[4]

Some working-class libraries were frankly philanthropic. An early example was the Public Library founded at Dundee in 1796, which was said to be intended chiefly "for the working

---

[1] Examples are Castle Eden, Westgate and Wolsingham (Co. Durham); Corbridge and Haydonbridge (Northd.); Mansfield (Notts.); and Tamworth (Staffs.), all listed by Hudson. Hampstead had a Library at 2s. 6d. a quarter and an Artizans' Reading Room at 2s. a quarter. The Village Library founded in 1833 at Dukinfield (a small industrial township in Cheshire) must also be counted in this group, in spite of its name. It was run on the basis of 1d. a week subscription and contributions from honorary members.

[2] *1849 Report*, p. 80.

[3] *Op. cit.*, p. 87. Six such libraries were formed between 1835 and 1844, five in public houses and one in a temperance institute – W. H. Wylie. *Old and New Nottingham* (1853), pp. 350–1.

[4] *1849 Report*, pp. 157–8.

poor".[1] In this aim, however, it was unsuccessful, and by 1817, with a subscription of 15s. per annum, it had become definitely a middle-class affair. The Library for Tradesmen, Apprentices and Others at Hitchin was established by a group of Quakers in 1824, and managed by John Thompson, a Quaker tailor. It was open in the evenings from 6 to 8 at a subscription of 2d. per month, and was moderately successful until 1832, when it was taken over by the Society for Bettering the Condition of the Poor, and renamed the Working Man's Library. Under these new auspices, however, it did not flourish, and it was transferred to the newly formed Mechanics' Institute in 1835.[2]

Norwich, which over the centuries has been a pioneer in so many forms of library provision, made its contribution here also. The Norwich Penny Library, founded in 1824 "for the purpose of supplying children and the poor with instructive literature",[3] was open daily from 11 to 2, and at its inception was able to offer a choice of 1,000 volumes at 1d. per week. It became very popular, and by 1843, when it was taken over by the Mechanics' Institute, it had accumulated 2,000 volumes.

An unusual venture in this field was the Society for the Improvement of the Working Men of Glamorgan, founded in 1831. This was an itinerating library – almost the only example of this kind of organization south of the Border.[4] It had its headquarters at Cowbridge, and branches at Bridgend, Cardiff, Llantwit, Neath and Swansea; and the scheme provided for the issue to each branch of a collection of twenty-five books, to be exchanged every six months. A newspaper account of the inaugural meeting makes it clear that the scheme was connected with the agricultural unrest that was prevalent at this time, its first object being defined as:

"By the circulation of tracts in English and Welsh, to diffuse a general knowledge of the circumstances on which the well-being of the community depends – to point out the effects of the institution of

---

[1] D. M. Torbet, *The Growth of Municipal Libraries in Dundee* (F.L.A. thesis 1953, Library Assoc.), p. 10.

[2] R. F. Ashby, *A Small Town's Libraries in the Early 19th Century*, (F.L.A. thesis 1949, Library Assoc.), p. 5.

[3] N. G. Wiltshire, *The Continuity of the Library Tradition in an English Provincial Town* (F.L.A. thesis 1957, Library Assoc.), p. 35.

[4] There was another at Chichester – see below, p. 234.

property, the principles which regulate the price of labour, and the manner in which that price is affected by machinery."[1]

This was a direct imitation of the plan followed in the Lothians by Samuel Brown, and though the libraries in this case were not primarily religious the local clergy acted as librarians and advisers. Membership of the Society cost 5s. per annum; for borrowers the charge was 2d. per fortnight. Books were presented by the Society for the Diffusion of Useful Knowledge, and the Cowbridge Society itself published a dozen pamphlets. Unfortunately there is no record of its activity after 1832.

BOOK CLUBS

Concerning the book clubs of this period we are unfortunately very ill-informed, partly because it is of the nature of such organizations to be ephemeral and leave little record behind, and partly because no adequate search has yet been made for such records as may remain. We can only say, therefore, that they seem to have been numerous, both in England and in Scotland. Casual references to them are fairly frequent, e.g. the entry for Lochwinnoch in the *New Statistical Account of Scotland* (1845), after describing the establishment of parochial libraries and a working men's library, remarks: "Long before the existence of any of these libraries there were book-clubs, which interfere with the prosperity of the parochial institutions."[2] What is lacking, however, is detailed information regarding actual clubs.

One Scottish club is referred to briefly in the Report of the Select Committee:

"At the town of Peterhead, which has a population of 6,000 people, there is a very handsome library, entirely supported by voluntary subscription, containing from time to time 2,000 or 3,000 volumes. The manner in which it is managed is this: books are purchased and read, and then they are disposed of, and new ones purchased, partly

---

[1] *Monmouthsire Merlin*, 5th February, 1831. The details of the organization are taken from a report in the *Cambrian*, 1st October, 1831. I am indebted for information on this little-known experiment to Mr. T. Evans, of Llansaint, Kidwelly, and to Mr. T. J. Hopkins of the Cardiff Central Library.
[2] Vol. VII, Renfrewshire, p. 108.

out of the funds produced from the sale of the books already read, and partly from the contributions of members; the subscription, I think, is one guinea a year."[1]

This sounds like a middle-class venture and must have been on a large scale. It was founded in 1800. We may compare the club founded thirteen years later at St. Helens in Lancashire – also a middle-class affair, but limited to twenty members. The rules adopted in 1828 follow the customary eighteenth-century pattern, and include the following:

"1. There shall be an Annual Meeting on the Friday nearest the full moon, in March, when the books shall be sold, and every member not attending such meeting shall be subject to a fine of ten shillings. This rule not to extend to Ladies. . . .

"7. At the Annual Meeting, the majority of Members then present shall fix what periodical publications shall be circulated in the Society. . . .

"8. Any Member may order what book he or she chooses, such book not exceeding two guineas in value, and the Member so ordering the book being bound to pay half the cost, if no one bid a higher price for it at the Annual Sale. . . .

"11. No novel or professional book be introduced into the Society, unless approved of at an Annual Meeting, except those published by the Author of *Waverley*, which may be introduced without the acquiescence of the Members. . . .

"13. Five days be the time allowed for the perusal of each book . . . and any one detaining a book beyond the time limited shall forfeit two pence per day."[2]

This club survived until the early years of the Second World War. Another long-lived English club was the Sheffield Book Society, founded by six gentlemen in 1806, and limited to twenty members. It had monthly meetings and an annual dinner and auction, and lasted until about 1951.[3]

An anonymous correspondent of the *Monthly Magazine* attempted in 1821 to compile statistics of "Book Societies and Literary Institutions of every description" in the United King-

---

[1] *1849 Report*, p. 201.
[2] F. Crooks, "The St. Helens Book Club", in *Trans. Hist. Soc. of Lancs. and Ches.*, Vol. CX (Liverpool 1958), pp. 155–6.
[3] W. S. Porter, *Sheffield Literary and Philosophical Society: a Centenary Retrospect* (Sheffield 1922), pp. 5–6.

dom.[1] His figures, though not always easy to interpret, are of considerable interest. He estimated that there were "at present not less than 6,500 of these useful institutions of various degrees, and for various purposes . . . and that . . . above 1,000 new ones have been formed within the last three years". To make up his grand total he counts, to begin with, about 260 "permanent libraries", a term which evidently refers in the main to subscription libraries, though it may include some institutional libraries – literary and philosophical societies and the like. Next come "not less than 500" book societies which sell their books periodically, i.e. book clubs: a little later he uses a figure of 600 for this group. In addition he reckons 750 magazine societies, "by which ten or twelve persons club their pound or guinea, to purchase and circulate the best periodical works", and "not less than 5,000" newspaper societies.

This last figure, inconsistently, does not refer to the United Kingdom only, but to societies scattered "in every parish and hamlet of the empire". They represented a type of organization which was common before the reduction of the newspaper tax in 1836: "seven, eight, or nine persons club their sixpence a week to take in and circulate from one to the other, a London, and one, two, or three provincial papers. In poor districts, twelve or fourteen club their weekly penny for one or two of their favourite provincial papers, which they wear out in passing from hand to hand."

It would obviously be unwise to place too much reliance on figures such as these. What is interesting and significant, for our present purpose, is the author's impression that book clubs were twice as numerous as subscription libraries. Probably this was about the peak period of their popularity, for within a few years, especially in Lancashire and Yorkshire, mechanics' institutes sprang up to meet the same kind of need.

COMMERCIAL LIBRARIES

Commercial circulating libraries of all kinds continued to flourish. John Feltham probably exaggerated when he declared in 1803 that "every intelligent village throughout the nation

[1] Vol. LI (1821), pp. 397–8.

now possesses its Circulating Library",[1] but the anonymous contributor to the *Monthly Magazine* computed that there were in the United Kingdom at least 1,500 of them, supported on the average by seventy subscribers. "These", he commented piously, "supply novels and high-seasoned productions for sickly or perverted appetites; and as far as they exhibit the passions and foibles of mankind, amend the heart, and extend the influence of sentiment and sensibility, they must be regarded as useful establishments."[2]

A notable example was to be found in Aberdeen. The first private subscription library here does not seem to have been founded until 1804, but the commercial libraries traced their history back to 1765, and by 1811 the largest of them, the United Public Library, was said to have a collection of some 52,000 volumes – twice as many as any private subscription library in the country at that period. A contemporary remarks that in addition to the new and popular works constantly issuing from the press,

"There are also many old and valuable books to be found in this library, which altogether contains a greater collection of works of merit than any similar provincial institution in the kingdom."[3]

As in the eighteenth century, circulating libraries were of all kinds, large and small, good and bad. At the one extreme were reputable establishments such as this at Aberdeen, or Mudie's Select Library in London, which was founded in 1842, and became before long a national institution;[4] in towns such as Brighton and Bath the best circulating libraries were places of fashionable resort, with evening concerts and card-parties. At the other extreme were the small shop libraries conducted as a side-line by stationers, tobacconists, confectioners, barbers, and the like, and hiring out the products of the Minerva Press and similar popular literature at 1d. a volume. Thirty-eight of these

[1] *A Picture of London for 1803*, p. 238, quoted G. K. Scott, *English Public Libraries in the Provinces, 1750–1850* (F.L.A. thesis, Library Assoc. 1951), p. 49.

[2] *Monthly Magazine*, Vol. LI (1821), p. 398. Cf. below, App. IV, on circulating libraries in Hull.

[3] W. Thom, *The History of Aberdeen*, Vol. II (1811), p. 207.

[4] The national reputation of Mudie's really dates from the 'fifties. The other well-known circulating libraries – W. H. Smith's, Boot's, and the Times Book Club – came later still.

were counted in 1838 in three Westminster parishes alone. Thomas Cooper, as a boy in Gainsborough (before he discovered the dusty treasures of old Nathaniel Robinson's library), made use of a circulating library kept by Mrs. Trevor, stationer, from whose shelves he drew

"the enchanting 'Arabian Nights', and odd plays of Shakespeare, Dryden, and Otway, and Cook's Voyages, and the Old English Baron; and the Castle of Otranto, and Guiscard; and the Bravo of Venice; and Hardenbras and Haverill; and Valentine's Eve; and the Castles of Athlin and Dunbayne; and the Scottish Chiefs – and a heap of other romances. . . . "

Later, by the kindness of the same lady, he was able to have the use, for a nominal subscription of 10s. a year, of the books belonging to a gentlemen's circulating library which she conducted at an annual subscription of £2 2s.[1]

Among commercial libraries we may also reckon the libraries which, in London at least, were occasionally provided in public houses, and quite often provided in coffee-houses. The public houses regularly supplied newspapers, and Hudson records that "In several of the suburban districts a few books are being introduced . . . for the use of parlour visitors."[2] It was, however, he tells us, the coffee-houses which made the only effective provision for the education of the London working man. William Lovett, in evidence before the 1849 Committee, gave an account of these institutions, which had sprung up in large numbers since the early years of the century to meet the needs of working people. By this date there were about 2,000 of them, and Lovett reported:

" . . . you may go into those places, and see a great number of the working classes reading; I am told that somewhere about 500 of them have libraries connected with them . . . there is one especially in Long Acre, 'Potter's Coffee-house', I think it is called, where they have 2,000 volumes, it is said; and there are other parts of London where they have also large libraries."[3]

Under the heading of commercial libraries we may also

---

[1] T. Cooper, *Life* (1872, 4th edn. 1873), pp. 34, 52. Cf. above, p. 196.
[2] J. W. Hudson, *History of Adult Education* (1851), p. 211.
[3] *1849 Report*, p. 177. For other contemporary evidence to the same effect see L. James, *Fiction for the Working Man, 1830–1850* (1963), p. 7.

include a London curiosity – the provision of libraries in omni-buses. The origin of the idea may be attributed to George Shillibeer, who ran the first London omnibus in 1829, and sup-plied his patrons with newspapers and magazines. A rival proprietor named Cloud, who in the early 'thirties ran a service from the Haymarket to Hammersmith and Chelsea, went one better by providing a selection of books by well-known authors:

"A little bookcase, well filled, was fixed in each of his omnibuses at the end near the horses. Books were expensive in those days, and many people rode to Hammersmith and back for the sole purpose of reading a particular one which they knew to be in the omnibus library. But this admirable innovation was shamefully abused by the passengers, who appeared to consider it no sin to purloin the volumes. Disgusted at the dishonesty of his patrons, Mr. Cloud announced publicly that, in consequence of the thefts, his libraries would be discontinued."[1]

INSTITUTIONAL LIBRARIES

In spite of all the developments that have been described so far, the main advance in library provision during these fifty years was through libraries attached to cultural and educational institutions. These institutional libraries were already numerous in 1800, and from the 1820s onwards they proliferated with astonishing rapidity.

The middle-class cultural societies, which formed the oldest group, need not be described in detail, for they functioned in much the same way as similar societies today – indeed many of them are still with us. Their prototypes were the Royal Society, founded in 1660 and still in 1800 more of a gentlemen's club than a learned society; and the Society of Antiquaries, founded originally about 1586 and revived after a lapse of over a hundred years in 1717. By the middle of the nineteenth century these pioneering bodies had been supplemented by a whole host of societies, both specialist and non-specialist, national and local. Many of the specialist societies, e.g. the Medical Societies of Edinburgh (1734) and London (1773), were professional in character, but others, especially in the provinces, still offered

---

[1] H. C. Moore, *Omnibuses and Cabs* (1901), p. 24. This was probably George Cloud, who had a coachyard in Hammersmith. I am indebted for information on this point to Mr. G. F. A. Wilmot of the London University Extra-Mural Department.

scope for the intelligent amateur: among such (to choose a few examples almost at random) were the Glasgow Philosophical Society (1802), the Newcastle Antiquarian Society (1813), the Cambrian Geological Institute at Swansea (1821), the Orkney Natural History Society (1837), and the Sussex Archaeological Society (1846).

Then there were societies of a more general cultural character, covering a range of subjects literary, historical and scientific. We have seen that from a quite early date in the eighteenth century there were small societies of this character at Spalding and other centres in the eastern counties.[1] These were mainly literary and antiquarian in their interests. The Society of Cymmrodorion was founded in London in 1751 to study Welsh literature and antiquities. There were Literary Societies at Glasgow in 1752 and at Warrington in 1758. Perth had a Literary and Antiquarian Society in 1784. The Lunar Society at Birmingham (1775) was predominantly scientific in character,[2] but pointed the way to the Manchester Literary and Philosophical Society (1781) which provided the pattern for numerous societies, commonly under the same or some similar name, in the English provincial towns.

The Newcastle Literary and Philosophical Society was the second institution of the kind, in 1793, and in the first quarter of the nineteenth century we have Warrington (1811), Liverpool and Plymouth (1812), Truro (1818), Leeds (1820), Sheffield and Hull (1822), Whitby (1823), Bristol and Nottingham (1824), and Bath (1825). Others followed later in the century. In the capital, bodies such as the London Institution (1805), the Philomathic Institution (1807), and the Russell Institution (1808), fulfilled a similar function. The general purpose of nearly all of these societies was similar to that stated by the Leeds Philosophical and Literary Society, namely "the promotion of Science and Literature, by the reading of Papers, the delivering of Lectures, the formation of a Museum, the collection of a Library, and the establishment of a Laboratory fitted up with Apparatus".[3]

[1] See above, p. 98.
[2] See above, p. 131. It was so called because, like so many societies of this period, it usually met at the time of the full moon.
[3] A. Hume, *Learned Societies and Printing Clubs of the United Kingdom* (1847), p. 13.

There were also some middle-class institutions of a more specifically educational character. The Royal Institution in London, though thanks to men such as Davy and Faraday it afterwards earned a reputation primarily as a centre of research, was originally founded in 1799 to diffuse a knowledge of applied science. The Royal Institutions at Liverpool (1814) and Manchester (1823) were also designed as teaching institutions, but their scope was broader – "the promotion of literature, science and the arts".[1]

Practically all these institutions made the formation of a library one of their major objectives. The libraries were not as a rule large, but they were usually well selected, and from the point of view of access they were on much the same footing as the gentlemen's subscription libraries. A notable example was the library of the Newcastle Literary and Philosophical Society, which by 1829 amounted to over 9,000 volumes, carefully arranged and adequately catalogued, with a reference room and a lending department. It was designed primarily as a scholars' library, with considerable emphasis upon science and scientific periodicals. In the early days there were the same difficulties about the admission of novels and works of religious controversy that we have seen in the case of the subscription libraries, and it was not until 1846 that the committee seriously took in hand the task of providing for those members whose tastes lay in the direction of more popular literature. The annual report of 1842 described the library as "the bond which has held the Society together for so many years, and which has enabled it to struggle through so many difficulties . . . every day's experience shows that it is by those persons who subscribe for the books the institution is principally supported".[2]

The 1820s saw a flood of new institutions, very varied in character, but having this in common, that they were designed for the education (or in some cases indoctrination) of the working and lower middle classes. In practice, as is the way of adult educational institutions, they nearly all tended to cater for

---

[1] The Royal Institution of Cornwall at Truro (1818), and the Royal Institution of South Wales at Swansea (1835), were literary and philosophical societies.

[2] R. S. Watson, *The History of the Literary and Philosophical Society of Newcastle-upon-Tyne* (1897), p. 186.

groups slightly higher in the social scale than those for which they were intended. The mechanics' institutes, under this and other names, were at the centre of this complex of institutions, and in a way bridged the gap between the classes, for they catered in the main for the skilled workers and for clerks and shopkeepers who ranked with the lower middle classes.[1] They were flanked on the one side by literary and scientific institutes or athenaeums meeting the social and educational needs of the commercial and professional classes, and by mutual improvement societies, lyceums and other bodies which directed their appeal with more or less success to the rank and file of the workers.[2] All these institutions had their libraries, similar in character to those of the mechanics' institutes, which will be dealt with in more detail below.

The mechanics' institutes were, in the modern phrase, part of the establishment, and being dependent in a considerable degree on the financial support of the well-to-do they were usually very careful to avoid controversial political and religious issues. For the more Radical wing of the working class this was not good enough, and all the various working-class reform movements of this period made their own arrangements for education through lectures, classes, readings and discussions. The library provision they were able to make was exceedingly limited in comparison with that of the institutes, but most of them made some provision for the circulation of books, and especially current newspapers and periodicals, and some kind of library or reading room was a common feature.

The Radical agitation took different forms, both political and economic, at various times. The Hampden Clubs, Unions of Political Protestants, and the like which flourished in the years immediately following the Napoleonic Wars, were organizations to agitate for political reform. They adopted from the Methodists the plan of the weekly class-meeting and the small weekly subscription, part of which went towards the purchase of Cobbett's *Political Register*, Sherwin's *Political Register*, Wooler's *Black Dwarf*, and other Radical journals, besides

---

[1] Cf. above, pp. 187–8, 190.

[2] The nomenclature is, however, exceedingly confusing: "literary and scientific institute", "athenaeum", and "lyceum" were sometimes just alternative names for mechanics' institutes. See also above, p. 211, note 4.

more solid fare such as Bentham's *Reform Catechism*. One of the notorious Six Acts of 1819, for the repression of this agitation, repeated an earlier prohibition of 1799 on unauthorized reading rooms open to the public.

In the 1820s the working-class reformers turned towards co-operation and trade unionism as a remedy for their ills. All the early co-operative societies of this period regarded education as one of their important functions, and libraries were not neglected. Dr. William King, a Brighton physician and a well-known co-operator, mentioned the point specifically:

> "But above all things . . . let Co-operators compete with each other in the improvement of their minds; let them form classes for this purpose; let them have common reading-rooms and libraries. . . ."[1]

The Reform Bill of 1832 brought a revival of political agitation, which persisted after the Bill was passed and led directly to the Chartist movement. The complex story of that movement, which came to a head in 1839–42 and had a brief revival in 1848, cannot be told here, but we cannot fail to note the strong element of educational idealism which was represented by leaders such as William Lovett, Henry Hetherington, and Thomas Cooper. The London Working Men's Association, created by Lovett and Hetherington in 1836, included in its aims the formation of "a library of reference and useful information".[2] Later, Chartist reading rooms, with newspapers and a small collection of books, became common in many parts of the country. In 1840 a tract entitled *Chartism*, written by Lovett and John Collins in Warwick gaol, put forward a scheme for the establishment throughout the country of *"Public Halls or Schools for the People"*, for the education of children and adults,

---

[1] *The Co-operator*, 1st December, 1829, repr. in T. W. Mercer, *Co-operation's Prophet* (Manchester 1947), p. 130. These early co-operative societies were short-lived, and the main contribution of co-operative society libraries came in the second half of the nineteenth century. The library of the Rochdale Co-operative Society – the pioneering society of the modern co-operative movement – had its beginnings only in 1849. See A. Greenwood, *The Educational Department of the Rochdale Equitable Pioneers' Society* (Manchester 1877), p. 4; and C. Stott, "Early Rochdale Libraries", in *Trans. Rochdale Lit. and Sci. Soc.*, Vol. XVIII, (1932–34). Stott's paper (p. 105) also has a reference to an early trade union library, formed by the Rochdale Weavers' Society in 1832.

[2] W. Lovett, *Life and Struggles* (1876, new edn., ed. R. H. Tawney, 1920), Vol. I, p. 95.

and envisaged also small district "circulating libraries, from a hundred to two hundred volumes each, containing the most useful works on politics, morals, the sciences, history, and such instructive and entertaining works as may be generally approved of. Such libraries to . . . be sent *in rotation* from one town or village in the district to another, and to be lent freely to the members."[1]

One such hall, the National Hall at Holborn, was actually established in 1842 under Lovett's direction, and duly included a "coffee-room and library".[2]

Many of the Chartists were also associated with the millennial Socialist movement of Robert Owen, which took shape as a national organization in 1837, appointed "social missionaries" to carry out propaganda, and began to erect "Social Institutions" or "Halls of Science" in the manufacturing towns of the north and midlands. Information concerning these is scanty, but we cannot doubt that most of them at least attempted to provide a library and reading room. Certainly this was the case with the largest and most expensive of them, the Hall of Science in Liverpool, which was erected in 1839 at a cost of £5,000, and closed in 1842.[3]

Even this is not the end of the story of these institutional libraries. We find libraries associated with Oddfellows' Institutes, benefit societies, farmers' clubs, Y.M.C.A.s – all kinds of institutions. The simple fact is that at a time when there was a great and increasing public demand for books, and when there was no public library service, almost every political, economic, religious, social and educational group regarded it as a duty to make some library provision for its members. The resulting libraries were often pitiably inadequate, but the universality of such provision is an impressive fact.

MECHANICS' INSTITUTE LIBRARIES

The libraries of the mechanics' institutes attracted a good deal of attention in the 1849 Committee, and have been much written about since, partly because they were so numerous and

[1] *Op. cit.*, Vol. II, p. 254.
[2] *Op. cit.*, Vol. II, p. 293. Cf. *1849 Report*, pp. 179–80.
[3] R. B. Rose, "John Finch", in *Trans. Hist. Soc. of Lancs. and Ches.*, Vol. CIX (Liverpool 1957), pp. 174–5.

partly because they are so much better documented than most pre-1850 libraries.

The origins of this movement have already been sufficiently indicated.[1] Its development, though sporadic at first, and liable to recessions in years when trade was bad, gathered momentum rapidly in the 1840s, and seems to have reached a peak round about 1860. The heaviest concentration was, as might be expected, in the industrial areas of the north of England, the midlands, South Wales, and central Scotland. Lancashire and the West Riding of Yorkshire alone accounted for more than a quarter of the total in 1851, but by this time they were to be found in almost every sizeable town in England, and often in quite small villages. Of the total of about 700 institutes at this date about thirty were in Wales, and about fifty in Scotland.

The institutes varied in size, of course, very greatly. At one end of the scale were large institutes such as Leeds, Liverpool, Manchester, and the Greenwich Society for the Diffusion of Useful Knowledge, with substantial buildings and more than 1,000 members apiece – Leeds, with 1,850, was the largest; at the other were the tiny rural institutes with a score or so of members, meeting in borrowed premises. Nearly four-fifths of the number had 200 members or less.

One of the essential functions of almost every institute was a library. There were other functions – lectures, classes, perhaps a museum and a collection of scientific apparatus – and these met with varying success, but generally speaking it was the library which became the heart and core of the institute. In 1849 Samuel Smiles testified of the Yorkshire mechanics' institutes that it was "necessary to have a library to keep the institution together",[2] and the same was true in other parts of the country. The size of the library, of course, depended on the resources of the institute concerned. There were a few fairly large libraries: Liverpool, in 1851, had 15,300 volumes, Man-

---

[1] See above, pp. 187–8, 190.
[2] *1849 Report*, p. 124. Cf. Langley's evidence: "if it were not for the libraries they would cease to exist" (p. 153). At Dundee the Directors of the Watt Institution stated in their Report for 1835 that they "have long been of the opinion that the Library is the most useful portion of such institutions as that over which they preside". – D. M. Torbet, *The Growth of Municipal Libraries in Dundee* (F.L.A. thesis, 1953, Library Assoc.).

chester 13,000, Northampton 9,000, Newcastle 8,250, Leeds
7,700, Greenwich 7,500, London and Glasgow 6,000 each; but
the total holdings of the 700 institutes referred to amounted to
some 655,000 volumes – an average of less than 1,000 per
institute. Some had only a few hundred.[1]

The mechanics' institute libraries suffered greatly from gifts.[2]
They suffered even more from the misguided attentions of
middle-class supporters who, misled perhaps by the astonishing
achievements of the gifted, overestimated the reading ability
of the ordinary working man. In the early years it was believed
that the institutes would concentrate upon systematic courses
in science, and the libraries were heavily biased in this direction.
Besides excluding works of political and religious controversy,
many institutes also excluded fiction, and Leeds even excluded
history and biography. As the illusion about scientific education
faded, library policy became more liberal and more adapted to
the needs of the members, but the original puritanical attitude
towards fiction long persisted.

B. F. Duppa, whose *Manual for Mechanics' Institutions* was
published by the Society for the Diffusion of Useful Knowledge
in 1839, has some sensible remarks about the difficulty the
ordinary man has in approaching a large collection of books,
and upon the importance of detailed catalogues:[3] but he obviously
disapproves of all reading which is not directed to serious and
consecutive study: "miscellaneous perusal of books", he declares,
"tends to weaken the intellect".[4] The list of books he recom-
mends begins with Butler's *Analogy*, Aristotle's *Ethics and
Politics*, Bacon's *Essays*, Bentham's *Morals and Legislation* and
Book of Fallacies, Butler's *Works*, and Blackstone's *Commentaries*.

For the later years of this period we have for the first time

---

[1] For these figures see T. Kelly, *George Birkbeck* (Liverpool 1957), p. 267.
Very similar conclusions are reached by W. A. Munford in *English
Libraries 1800–1850* (1958), p. 54.

[2] "Many of the books are gift books, turned out of people's shelves . . .
so that, out of 1,000 volumes, perhaps there may be only 400 or 500
useful ones. The rest are, many of them, only annual registers and old
religious magazines that are never taken down from the shelves." –
George Dawson, *1849 Report*, p. 79. See also Smiles's evidence, p. 127.

[3] "The most useful of all things", he remarks optimistically, "would be a
full catalogue of all the subjects to be found in all the books of a library,
referring to the volume and page of each work" (p. 51).

[4] p. 49.

statistics of book issues.[1] J. B. Langley, in 1849, on the basis of information he had collected regarding mechanics' institutes and similar bodies in England and Wales, thought that on the average annual issues were about three times the number of books in stock.[2] Smiles reported that in the Yorkshire Union the issues varied from one to twelve times the books in stock.[3] These proportions, however, are not very meaningful, since the issues were clearly related to the number of members and the size of the bookstock. It is perhaps more interesting, as evidence of the extent to which these libraries were used, to look at the number of issues per annum per member.

The most comprehensive set of figures for this purpose is to be found in the table appended to Hudson's *History of Adult Education* (1851). Unfortunately these figures are not very reliable, since in most cases the figure for issues is given in round hundreds or even thousands, and may be no more than guesswork. If, however, we select only those institutes (about a hundred in number) for which the figures have the appearance of accuracy, we find the number of issues per member usually ranges between 10 and 40 per annum. It is noticeable that where the book stock exceeds 2,000, the number of issues never falls below 20 per member; whereas in small institutes with a stock of only a few hundred books (e.g. many of the Yorkshire institutes), the figure is often below 10. Bad management may have been part of the reason, but we can hardly doubt that the main reason was a shortage of suitable books. Sometimes when an institute was new, and the books unfamiliar, borrowings were high. A striking example recorded by Hudson is the New Mechanics' Institute at Horsforth in the West Riding, which with 50 members and 400 books claimed an annual issue of 4,735 – nearly 95 books per member. The next highest figure is that shown for the Winlaton Literary and Mechanics' Institute in Co. Durham, which had 90 members, 1,400 books, and an annual issue of 5,350, giving an average of over 59 issues per member.

On the whole, therefore, we may say that making due allowance for the quantity and quality of the books, the libraries of

[1] See Bibliographical Note at end of chapter.
[2] *1849 Report*, p. 156.
[3] *Op. cit.*, p. 128.

the mechanics' institutes were reasonably well used. If, however, we are tempted to regard them as a substitute for modern public libraries, we must remember that they were never free. The subscription might be as low as 1s. a quarter, but was more commonly 2s. 6d., and might even be 4s. or 5s. These were substantial charges at a time when £1 a week was a good wage for a working man, and many, e.g. cotton operatives and agricultural labourers, earned only half that amount. Huddersfield Mechanics' Institute, which prided itself on its working-class character, charged 3½d. a week, and this device of the weekly subscription was adopted by some other institutes also.

By 1850 the attempt to provide scientific libraries had long since been abandoned. In most institutes fiction, biography, travel and general literature were now the order of the day, with fiction the most popular of all. By contemporaries this emphasis on fiction was universally deplored, and witnesses before the 1849 Committee did their best to demonstrate that the taste for non-fiction was increasing. The same attitude is not unknown in more modern library reports, and has never been better satirized than by Dickens in his description of the library of the Dulborough Mechanics' Institute in *The Uncommercial Traveller:*

" . . . there was such a painfully apologetic return of 62 offenders who had read Travels, Popular Biography, and mere Fiction descriptive of the aspirations of the hearts and souls of mere human creatures like themselves; and such an elaborate parade of 2 bright examples who had had down Euclid after the day's occupation and confinement; and 3 who had had down Metaphysics after ditto; and 1 who had had down Theology after ditto; and 4 who had worried Grammar, Political Economy, Botany, and Logarithms all at once after ditto; that I suspected the boasted class to be one man, who had been hired to do it."[1]

For an example of a large and well-conducted library we can turn to the Manchester Mechanics' Institute, founded in 1824. The library opened in the following year with 823 volumes: by 1850 it had 12,000. At the outset the Institute had to rely on donations, but as membership increased books were purchased on a substantial scale. From the beginning the library

[1] *The Uncommercial Traveller* (1861), Ch. xii. "Dulborough" was Chatham, Dickens's birthplace.

was a general one, embracing science, history, and "polite literature". By 1849 fiction formed the largest section. By 1835 the library room could no longer cope with the demand: the library was therefore transferred to a room formerly used as a gymnasium, the original library being converted into a reading room with periodicals and a small reference collection. From 1838–39 the library was open daily, except Sundays, from 10 a.m. to 9.30 p.m. It was evidently very popular, and annual issues rose to a peak of 54 volumes per member in 1848.

An important controversy arose in 1840 over a proposal to establish a newspaper reading room. The same problem was agitating mechanics' institutes in many parts of the country about this time. Hitherto the institutes, unlike the private subscription libraries, had normally provided their members only with books and periodicals, not with newspapers. Since even after the reduction of the newspaper tax in 1836 newspapers still commonly retailed at 5d., this meant that the working man who wished to read a paper normally resorted to a public house or coffee-house. If he were more serious he might join a newspaper club or a cheap subscription reading room.

The provision of a newsroom became general practice in the institutes in the 'forties, but in Manchester and elsewhere the principle was not conceded without heated discussion. The objection was partly on the ground of expense and partly because it was thought that newspapers would bring controversy and ill feeling. In Manchester the decision to establish a newsroom was taken after a petition had been received from four hundred members; but until 1845 those using it were required to pay an extra subscription of 4s. a year. Thereafter it was free to all members. "Both London and provincial newspapers were supplied, and also Irish and Scottish papers. Papers from France, New York, and Jamaica were received regularly by the packets, and several commercial publications provided."[1]

Two smaller mechanics' institute libraries may be more briefly mentioned. The main effort of the Huddersfield Mechanics' Institute, founded in 1841, was concentrated upon class-teaching, but its library (1,700 books in 1850), was in

---

[1] M. Tylecote, *The Mechanics' Institutes of Lancashire and Yorkshire before 1851* (Manchester 1957), p. 156.

great demand. It was open on two evenings a week, and staffed by honorary librarians, who reported:

"It has also been gratifying to us to see the animation that exists among the members on the nights the library is open; finding work for three and sometimes four persons to attend to them. It is no unusual occurrence to see twenty of the juvenile members, calling out the number of the volume they want at one time."[1]

A reading room for newspapers and periodicals, open every weekday evening, was added in 1844, and was "constantly full of readers".[2]

The Chichester Mechanics' Institute, situated in the midst of an agricultural region, is specially commended in an account written in 1837 for its active library policy. The Institute had at this time over 400 members, and its library amounted only to 1,000 volumes, but it made its influence felt over a wide area. Branches were established, under the management of committees of local farmers, in the neighbouring hamlets of Bognor and Selsey, and each of these branches, in addition to having occasional lectures, periodically received a box of books from the Institute library.[3] This missionary endeavour anticipated the travelling libraries which were established by mechanics' institutes in the North of England in the second half of the century.

At Peebles, where a mechanics' institute "for the delivery of popular lectures on various scientific subjects" was started in 1832, and carried on with only moderate success, it was resolved in 1847 "to re-model the institution, and make the library its prominent feature". By 1849, 730 volumes had been assembled, largely from gifts, and the number of readers was said to be increasing. The secretary wrote in typical Victorian vein regarding the effect of the library on the morals of the young men of Peebles:

"The young men are in general exemplary in their conduct. The clerks in offices present a striking contrast to their predecessors. The most of them are ardent readers, and a knot of them meet weekly for mutual instruction in the principles of their profession. They have

[1] *Op. cit.*, p. 217.　　　　　　　[2] *Op. cit.*, p. 218.
[3] C. W. Baker, "Mechanics' Institutions and Libraries", in Central Society of Education, *First Publication* (1837), p. 236.

thereby every chance of becoming useful and intelligent members of society, instead of a curse to all connected with them. Another body of young men meet periodically, and discuss literary topics and questions in ethics. In short a wholesome spirit appears to pervade the youth, which must eventually be productive of good."[1]

All in all, after making every allowance for the weakness and inadequacies of the mechanics' institute libraries, we are bound to recognize that they made a substantial addition to the facilities available to the reading public. Nor was their contribution restricted to the years before 1850: it continued well on into the latter part of the century, in some cases even into the present century, and in many instances laid the foundation for the free public libraries we know today.

Closely allied to the mechanics' institute libraries were the factory libraries which became increasingly common towards the middle of the century. Many mechanics' institutes, of course, were associated with particular industries and even particular firms.[2] Elsewhere philanthropic employers frequently sponsored some kind of institute or mutual improvement society offering a variety of social and educational amenities, and these amenities nearly always included a library. At Rochdale, for example, John Bright and Bros. provided a library at 1d. a week in the Fieldhouse Institute, which was founded for their employers in 1832 and existed till 1869.[3] At Ipswich in 1836 a Mental Improvement Society, mainly for library purposes, was established in connection with Messrs. Ransomes and May's foundry.[4] In Dundee there was a library at Brown's spinning-mills.

At Chorlton-on-Medlock, Manchester, the mill-workers of W. & D. Morris founded in 1845 a mutual improvement society which according to Hudson had "one of the best factory libraries in the kingdom":

"The library has about seven hundred and fifty volumes, to which the subscription is one halfpenny per week, and to the newsroom and library one penny per week subscription. The news and reading room is open all day, so that at meal times, or when any of the hands are

[1] *1849 Report*, pp. 251–2.
[2] For examples see T. Kelly, *George Birkbeck* (Liverpool 1957), p. 262.
[3] C. Stott, "Early Rochdale Libraries", in *Trans. Rochdale Lit.* and *Sci. Soc.* Vol. XVIII (1932–34), pp. 106–7.
[4] J. Glyde, jun., *The Moral, Social and Religious Condition of Ipswich* (Ipswich 1850), pp. 179–80.

waiting for work, they may pass their time in reading the various newspapers and periodicals taken in."[1]

Many other examples could be given, especially from the north of England. In 1847 we hear of a society

"the object of which was to introduce libraries into manufactories, to further the social and moral improvement of the workmen, imposing one condition only: that no books of a sectarian or demoralising character should be afterwards admitted."[2]

Two years later Dawson reported a movement of a similar kind in Manchester:

"A bookseller told me that in Manchester there is a great demand for books, to go to form factory libraries. He attributed it to a book published in Manchester, which came out and was reviewed, as since that he had had a great demand for books to go to factory libraries. It was a novel or tale of Manchester life, which attracted great attention."[3]

The book here referred to must surely have been Mrs. Elizabeth Gaskell's *Mary Barton: a Tale of Manchester Life*, which was published towards the latter end of 1848, and which not only dealt sympathetically with the cause of the distressed Lancashire operatives, but also drew attention to the uncommon accomplishments of some of them in mathematics and natural history. Throughout the manufacturing districts of Lancashire were to be found, here and there, men of real scholarship:

"In the neighbourhood of Oldham there are weavers, common handloom weavers, who throw the shuttle with unceasing sound, though Newton's 'Principia' lie open on the loom. . . . There are botanists among them, equally familiar with either the Linnaean or the Natural system, who know the name and habitat of every plant within a day's walk from their dwellings. . . . There are entomologists, who may be seen with a rude-looking net, ready to catch any winged insect, or a kind of dredge, with which they rake the green and slimy pools; practical, shrewd, hard-working men, who pore over each new specimen with real scientific delight."[4]

[1] J. W. Hudson, *History of Adult Education* (1851), pp. 191–2.
[2] G. R. Humphery, "On Workmen's, or Factory, Libraries", in *Monthly Notes of the Library Association*, Vol. II (1881), p. 54.
[3] *1849 Report*, p. 89.
[4] *Mary Barton*, Ch. v. The Manchester weavers, in 1718, formed a Mathematical Society on lines similar to that formed at Spitalfields in

Mrs. Gaskell's book is said to have angered some of the master-manufacturers, but in others it evidently struck a chord of sympathy.

CONCLUSION

In paying this tribute to the mechanics' institutes and similar bodies we must not forget all the other forms of library provision which have been detailed in this long chapter. The oft-quoted remark of George Dawson to the 1849 Committee that "we give the people of this country an appetite to read, and supply them with nothing",[1] was no more than a rhetorical exaggeration. The fact is that, in the expressive Scottish phrase, the whole country was "hotching" with libraries.[2] It remains true, however, that good libraries were rare, and good free libraries almost non-existent.

It was to find a remedy for this situation that the Select Committee on Public Libraries was set up. In the course of its deliberations it discovered that two enterprising local authorities had already taken steps to establish rate-aided libraries. Warrington, in 1848, had brought together the fine museum collected by the local Natural History Society, and the books of the old Warrington Subscription Library, to form a public museum and library supported from the rates under the terms of the Museums Act of 1845, which permitted local authorities to levy $\frac{1}{2}$d. rate for the support of a public museum. Salford, in 1849, had just set about doing the same thing.[3] Whether, as Warrington

the previous year (see above, p. 128). The Oldham Mathematical Society was an offshoot, formed in 1794.

[1] *1849 Report*, p. 85.

[2] See, for example, the survey of library provision in Hull, below, App. IV.

[3] A similar arrangement had been made, even earlier, at Canterbury, where in 1847 the Corporation purchased for public use the Museum and Library of the Philosophical and Literary Institution. Members of the public could borrow books at 1d. per volume, but until at least 1853 only on production of an order from a member of the Museum Committee. (Information from Mr. F. Higenbottam, City Librarian—cf. J. J. Ogle, *The Free Library* (1897), p. 11.)

Another civic enterprise, though not quite on the same footing, was the new Guildhall Library in London, opened in 1828 as a repository of "all matters relating to this City". It was supported, not from the rates, but from the Corporation's Privy Purse, and until 1873 was open only to members of the Corporation and accredited students – R. Irwin and R. Staveley (eds.), *The Libraries of London* (1949, 2nd edn. 1961), p. 123.

contended, books could legitimately be included in the contents of a museum, was a doubtful point, but these pioneering ventures pointed the way to the right solution – the rate-aided public library, which was duly provided for in the Public Libraries Act of 1850.

This Act is sometimes spoken of as though it were a magic wand which brought a national public library service into being overnight. Nothing could be further from the truth. The powers given by the Áct were exceedingly limited and inadequate; they were, moreover, permissive not compulsory. It was only after long and often bitter struggles, and much supplementary legislation, that the library service as we know it came into existence. Many towns were still without public libraries even in 1900, and the county libraries were a creation of the Public Libraries Act of 1919. All these developments, however, form a story in themselves, and must be reserved for another volume.

Bibliographical Note

For the general background see R. D. Altick, *The English Common Reader* (Chicago 1957), and T. Kelly, *A History of Adult Education in Great Britain* (Liverpool 1962), Chs. viii–xi. On literacy see also T. Kelly, *George Birkbeck* (Liverpool 1957), App. X, and authorities there cited; and for the literature of the period R. K. Webb, *The British Working Class Reader, 1790–1848* (1955), and L. James, *Fiction for the Working Man* (1963). The early chapters of J. F. C. Harrison, *Learning and Living, 1790–1960* (1961), illustrate many facets of the period with special reference to the West Riding.

The *Report from the Select Committee on Public Libraries* (1849), is an indispensable source (the later Reports of the Committee, for 1850, 1851, and 1852, are mainly concerned with statistics of foreign libraries). The older histories of public libraries are not very helpful on this period, but a few details may be gleaned from E. Edwards, *Memoirs of Libraries*, 2 v. (1859), and there are brief accounts in J. J. Ogle, *The Free Library* (1897), Ch. i, and J. Minto, *A History of the Public Library Movement* (1932). *English Libraries 1800–1850* (Univ. Coll. London 1958) includes papers by C. B. Oldman on "Sir Anthony Panizzi and the British Museum", W. A. Munford on "George Birkbeck and the Mechanics' Institutes", and S. Nowell-Smith on "Carlyle and the London Library". J. W. Hudson, *History of Adult Education* (1851), deals mainly with mechanics' institutes, but also includes valuable material relating to other libraries. G. K. Scott,

English Public and Semi-Public Libraries in the Provinces, 1750–1850 (F.L.A. thesis 1951, Library Association) brings together references concerning various kinds of libraries from many scattered sources.

For this period much useful information regarding libraries of all kinds may be obtained from local guide-books and directories, and from S. Lewis, *Topographical Dictionary* (*England*, 1831, 7th edn. 1849; *Wales*, 1833, 4th edn. 1849; *Scotland*, 1846, 2nd edn. 1851). For London see also R. A. Rye, *Students' Guide to the Libraries of London* (1908, 3rd edn. 1927). For Scotland the *New Statistical Account* (1845) continues to be useful; see also the works by Anderson and Shirley cited at the end of Ch. vi; and P. K. Livingstone, *Kirkcaldy and its Libraries* (Kirkcaldy 1950).

For the cathedral libraries see the references at the end of Ch. iii, to which may be added the *History of Brechin Diocesan Library* (Brechin 1928).

For town and parish libraries see the references at the end of Chs. iv and v, to which may be added E. D. Mackerness, "The Castleton Parish Library", in *Journal of the Derbyshire Archaeological and Natural History Society*, Vol. LXXVII (1957); P. Morgan, "Wigan's Library, Bewdley", in *Transactions of the Worcestershire Archaeological Society*, N.S., Vol. XXXV (1958); and W. E. Alder-Bennett, "St. John's Library, Keswick", in *Library Association Record*, Vol. LXI (1959). Itinerating libraries are described in [S. Brown] *Some Account of the Itinerating Libraries and their Founder* (Edinburgh 1856). W. R. Aitken, *A History of the Public Library Movement in Scotland* (Ph.D. thesis, Edinburgh University 1956), gives details of those in the Highlands.

For subscription libraries see the references at the end of Ch. vi. The origins of the London Library are fully described in F. Harrison, *Carlyle and the London Library* (1907), and more briefly in the paper by S. Nowell-Smith referred to above. J. Taylor, "A Nineteenth Century Experiment in Adult Education", in *Adult Education*, Vol. XI (1938–39), deals with the Sheffield Mechanics' and Apprentices' Library. For Mudie's see the essay in H. Curwen, *A History of Booksellers* (1873); and A. Waugh, *A Hundred Years of Publishing* (1930), Ch. viii.

Detailed accounts of the mechanics' institutes are to be found in T. Kelly, *George Birkbeck* (Liverpool 1957), and M. Tylecote, *The Mechanics' Institutes of Lancashire and Yorkshire before 1851* (Manchester 1957). See also the appendix on this subject in W. A. Munford's *Penny Rate* (1951), and the paper by the same author in *English Libraries, 1800–1950*, referred to above. A. R. Thompson, "The Use of Libraries by the Working Class in Scotland in the Early

Nineteenth Century", in *Scottish Historical Review*, Vol. XLII (1963), illustrates the position in certain Scottish institutes. For contemporary opinion see the work by Hudson already cited, and also C. W. Baker, "Mechanics' Institutions and Libraries", in Central Society of Education, *First Publication* (1837); [B. F. Duppa], *A Manual for Mechanics' Institutions* (Society for the Diffusion of Useful Knowledge 1841); and J. Hole, *An Essay on the History and Management of Literary, Scientific and Mechanics' Institutions* (Society of Arts 1853). Details of book issues are to be found in Coates and Hudson, and also in Apps. 2 and 3 of the Report of the Select Committee of 1849 (see above).

Library Nomenclature

THE present history demonstrates how loosely names were used for the various kinds of libraries existing before 1850. The term "public library" may refer to a university library, a cathedral library, an endowed parochial library, or a subscription library; and the term "circulating library" may apply equally to a large private subscription library or to a small shop library. This was natural enough when most libraries were local and individual ventures without any kind of central direction. For the modern library historian, however, the position is different. His task is to identify, classify, look for national patterns. He must, therefore, seek some consistent terminology, even if it is sometimes at variance with contemporary usage. This I have tried to do, and it may be well to indicate some of the definitions I have had in mind.

Public Libraries

A public library, I think, can be sufficiently defined as a library freely accessible to the public, without charge, and with such safeguards only as are necessary to ensure that the books are protected against damage and misuse. This definition includes the modern national and rate-aided libraries, which are public in the additional sense of being maintained from public funds. It also includes a number of the older endowed libraries, e.g. Chetham's Library, Manchester. Most of the pre-1850 libraries, however, fail to qualify. For these there is no general name, but I have found it useful to group them into three broad divisions – institutional, endowed, and subscription.

Institutional Libraries

I have applied this term to libraries which are an integral part of an institution which exists also to serve other purposes, and which are founded and maintained from the general revenues of the establishment. Monastic, cathedral, and university libraries fall under this heading; so, in later times, do the libraries of mechanics' institutes and literary and philosophical societies.

Endowed Libraries

These are libraries created (and sometimes maintained), by the gift of an individual or group of individuals. The commonest type was the *parochial* library, placed by the founder under the control of the parochial authorities, but endowed libraries might also be *independent* (e.g. Innerpeffray), *scholastic* (e.g. Shrewsbury), *municipal* (e.g. Norwich), or *municipal and parochial* at the same time (e.g. Newcastle). Those which were ecclesiastical in character might also serve a larger area than the parish: they might serve a *deanery* (e.g. Bedford), or an *archdeaconry* (e.g. Huntingdon), or even a *diocese* (e.g. Bishop Cosin's Library, Durham).

The *Bray Libraries*, where they were not lending libraries, must be classified as parochial: the lending libraries, including the four Welsh diocesan libraries, covered a wider area and were not necessarily based on a parish church.

The line between endowed and other libraries is not always easy to draw, and libraries which begin as endowed libraries may develop in time into institutional or even subscription libraries. None the less the endowed library is, I think, sufficiently distinctive to justify a separate name.

Subscription Libraries

In its widest sense this term can reasonably be used to cover all libraries of which the costs are met by the subscriptions of the users.[1] Three main types of such libraries can be distinguished, however, and the name "subscription library" is most commonly applied to the first. The three types are:

(i) *Private Subscription Libraries.* The characteristic of these was that they aimed at a permanent collection. They might be either *proprietary libraries*, i.e. joint stock enterprises in which each user, in addition to paying an annual subscription, purchased a share in the property; or *non-proprietary libraries*, relying on annual subscriptions only. Contemporary names included Subscription Library, Public Library, Circulating Library, Permanent Library, Library Society, Book Society, and Literary Society.

(ii) *Book Clubs.* These were non-proprietary subscription libraries in which the books were disposed of when they had been read, so that no substantial permanent library was accumulated. Many of them also had a strong social element, with regular meetings for convivial purposes as well as for the distribution of books.[2] Book Club, Book

---

[1] Dr. P. Kaufman uses in this general sense the term "community lending libraries", which is convenient but lacks any sanction in contemporary usage. See his article, "Community Lending Libraries in Eighteenth-Century Ireland and Wales", in *Library Quarterly*, Vol. XXXIII (1963), p. 299 n.l.

[2] Dr. Kaufman, "English Book Clubs" (*Libri*, Vol XIV, 1964), regards this club element, rather than the nature of the book collection, as the distinguishing feature of the book club.

Society, and Reading Society were the commonest contemporary names. There were pamphlet clubs, magazine clubs, and newspaper clubs as well as book clubs.

(iii) *Circulating Libraries.* I have restricted the use of this term to commercial subscription libraries conducted for profit.

Philanthropic Libraries

Although all types of pre-1850 libraries can be classified under one or other of the three headings, institutional, endowed and subscription, there is one group of libraries, belonging mainly to the nineteenth century, for which it may be useful to have a special name. I refer to the various subsidised libraries for working people: *Working Men's Libraries, Mechanics' and Apprentices' Libraries, Village Libraries, Parish Libraries, Penny Libraries, Itinerating Libraries* and the like. Most of these operated on the basis of a nominal subscription by the user, but the main cost – sometimes, as in the case of the early Itinerating Libraries of East Lothian, the entire cost – was borne by the contributions of the well-to-do. These libraries thus have an element of endowment as well as subscription; and since their common feature is their philanthropic character, they could conveniently be classified as Philanthropic Libraries.

"Parish" and "Parochial"

It is, I think, useful to make a distinction between parochial libraries, i.e. libraries under the control of the parochial authorities, and parish libraries, i.e. libraries designed for the use of inhabitants of the parish. Many parochial libraries were also parish libraries, and in Scotland this seems to have been almost a general rule, but a parish library was not necessarily parochial, nor was a parochial library necessarily for the use of the parish.

Checklist of Endowed Libraries Founded Before 1800

(other than Bray Libraries)

THIS is a first attempt at a comprehensive list of all endowed libraries founded between the Reformation and 1800. I have excluded only the Bray libraries, which are separately listed in Appendix III, and what are sometimes known as "desk libraries", i.e. the small parochial collections of books such as the *Book of Homilies*, Jewel's *Apology*, and Foxe's *Book of Martyrs*, which were acquired by prescription during the century following the Reformation (cf. above, p. 81).

I have endeavoured to establish, for each library listed (a) the date of foundation or bequest; (b) the number of volumes remaining, and their location. The names of the larger libraries, i.e. those known to have contained over 1,000 volumes, are printed in small capitals. The letter *p* preceding an entry indicates that the library concerned was under parochial control (using this term loosely to include control either by a parish church or by a chapel attached to a parish church); the letter *m* indicates municipal control; and the letters *pm* indicate either joint parochial and municipal control, or parochial and municipal control at different times. The letter *l* indicates a lending library. Unless otherwise stated, surviving volumes are in the possession of the original foundation.

Libraries marked * are included in the alphabetical list in the volume on *Parochial Libraries* published by the Central Council for the Care of Churches (1959), to which reference may be made for further details. Some other parochial libraries have been brought to my attention privately by the editor of that volume, Mr. N. R. Ker. In other instances I have indicated the source of my information in the footnotes.

The following abbreviations have been used in addition to those mentioned above: f., founded; b., bequeathed; rec., recorded; P.L., Public Library. In the case of bequests the date given is that of the death of the testator, which of course might be a year or two before the actual establishment of the library.

ENGLAND

Bedfordshire

pl   Bedford (St. John), f. 1700; *c.* 550 v. remain in P.L.

p   Bromham (St. Owen), f. 1740; *c.* 800 v. remain.

p   Cranfield (St. Peter and St. Paul), rec. 1715; none remain.

Berkshire

*p Buckland (All Saints), f. 17th cent.?; 17 v. remain in Old Manor Ho.

*p Denchworth (St. James), f. 1693; 150 v. remain.

*p Hurley (St. Mary), f. by 1634; none remain.
Reading, f. *c.* 1727(?)[1]

Buckinghamshire

*p Langley Marish (St. Mary), f. 1623; *c.* 250 v. remain.

*p Mentmore (St. Mary), f. or b. 1743; *c.* 120 v. remain with Berks. Archaeol. Soc. Aylesbury.

*p Newport Pagnell (St. Peter and St. Paul), b. 1731; none remain.[2]

*p Willen (St. Mary Magd.), b. 1695; destroyed by fire 1946.

Cambridgeshire

*p Bassingbourne (St. Peter), f. 1717; *c.* 800 v. remain.

*p Chippenham (St. Andrew), rec. 1750; none remain.

p Ely (St. Mary), rec. 1711;[3] none remain.

*p GRAVELEY (St. Botolph), b. 1766; *c.* 1,400 v. remain in London Univ. Lib.

*pm WISBECH (St. Peter and St. Paul), f. 1653–54; *c.* 1,100 v. remain in Museum.

Cheshire

*p Halton (Chapel), f. 1733; *c.* 400 v. remain.

*pl Nantwich (St. Mary and St. Nicholas), f. *c.* 1700;[4] 165 v. remain.

*p Woodchurch (Holy Cross), f. by 1727; 45 v. remain. Cf. App. III(c).

Cornwall

*p Lanteglos-by-Camelford (St. Santy and St. Advent), b. 1747; 209 books remain.

[1] "A public library at Reading" – S.P.C.K. MSS., *Minutes of Bray Trustees*, 23rd August, 1727; cf. *Abstracts of Correspondence*, Vol. XIV, No. 9451, 3rd September, 1727.

[2] The 3 v. recorded in *Parochial Libraries* are clearly remains of a "desk library".

[3] A good library here is recorded in S.P.C.K. MSS., *Minutes of Bray Trustees*, 16th July, 1711: "all that will may have the free use of it."

[4] *Parochial Libraries* says *c.* 1704, but a grant for a lending library here is included in Bray's Accounts 1695–99 (see below, App. III(b)), and the existence of such a library in 1700 is recorded in a letter to the S.P.C.K. in E. McClure, *A Chapter in English Church History* (1888), p. 309.

*p Newquay (St. Michael), prob. 17th cent.; 23 v. remain.
*p Tideford (Chapel), prob. 18th cent.; none remain.

Cumberland

*p Ainstable (St. Michael), f. 1687;[1] 4 v. remain.
*p Burgh-by-Sands (St. Michael), f. 1687;[1] none remain. Cf. App. III(c).
*p Crosby-on-Eden (St. John), f. 1687;[1] none remain.
*p Dalston (St. Michael), f. 1687;[1] 9 v. remain.
*p Dearham, f. 1687;[1] none remain.
*p Isel (St. Michael), f. 1687;[1] none remain.
*p Thursby (St. Andrew), f. 1687;[1] none remain.
*p Wigton (St. Mary), f. 1687;[1] none remain. Cf. App. III(b) and (c).

Derbyshire

*p Earl Sterndale (Chapel), b. 1712; none remain.
*p Norton (St. James), b. 1749; c. 390 v. remain in Sheffield P.L.
*pl Repton (St. Wyston), f. 1622; none remain.[2]

Devon

*pm Barnstaple (St. Peter and St. Paul), f. 1664; c. 350 v. remain in Roborough Lib. Exeter.
*p Bratton Fleming (St. Peter), b. 1749; none remain.
*p CREDITON (Holy Cross), b. 1721; 1,250 v. remain.
*p Heanton (St. Augustine), projected 1719.[3]
*p Ottery St. Mary (Holy Cross), first rec. 1672; c. 250 v. remain.
*l Plymouth (St. Andrew), rec. 1700;[4] none remain.
*p Plymtree (St. John the B.), b. 1796 (?); c. 300 v. remain.
*p Tiverton (St. Peter), b. 1715; over 300 v. remain.
*p Totnes (St. Mary), f. 1619; c. 300 v. remain.

Dorset

*p Gillingham (B.V.M.), b. 1718; c. 300 v. remain.
*p Milton Abbas (St. Mary and St. Sampson), f. by 1680; 7 v. remain.
*p Wimborne Minster (St. Cuthberga), b. 1685; c. 240 v. remain.

[1] These eight libraries were founded under the bequest of Barnabas Oley (†1685) see above, p. 105. The Wigton parish records show that a bequest of books was also received in 1687 from another source.
[2] See above, pp. 82–3
[3] S.P.C.K. MSS., *Abstracts of Correspondence*, Vol. X, No. 6207, 25th November, 1719.
[4] Perhaps originally a parochial library, this was revived as a lending library by Bray in 1700 (see above, p. 106).

Durham

Durham (Bishop Cosin's Lib.). Diocesan, f. 1669 by John Cosin Bp. of Durham; 6,000 v. remain.

*p Durham (St. Oswald), b. 1701; sold 1929/39.

*p Stockton-on-Tees (St. Thomas), b. prob. before 1750; none remain.

Essex

*p Chelmsford (St. Mary's, now Cathedral), f. 1679; *c.* 2,000 v. remain.

m Colchester, b. 1631; *c.* 850 v. remain in P.L.[1]

pml Harwich (St. Nicholas), f. *c.* 1710;[2] none remain.

*p Hatfield Broad Oak (St. Mary), f. *c.* 1708; *c.* 300 v. remain.

*l Maldon, b. 1704; now *c.* 5,000 v.[3]

*p Sible Hedingham (St. Mary), b. 1733; sold 1918.

*p Stansted Mount-Fitchett (St. Mary), first rec. early 18th cent., none remain.

*pl Witham (St. Nicholas), first rec. 1751; none remain.

Gloucestershire

*p Newent (B.V.M.), b. by will of 1737; none remain.

*p Stonehouse (St. Cyril), b. 1763; 786 v. remain in Sec. Mod. School.

*p Tortworth (St. Leonard), b. 1757; *c.* 650 v. remain.

*p Wotton-under-Edge (St. Mary), b. 1710; *c.* 300 v. remain.

Hampshire

*p Basingstoke (St. Michael), first rec. 1703/5; *c.* 110 v. remain.

*p Southampton (St. Michael), f. by 1646; none remain. Cf. App. III(c).

*pl Whitchurch (All Saints), b. 1731, sold 1927; 2 v. remain. Cf. App. III(c).

---

[1] See above, pp. 75, 98.

[2] The Corporation fitted up a room in the church for a lending library, which was in operation by 1711 – S.P.C.K. MSS., *Abstracts of Correspondence*, Vol. I, No. 1825, 3rd November, 1709; Vol. II, No. 1946, 29th December, 1709; Vol. III, No. 2791, 25th September, 1711. St. Nicholas' was the parish church, but it is possible that the library was at All Saints', the S.P.C.K. correspondent, Rev. William Curtis, being incumbent of both parishes.

[3] S. G. Deed (ed.), *Catalogue of the Plume Library*, Maldon (Maldon 1959). Though designed for the clergy, this was not strictly speaking a parochial library: it was (and is) under the control of a body of trustees and housed separately from the parish church.

Herefordshire

*p   Hereford (All Saints), b. 1715; *c.* 300 v. remain.
*p   Withington (St. Peter), rec. 1717; none remain.

Hertfordshire

*p   Bushey (St. James), f. 18th cent. (?); some remain at Community of the Resurrection, Mirfield, Yorks.
p   Eastwick (St. Botolph), f. by 1765.
*p   Royston (St. John the B.), f. by 1768; remnants sold 1953, 9 v. remain in Bodleian Lib.

Huntingdonshire

*p   Broughton (All Saints), f. by 1737; 18 v. remain, *c.* 600 v. sold 1958 to Camb. Univ. Lib.
l   HUNTINGDON (Archdeaconry Lib.), f. by 1716;[1] now *c.* 500 v.
*p   Offord Cluny (All Saints), b. 1765; 17 v. remain.
*p   St. Neots (St. Mary), f. by 1783;[2] *c.* 90 v. remain.
*p   STANGROUND (St. John the B.), b. 1755; sold by 1950.

Kent

Canterbury, f. 1740;[3] a few remain in Eastbridge Hospital and P.L.
*p   Crundale (St. Mary), b. 1728; *c.* 900 v. remain at Godmersham Vicarage.
*p   Doddington (St. John the B.), f. 1743; *c.* 385 v. remain.
Lewisham (Grammar School), f. 1652;[4] *c.* 380 v. remain at Leathersellers' Hall, London.
*pl   Maidstone (All Saints), f. by 1716;[5] *c.* 700 v. remain in Museum.
*p   Thurnham (St. Mary), rec. 1751; none remain.
*p   Westerham (St. Mary), f. 1765; none remain.

---

[1] By William Wake (afterwards Archbishop of Canterbury) while Bishop of Lincoln 1705–16. Originally in the Bishop's Palace at Buckden, transferred 1837–38 to Huntingdon, where the present library was erected 1890. For a projected library at Huntingdon before 1705 see App. III(b).

[2] Augmenting an earlier Bray collection – see App. III(b) and (d).

[3] In the Eastbridge Hospital, for the use of "Religious Societies and other well disposed persons", under a charity created by Edwin Belke of London – S.P.C.K. MSS., *Miscellaneous Letters, 1740–41*, 14th August, and 13th November, 1740. The Rules and Catalogue (78 v.) are now in the custody of the Canterbury City Archivist.

[4] See above, pp. 76–7.

[5] Augm. 1735 by purchase of part of Bray's library (see above, p. 97, note 2).

Lancashire

*p   Astley (Chapel), f. by 1734; *c.* 200 v. remain.

*p   Bolton (St. Peter), b. 1653;[1] 56 v. remain at Bolton School.

*p   Bury (St. Mary), f. by 1634; at least 3 v. remain at Grammar School.

*pl Cartmel (St. Mary), b. 1697; *c.* 300 v. remain.

*p   Coniston (Chapel), f. 1699; destroyed *c.* 1957.

*p   Gorton (St. James), b. 1653;[1] 45 v. remain.

*p   Liverpool (St. Peter), f. 1715; destroyed during Second World War.

*p   Manchester (St. Mary's, now Cathedral), f. 1636;[2] sold *c.* 1829. MANCHESTER (Chetham's Lib.), b. 1653; now *c.* 70,000 v.[3]

m   PRESTON (Shepherd's Lib.), b. 1761; now *c.* 10,000 v. in P.L.[4]

*p   Ribchester (St. Wilfrid), b. 1684; 1 v. remains.

*p   Rivington (Chapel), rec. 18th cent.; none remain.

*p   Turton (Chapel), b. 1653;[1] 51 v. remain.

*p   Walmsley (Chapel), b. 1653, but the legacy seems to have gone instead to Turton.[1]

Leicestershire

*p   ASHBY DE LA ZOUCH (St. Helen), f. by 1714; *c.* 800 v. remain.

*p   Cole Orton (St. Mary), f. by 1800; *c.* 500 v. remain in Co. Lib.

*p   Frisby-on-the-Wreak (St. Thomas à Becket), b. *c.* 1655; none remain.

*pm LEICESTER (St. Martin), f. by 1587; *c.* 900 v. remain in Guildhall

*p   Loughborough (All Saints), b. 1785; *c.* 600 v. remain, inc. 100 v. at Loughborough Coll. of Further Educ.

Lincolnshire

*p   Barton-on-Humber (St. Mary), rec. 1707; none remain.

*p   BOSTON (St. Botolph), f. *c.* 1634; *c.* 1,500 v. remain. Gainsborough, b. 1731; town lib. kept in schoolmaster's house; appar. none remain.[5] Cf. App. III(b).

*pm GRANTHAM (St. Wulfram), really two libs., a parochial lib. f. 1598, of which *c.* 250 v. remain; and a munic. lib. of *c.* 700 v., b. 1765 and kept in the church till transf. to P.L. 1929.

*p   Sleaford (St. Denis), b. 1703; 20 v. remain.

*pl Spalding (St. Mary and St. Nicholas), f. 1637; *c.* 600 v. remain with Spalding Gentlemen's Soc.[6]

---

[1] Chetham bequest: see above, pp. 83-4.
Augmented by Chetham bequest 1653.

See above, pp. 77-80.   [4] See above, pp. 91, 94.

See above, p. 91.   [6] See above, p. 98.

*p   Stamford (St. Mary), f. by 1626; *c.* 150 v. remain.

*p   Swinderby (All Saints), b. 1741; none remain.

London

*pl   St. Botolph, Aldgate, f. by 1730;[1] none remain.

*p   St. George the Martyr, Bloomsbury, f. early 18th cent. (?); sold 1862.

*p   St. Leonard, Shoreditch, b. 1763; *c.* 650 v. remain in P.L.

*p   ST. MARTIN IN THE FIELDS, Westminster (Archbishop Tenison's Lib.), f. 1684; sold 1861.

     DR. WILLIAMS'S LIBRARY, f. 1729; now *c.* 100,000 v.[2]

Middlesex

p   East Bedfont (St. Mary), f. *c.* 1731; 16 v. remain.

p   Feltham (St. Dunstan), f. *c.* 1731.

*p   Hillingdon (St. John the B.), b. 1721; destroyed 1934/49; 1 v. remains.

p   Hounslow (Chapel), f. *c.* 1731. Cf. App. III(d) Introd.

Norfolk

*p   Fersfield (St. Andrew), rec. 1736; none remain.

*p   Great Yarmouth (St. Nicholas), prob. f. 17th cent.; *c.* 320 v. remain.

*pml   KING'S LYNN (St. Margaret), f. 1631; 1,880 v. remain, some in P.L.

*p   King's Lynn (St. Nicholas), f. 1617, later amalg. with St. Margaret's.

m   NORWICH (City Lib.), f. 1608; *c.* 2,000 v. remain in P.L.[3]

*p   Norwich (St. Andrew), f. 1586; none remain.[4]

*p   Norwich (St. Peter Mancroft), f. by 1629; 2 MSS. remain.

p   Ormesby (St. Margaret), f. 1720.

*p   Reepham (St. Mary), date unknown, but some 17th cent. works sold *c.* 1843; none remain.

---

[1] Bray's grant towards a parochial library at Aldgate, 1695–99 (see App. III(b)) probably refers to this parish, of which he afterwards became Rector. The books from his own library subsequently recorded there may have been those bequeathed by him to the church in 1730 for the use of probationary missionaries. The collection was afterwards treated by the Bray Associates as a Bray library, and transferred in 1872 to Stratford, Essex.

[2] See above, pp. 92, 194.

[3] See above, pp. 74-5.

[4] See above, pp. 71-2.

*p Rougham (St. Mary), f. 1714; none remain.
*p Shipdham (St. Mary), b. 1764; 490 v. remain in Norwich P.L.
*p Swaffham (St. Peter and St. Paul), b. 1622 (?); c. 400 v. remain.

Northamptonshire

pl Ashton, nr. Oundle (Chapel), rec. 1718;[1] none remain.
p Daventry (Holy Cross), f. early 18th cent.; 85 v. remain.
*p Finedon (St. Mary), f. 1788; c. 1,000 v. remain.
*l King's Cliffe (All Saints), f. 1752; c. 550 v. remain in a house in the village.
*p Northampton (All Saints), f. by 1701, consid. augm. 1777; none remain. Cf. App. III(b).
p Welford (St. Mary), f. 1703.[2]

Northumberland

l Bamburgh, f. 1778; 6,400 v. remain in Durham Univ. Lib., and 2,100 v. in Durham Cath. Lib.[3]
*p Corbridge (St. Andrew), f. 1729; none remain.
*pm Newcastle-upon-Tyne (St. Nicholas), f. by 1597, consid. augm. by Rev. R. Thomlinson (1735–45); c. 300 v. remain in the church, and over 4,000 v. of the Thomlinson collection in P.L.[4]

Nottinghamshire

*p Costock (St. Giles), b. 1701; none remain.
*p Elston (All Saints), b. 1732 (?); c. 24 v. remain in Co. Lib., Nottingham.
*pm Newark-upon-Trent (St. Mary Magd.), b. 1698; c. 1,300 v. remain.

[1] This is probably the Ashton referred to in S.P.C.K. MSS., *Abstracts of Correspondence*, Vol. VIII, No. 5646, 21st July, 1718, where a correspondent from Great Gidding describes "a sort of lending library established by the pious gentlewoman who built the chapel". A schoolhouse, which served also as a chapel, was erected by Elizabeth Creed in 1708 – *Report of the Charity Commissioners*, Vol. XXIII (1832), pp. 357–61.
[2] *Topographer*, Vol. III (1790), p. 303.
[3] This library is known from the name of its principal founder, Dr. John Sharp, as the Sharp Library. The University Library holds the older books and the Cathedral Library the modern books, which are still being added to and which form a library for the use of the clergy of the dioceses of Durham and Newcastle. The Cathedral Library has also taken over from Bamburgh Castle 200 volumes of music.
[4] See above, pp. 73–4, 96–7.

NOTTINGHAM (Bluecoat School), f. 1744;[1] appar. none remain.
p SOUTHWELL (St. Mary, now Cathedral), f. *c.* 1705; now *c.* 3,000 v.

Oxfordshire

*p Bicester (St. Eadburg), f. by 1691; appar. a school and parochial lib., housed in adjoining Grammar School till 1862; none remain.
*p Bloxham (St. Mary), f. 17th cent. (?); *c.* 40 v. remain.
*pl Henley-on-Thames (St. Mary), b. 1737; *c.* 800 v. remain at Christ Church, Oxford, and Reading Univ. Lib.[2]
*p Shiplake (St. Peter and St. Paul), rec. 1661; none remain.
*p Wendlebury (St. Giles), b. 1764; destroyed in present century.

Rutlandshire

*p Oakham (All Saints), f. 1616; 118 v. remain.

Shropshire

Bishop's Castle, f. *c.* 1700.[3]
pl BRIDGNORTH (St. Leonard), b. 1743,[4] subsn. lib. in 19th cent.; *c.* 3,000 v. remain.
*p Chirbury (St. Michael), b. 1677; 180 v. remain. Cf. App. III(b) and Introd. to III(d).
p Church Pulverbalch (St. Edith). *See* Wentnor, and cf. App. III(b).
*p Ludlow (St. Lawrence), rec. 1557; 1 v. remains in Bodleian Lib. Cf. App. III(b).
p Mindtown (St. John the B.). *See* Wentnor, and cf. App. III(b).
*p More (St. Peter), f. 1680; *c.* 250 v. remain.
p Norbury (All Saints). *See* Wentnor, and cf. App. III(b).
p Preston Gobalds (St. Martin), f. by 1798 (?); *c.* 60 v. remain

---

[1] Founded by Rev. William Standfast and transferred 1816 to the newly founded Nottingham Subscription Library – see J. Russell. *A History of the Nottingham Subscription Library* (Nottingham 1916), pp. 49–58. This library still exists at Bromley House.

[2] See above, p. 93.

[3] A private [i.e. non-parochial] library "for the use of neighbours", founded by Chas. Mason, M.P. *ante* 1705 (*Parochial Libraries*, p. 22n.). Mason became M.P. for Bishop's Castle in 1695, so this may be identical with the lending library aided by Bray (see App. III(b)).

[4] Bequeathed by Rev. Hugh Stackhouse to the Society of Clergymen in and about Bridgnorth. The foundation deed of 1743 (Brit. Mus. Add. MS. 28732) gives the rules for borrowing, and suggests that the Society may already have possessed a library, perhaps on the lines of those formed at Doncaster and elsewhere about this time (see above, p. 98). The future disposal of the library is at present under consideration.

l   SHREWSBURY (School), f. 1596;[1] *c.* 7,000 v. remain, inc. 100 MSS.

*p   Tong (St. Bartholomew), f. 1697;[2] over 400 v. remain.

*p   Wentnor (St. Michael), b. 1788; 108 v. remain in Co. Lib.[3]

*p   WHITCHURCH (St. Alkmund), f. 1717, much augm. 1829; over 1,000 v. remain.

Somerset

*p   Bath (St. Peter and St. Paul), f. *c.* 1619; *c.* 300 v. remain in P.L.

*p   Bishop's Lydyeard (St. Mary), b. 1733; none remain.

m   BRISTOL (City Lib.), f. 1615; *c.* 1,500 v. remain in P.L.[4]

*p   Cudworth (St. Michael), b. 1695; none remain.

*p   Martock (All Saints), b. 1695; 13 v. remain in Wells Cath. Lib.

Staffordshire

*p   B.lston (Chapel), f. by 1705; none remain.

m   Tamworth, b. by will of 1686;[5] sold 1932.

Suffolk

*p   Assington (St. Edmund), b. 1690; *c.* 385 v. remain, in process of transfer to Cath. Lib., Bury St. Edmunds.

*p   Beccles (St. Michael), f. *c.* 1700; 148 v. remain,[6] in process of transfer to Cath. Lib., Bury St. Edmunds.

*p   BRENT ELEIGH (St. Mary), f. *c.* 1700; 10 MSS. remain in Bodleian Lib., Camb. Univ. Lib., and Fitzwilliam Mus.

*p   Bury St. Edmunds (St. James, now Cathedral), f. 1595; *c.* 475 v. remain.

*p   Coddenham (St. Mary), b. 1739; 360 v. now in Cath. Lib., Bury St. Edmunds.

---

[1] See above, p. 71.

[2] Originally housed at Tong Castle, home of the founder Lord Pierrepont; transferred 1725 to the vicarage, and later (by 1812), to the church.

[3] This library was founded at Wentnor by a curate who was also Rector of Mindtown. Miss O. S. Newman, County Librarian, tells me that according to the evidence of a former Rector of Wentnor the collection was at various times (because of the amalgamation of livings) at Church Pulverbatch and Norbury, perhaps also at Mindtown, before returning to its original home at Wentnor.

[4] See above, p. 75.

[5] Bequeathed by Rev. John Rawlett, a native of Tamworth, to be placed in the Grammar School as a nucleus of a public library. This may have been the library aided by Bray (App. III(b)).

[6] In the nineteenth century the books for a time formed part of a town library, but they were afterwards returned to the church.

*pml Ipswich (St. Mary Tower), b. by will of 1599; over 700 v. remain in P.L.

*p Lawshall (All Saints), b. 1704; 137 v. remain, in process of transfer to Cath. Lib., Bury St. Edmunds.

*p MILDEN (St. Peter), b. 1703; sold 1897/1907.

p Poslingford (St. Mary Virg.), rec. 1716; none remain.

*p Nayland (St. Stephen), f. 18th cent. (?); *c.* 100 v. remain.

*p Stoke-by-Nayland (St. Mary), f. by 1719; *c.* 120 v. remain.[1]

*p Woodbridge (St. Mary), b. 1773; *c.* 190 v. remain.

Surrey

p Chertsey (All Saints), f. *c.* 1731.

*p Compton (St. Nicholas), f. 17th cent. (?); none remain.

*p Effingham (St. Lawrence), b. 1724; 2 v. remain.

m? Guildford. Town Lib. rec. 1573, appropr. to Grammar School by 1600; over 400 v. remain.

*pl REIGATE (St. Mary Magd.), f. 1701; *c.* 2,000 v. remain.[2]

Sussex

*p Amberley (St. Michael), perhaps f. 1730 as a result of a bequest from Bray; 1 v. remains.

*p Heathfield (All Saints), b. 1740; *c.* 230 v. remain.

*p Lewes (St. Anne), b. 1717; sold 1823.[3]

Warwickshire

*p Birmingham (St. Martin), f. 1661; *c.* 12 v. remain in P.L.

*p Birmingham (St. Philip), f. 1733; 415 v. remain in P.L.

*pl Coleshill (St. Peter and St. Paul), rec. 1730;[4] none remain.

m Coventry, f. 1602 in Grammar School; sold 1908. Cf. App. III(b).

*p King's Norton (St. Nicholas), b. 1665; 876 v. remain in Birmingham P.L.

---

[1] Rev. Thos. Reeve, who is said to have given most of the books, was vicar 1685–1719, so this may have been the library aided by Bray (App. III(b)).

[2] E. McClure, *A Chapter in English Church History* (1888), pp. 132, 220, shows that this was a lending library.

[3] A lending library, perhaps the same, was projected here as early as 1708 – S.P.C.K. MSS., *Abstracts of Correspondence*, Vol. I, No. 1338.

[4] In 1730 Bray bequeathed thirty-one volumes of Aquinas and Lorinus to "the Lending or Publick Library of Coleshill". This may have been the library grant-aided by Bray in 1695–99. See App. III(b). A copy of Bray's will is in the U.S.P.G. archives.

*p   Sheldon (St. Giles), f. by 1705;[1] over 300 v. remain in Birmingham P.L.

*pl Warwick (St. Mary's), f. 1701; 1,385 v. remain, inc. 965 in Co. Record Off.[2]

*p   Wootton Wawen (St. Peter), b. 1652; 11 v. remain.

Westmorland

*p   Askham (St. Peter), f. 1687;[3] none remain.

*p   Bampton (St. Patrick), b. 1751; *c.* 650 v. remain. Cf. App. III(d).

*p   Beetham (St. Michael), f. 1795; *c.* 150 v. remain.

*p   Crosby Ravensworth (St. Lawrence), f. 1687;[3] none remain.

l   Kendal. Projected 1701.[4]

Wiltshire

p   Box (St. Thomas à B.), f. by 1727;[5] none remain.

*pm Marlborough (St. Mary), b. 1678; *c.* 600 v. remain at Marlborough Coll.

*p   Steeple Ashton (St. Mary), b. 1569, much augm. 1828; *c.* 250 v. remain.

Worcestershire

*p   Bromsgrove (St. John the B.), f. 17th cent. (?) ; *c.* 100 v. remain.[6]

*p   Norton-cum-Lenchwick (St. Egwin), b. 1784; old *c.* 1951, 1 v. remains.

Yorkshire

*p   Beverley (St. Mary), f. 1699; 32 v. remain.

*p   Bradfield (Chapel), b. 1720; 49 v. remain.

---

[1] Founded by Bray (Rector here 1690–1729), probably before 1700. He gave a grant for a library there in 1695–99, and afterwards bequeathed to the church his own library at Sheldon. Cf. App. III(a) and (b).

[2] The mediaeval library in the parvis, founded by the antiquary John Rous in 1464, survived until destroyed by fire in 1694. The 1701 library was assisted by a grant from Bray – see App. III(b).

[3] These two libraries were founded under the bequest of Barnabas Oley (†1685) see above, p. 105.

[4] The S.P.C.K. offered £10 for a lending library for the Archdeaconry of Richmond, Kendal being considered the best centre – E. McClure, *A Chapter in English Church History* (1888), pp. 126, 128.

[5] S.P.C.K. MSS., *Minutes of Bray Trustees*, 23rd August, 1727 (gift of surplus books).

[6] This may have been the lending library aided by Bray 1695–99. Cf. App. III(b).

*p   Bubwith (All Saints), b. by 1747; *c.* 7 v. remain in York Cath. Lib.

      Campsall (St. Mary Magd.), f. prob. early 18th cent.; 152 v. remain.

p   Dent (Chapel), f. by 1754; 9 v. remain.

*p   Doncaster (St. George), f. 1714;[1] destroyed by fire 1853.

*p   East Harlsey (St. Oswald), b. 1725; *c.* 600 v. remain.

*p   Ecclesfield (St. John the B.), f. 1549 (?); 2 v. remain.

p   Garsdale (Chapel), rec. 1778.

*p   Hackness (St. Peter), f. 1700; 115 v. remain.

*p   Halifax (St. John the B.), f. *c.* 1626, consid. augm. 1862; *c.* 660 v. remain. To be divided between York Minster Lib. and York Univ. Lib.

*p   Hull (Holy Trinity), f. 1665; 666 v. remain, all but one in Univ. Lib.

*p   Hull (St. Mary Lowgate), f. by 1682; *c.* 100 v. remain.

*p   Kildwick (St. Andrew), f. early 18th cent. (?); *c.* 70 v. remain.

*p   Ledsham (All Saints), f. 1730 (?)[2] None remain.

l   Leeds (Grammar School), f. 1692 as a public library, appropr. to School by 1815.[3]

p   Marske, nr. Richmond (St. Edmund), b. 1666; a few v. remain.

*p   North Grimston (St. Nicholas), b. 1671; none remain.

*p   Rotherham (All Saints), f. 1704; none remain.

*p   Sheffield (St. Peter), rec. 1705; none remain.

*p   SKIPTON (Holy Trinity), f. *c.* 1701; *c.* 1,700 v. remain in P.L.[4]

*p   Slaithwaite (Chapel), b. 1724; 25 v. remain.

*p   Stainton, nr. Guisborough (St. Peter), b. 1694; *c.* 300 v. remain in York Cath. Lib.

*p   Tankersley (St. Peter), b. 1615; 32 v. remain in Sheffield P.L.

*p   Womersley (St. Martin), f. *c.* 1700; none remain.

*p   Worsborough (Chapel), f. by 1695; some remain in old Grammar School lib. in vicarage.

*p   York (St. Mary Castlegate), f. *c.* 1705; none remain.

---

[1] Library of a Society of Clergymen, housed in the church: see above p. 98.

[2] The two boxes of books bequeathed by Bray in 1730 may have been the foundation of the library.

[3] A. C. Price, *A History of the Leeds Grammar School* (Leeds 1919), Ch. xiii.

[4] See *Catalogue of the Petyt Library*, Skipton (Coulthurst Trust, Gargrave 1964).

pl Llanbadarnfawr, Cards. (St. Padarn), f. 18th cent.;[1] none remain.

pl Presteigne, Radn. (St. Andrew), f. *c.* 1707;[2] none remain.

l Wrexham, Denb. Projected 1709.[3]

SCOTLAND[4]

Aberdeen, f. 1585, transf. 1632 to Marischal Coll., 93 v. remain in Univ. Lib.

DUMFRIES (Presbytery Lib.), f. 1706,[5] transf. 1885 to General Assembly Lib., Edinburgh.

DUNBLANE, Perthsh. (Diocesan Lib.), b. 1684; now *c.* 2,900 v.

pml DUNDEE, f. by 1598; 6 v. remain in P.L.

pm Edinburgh, b. 1580, transf. to Univ. 1584; *c.* 300 v. remain.

ml GLASGOW (Stirling's Lib.), b. 1791, organized as subsn. lib., *c.* 10,000 v. by 1850; 2 MSS. and all books prior to 1801 now in P.L.

m HADDINGTON, E. Lothian, b. 1729; 968 v. remain in Nat. Lib. of Scotland.

l INNERPEFFRAY, Perthsh., b. *c.* 1694; now nearly 4,000 v.

p Kirkwall, Orkney, b. 1683; *c.* 600 v. remain in Aberdeen Univ. Lib., and 1 v. in P.L.

l LAURENCEKIRK, Kincardinesh. (Brechin Diocesan Lib.), projected 1792 though not actually estab. till 1819; transf. to Brechin 1854; *c.* 7,000 v. remain in Dundee Univ. Lib.[6]

Linlithgow, (Presbytery Lib.), b. 1790; destroyed by fire 1845.

Lochmaben, Dumfriessh. (Schoolmaster's lib.), b. 1726.[7]

Logie, nr. Cupar, Fife, b. *c.* 1750; sold 1949.

p Rothesay, Bute, b. 1702; none remain.

p SALTOUN, E. Lothian, f. 1658; now *c.* 1,300 v.

p Tranent, E. Lothian, f. *c.* 1790.

[1] "A lending library for the parishioners", complementing a Bray parochial library founded 1710. For this and the later Bray lending library see App. III(d).
[2] S.P.C.K. MSS., *Minutes of General Meetings*, 15th August, 1706; *Abstracts of Correspondence*, Vol. I, No. 1370, 13th August, 1708.
[3] S.P.C.K. MSS., *Abstracts of Correspondence*, Vol. I, No. 1897, 18th November, 1709.
[4] Further particulars of most of the libraries here listed will be found in the relevant chapters above: see Index, *s.v.*
[5] Originally a Kirkwood library: see above, p. 114.
[6] Including *c.* 200 v. from the inn library established at Laurencekirk by Lord Gardenstone (above, p. 104).
[7] The bequest was absorbed into another endowment in 1882.

Checklist of Bray Libraries in Great Britain to 1850

(a) *Libraries founded or assisted by Bray personally, by gift or bequest*

These are included in the list of endowed libraries given in Appendix II: see *s.v.* Kent (Maidstone), London (St. Botolph Aldgate), Sussex (Amberley), Warwickshire (Coleshill and Sheldon), and Yorkshire (Ledsham).

(b) *Lending libraries (l) and parochial libraries (p) assisted by Bray from funds at his disposal (1695–99)*

All these except Plymouth are recorded in Bray's Accounts for these years, which are preserved in MS. in the archives of the United Society for the Propagation of the Gospel. The amount given is shown in brackets. For Plymouth see above, p. 106. Libraries marked * appear to be identical with libraries included in the alphabetical list in the volume on *Parochial Libraries* published in 1959 by the Central Council for the Care of Churches, and are included in Appendix II.

Berkshire
  l Newbury (£2 10s.).

Cheshire
  l "Bishop and Archdeacon of Chester" (£10).
  *l Nantwich (£10). Cf. App. II.

Cumberland
  l Carlisle (£1).
  l Kirkoswald (£1). See also below under (d).
  l Wigton (£1). See also below under (d), and cf. App. II.

Devon
  l Plymouth. Cf. App. II.

Dorset
  l Sherborne (£1 10s.).

Hampshire
  l Andover (£2 10s.).

Huntingdonshire
  l Buckden (£1).[1]
  l Huntingdon (£1). Cf. App. II.
  l Kimbolton (£1).
  l St. Ives (£1).
  l St. Neots (£1). Cf. App. II, and below under (d).

Kent
  l Deal (£2 10s.). See above, p. 106.

[1] A Bray library, possibly the same since no separate foundation is recorded, was removed from Buckden to Huntingdon in 1874.

258

l Gravesend (£2 10s.). See above, p. 000.

Lincolnshire
l Gainsborough (£2 10s.). See above, p. 000 and cf. App. II.

London
**p* St. Botolph's Aldgate (£1 5s.). Cf. App. II.

Northamptonshire
l Northampton (£1). Cf. App. II.[1]

Northumberland
l Deanery of Alnwick (£1 10s.).
l Deanery of Bamburgh (£1 10s.). Cf. App. II.
l Deanery of Corbridge (£1 10s.). Cf. App. II.
l Deanery of Morpeth (£1 10s.).

Shropshire
l Bishop's Castle (£1). Cf. App. II.
p Chirbury (£1). Cf. App. II and below under (d).
p Church Pulverbatch (15s.).[2]
l Ludlow (£2 10s.). Cf. App. II.
p Mindtown (15s.).[3]
p Norbury (15s.).
p Ratlinghope (15s.).
p Shelve (15s.).

Staffordshire
l Tamworth (£2). Cf. App. II.

Suffolk
**l* Stoke-by-Nayland (£2 10s). Cf. App. II.

Warwickshire
l Atherstone (£2 10s.).
**l* Coleshill (£5). Cf. App. II, and above under (a).
l Coventry (£1). Cf. App. II.
**p* Sheldon (£5). Cf. App. II, and above under (a).
**l* Warwick (£5). Cf. App. II.

Westmorland
l Shap (£1).

Worcestershire
**l* Bromsgrove (£2). Cf. App. II.

Montgomeryshire
p Buttington (15s.).
p Church Stoke (£6).
p Forden (15s.).
l Llanfyllin.[4]
l Llanidloes.[4]
l Montgomery.[4]
l Newtown.[4]
p Trelystan (?) (15s.).[5]
l Welshpool.[4]

Also ten poor vicarages in the diocese of Carlisle, for which the total sum was £7 10s.

---

[1] I have not asterisked this entry, since the particulars regarding the library recorded in App. II are so vague, but it is possible that the two are identical. [2] MS. *Poulderbatch*

[3] MS. *Mintown*. Minton, which also suggests itself as a possibility, is not a parish.

[4] The sum of £34 was divided among the libraries at Llanfyllin, Llanidloes, Montgomery, Newtown and Welshpool. The establishment of lending libraries at Montgomery and Newtown was still under discussion in 1708 – S.P.C.K., *Abstracts of Correspondence* (MS.), Vol. I, No. 1502, 27th November, 1708. [5] MS. *Trelytyn*.

(c) *Diocesan lending libraries founded by the S.P.C.K.* (*1708–11*)

Caernarvonshire	*Flintshire*
Bangor (Cathedral), 1710.	St. Asaph (Cathedral), 1711.
Carmarthenshire	*Glamorgan*
Carmarthen (for St. David's), 1708.[1]	Cowbridge (for Llandaff), 1711.[2] See also below under (d).

(d) *Lending libraries* (*l*) *and parochial libraries* (*p*) *established by the Trustees for Erecting Parochial Libraries* (*1705–30*), *and the Associates of Dr. Bray* (*after 1730*)

For the libraries established by the Trustees I have relied mainly on the alphabetical list in *Parochial Libraries:* libraries included there are marked *. For later libraries I have used the published Reports of the Associates, which begin in 1762, and which also include, though without giving dates, libraries founded during Bray's lifetime.[3]

Libraries after 1840 have no *l* or *p* prefixed, because from this time the founding of parochial libraries became exceptional, and the Reports no longer make any distinction. A few libraries founded before 1840 have also no distinguishing mark, because information as to their character is not available.

The Report for 1849 lists fifty-two libraries (mainly of the eighteenth century) as "either wholly lost, or reduced to a few tattered volumes", and the names of these are printed in italics. This statement should, however, be treated with some reserve: cf. below *s.v.* Darlington (Co. Durham), Flaxley (Gloucs.), and Llanrhos (Caerns.).

The Minutes of the Trustees (S.P.C.K. Archives), include conditional allocations of parochial libraries during the years 1727–29 to Biggleswade and Shidlington (Beds.), Abbotsbury and Melham [Melcombe Regis?] (Dorset), Grays and Havering Bower (Essex), Hounslow (Mx.), Chirbury (Shrops.), Lea Marston (Warw.), Colerne (Wilts.), Ledstone (Yorks.), and Welshpool (Montg.). In the absence of other evidence these have been excluded.

---

[1] Now in the Cathedral Library.
[2] Now in private hands at Ewenny Priory.
[3] The Reports first appeared under the title, *An Account of the Designs of the Associates of the late Dr. Bray with an Abstract of their Proceedings.* From 1824 the title changes to *An Account of the Institution established by the late Rev. Dr. Bray,* etc., and from 1841 to *Report for the Year . . . of the Institution established,* etc.

ENGLAND

Bedfordshire
p Streatley, c. 1729.[1]

Berkshire[2]
Hungerford, 1841.

Buckinghamshire
HighWycombe, 1849.
p Princes Risborough, 1816.

Cambridgeshire
p Burwell, 1729.[3]
*p Dullingham, 1712.
p Guilden Morden, 1817.

Cheshire
l Knutsford, 1780.
Macclesfield, 1843.
l Sandbach, 1810.
Stockport, 1843.
l Woodchurch, 1793.

Cornwall
*p Lostwithiel, 1710.
St. Columb Major, 1845.
p St. Mary's, Scilly, 1729.
Truro, 1842.

Cumberland
l Brampton, 1792.
*p Burgh-by-Sands, 1712. Cf. App. II.
l Cockermouth, 1762, augm. 1844.
p Crosthwaite, 1786.

l Keswick, 1786.
*p Kirkoswald, 1710. See also above under (b).
*p St. Bees, 1712, augm. 1818, 1842.
p Secmurthy, 1757.
p Thwaites, 1757.
p Ulpha, 1761.
p Waberthwaite, 1757.
p Wasdalehead, 1766, augm. 1805.
*pl Wigton, p. 1710, l. 1783. See also above under (b), and App. II.
p Wythop, 1757.

Derbyshire
Bakewell, 1843.
p Spondon, 1822.

Devon
*p Kingsbridge, 1711. Cf. App. II.
l Plymouth, 1840. Cf. App. II, and above under (b).
*p Slapton, 1710.
Tormoham (Torquay), 1849.

Dorset
*p Dorchester (All Saints), 1710.
p Rampisham, 1818.
Shaftesbury, 1846.

Durham
*p Darlington, 1711.[4]

---

[1] *Parochial Libraries*, p. 24 n.
[2] For the library at Reading, which was assisted by the Bray Trustees though not founded by them, see App. II.
[3] *Op. cit.*, p. 24.
[4] Recorded as missing in 1849, but see *Parochial Libraries*, *s.v.*

Essex
*p Newport, 1710, augm. 1834.
l Rochford, 1840.

Gloucestershire
*p Brookthorpe, 1712.
*p Flaxley, 1710.[1]
*p Oxenhall, 1710.

Hampshire
Portsmouth, 1843.
l Southampton, 1840. Cf. App. II.
*p Whitchurch, 1720. Cf. App. II.

Herefordshire
p Leominster, 1812.
l Ross, 1782.
*p Weobley, 1710.

Hertfordshire
l Aldbury, 1821.
St. Albans, 1848.

Huntingdonshire
p Alconbury, 1824.
*p St. Neots, 1711. Cf. App. II, and above under (b).

Isle of Wight
l Newport, 1834.

Kent
p Ashurst, 1823.
p Deptford (St. Nicholas), 1832.
*p Detling, 1710.
*p Preston-by-Wingham, 1710.

Lancashire
p Accrington, 1818.

p Admarsh, 1757, augm. 1835.
p Ainsworth, 1838.
Ashton-under Lyne, 1847.
p Ashworth, 1840.
p Bacup, 1807.
p Birch, 1837.
p Bolton-le-Sands, 1761.
p Bury (St. John's) 1823, augm. 1847. Cf. App. II.
p Cockerham, 1761.
p Dalton, 1757.
p Ellel, 1757.
p Field Broughton, 1766.
*p Flookburgh, 1725.
p Goodshaw, 1840.
p Gressingham, 1761.
p Haslingden, 1819.
p Hoole, 1761.
l Lancaster, 1764, augm. 1847.
p Leck, 1761.
Leigh, 1847.
p Lindale, 1761.
p Littledale, 1761.
p Lowick, 1757.
l Marsden, 1820.
p Milnrow, 1833.
l Newchurch-in-Pendle, 1826.
Oldham, 1846.
p Pilling, 1761.
*p Poulton-le-Fylde, 1720, augm. 1757.
l Preston, 1840.
p Silverdale, 1757.
p Staveley, 1757.
l Ulverston, 1753, augm. 1824.
Warrington, 1844.
Warton, 1846.
p Woodplumpton, 1757.

Leicestershire
*p Shepshed, 1720.

---

[1] Recorded as missing in 1849, but see *Parochial Libraries, s.v.*

London
    Bethnal Green, 1844.

Norfolk
p How, *c.* 1729.[1]
*pl North Walsham, p. 1710, l. 1788.

Northamptonshire
p East Haddon, 1817.
*p Irthlingborough, 1710.
*p Little Harrowden, 1711.
*p Oundle, 1711.
*p *Wollaston*, 1711.

Northumberland
*p Alnwick, 1711, augm. 1822. See also above under (b).
l Newcastle-upon-Tyne, 1840.

Nottinghamshire
p Eastwood, 1819.
l East Retford, 1836.

Oxfordshire
p Oxford, St. Peter-le-Bailey, by 1731.[2]

Shropshire
*p Dudleston, 1712.
p *Ford*, 1760.
l Oswestry, 1795.
*p St. Martin, 1721.
l Wenlock, 1799.

Somerset
*p Corston, 1710.
l Frome, 1840.
    Ilminster, 1848.
*p Kilmersdon, 1711.

p Norton St. Philip, 1821.
*p Stowey, 1720.

Staffordshire
*p Brewood, 1710.
p Burton-on-Trent, 1818.
l Cannock, 1812.
    Cheadle, 1848.
p King's Bromley, 1823.
l Lane End, 1814.
p Needwood, 1812.

Suffolk
*p Sudbury (*All Saints*), 1712.

Surrey
l Ewell, 1817.
    Guildford, 1842.

Warwickshire
*p Alcester, 1712.
*p Henley-in-Arden, 1710.
*p Over Whitacre, 1711.
*p Shustoke, 1727.

Westmorland
*pl Bampton, p. 1712, l. 1758. (School). Cf. App. II.
p Crook, 1757.
p *Croscake*, 1761.
p Grayrigg, 1766.
l Heversham, 1766, augm. 1804.[3]
p *Mallerstang*, 1761.
l Old Hutton (School), 1757.
p *Ravenstonedale*, 1761.
p *Selside*, 1757.
l Temple Sowerby, 1811.
p Witherslack, 1757.

---

[1] *Parochial Libraries*, p. 24 n.
[2] *Op. cit.*, p. 112. Not officially recorded as a Bray library.
[3] Deposited 1964 in the Newcastle University Library.

Wiltshire[1]

    Bradford-on-Avon, 1843.
    Devizes, 1841.
    Tilshead, 1813.
    Warminster, 1840.

Worcestershire

  l Bewdley, 1781.
  p Cradley, 1823.
 *p Elmley, 1712.
 *p Evesham, 1710.
 *p Feckenham, 1712.
 *p *Oldbury*, 1713.[2]

Yorkshire

  p *Askengarthdale*, 1761.
  p *Askrigg*, 1757.
 *p Bolterstone, 1711.
  l Bradford, 1830, augm. 1840.
 *p Bridlington, 1710.[3]
  l Dewsbury, 1831.
  p Friezland, 1800.
  l Great Driffield, 1835.

  p Hardrow, 1766.
    Huddersfield, 1841.
  l Hunmanby, 1811.
  l Illingworth (Halifax), 1840.
  p Ingleton, 1757.
    Leeds, 1845.
 *p Marske (nr. Guisborough), 1712.
  l Muker, 1821.
 *p *New Malton* (*St. Leonard's*), 1721.
    North Craven, 1850.
  l Old Malton, 1823.
  p Penistone, 1815.
  l Pudsey, 1818.
  l Redmire, 1785.
  p *Richmond* (*Trinity Chapel*), 1761.
 *p Skelton, 1720.
  p *South Cowton*, 1761.
  l Stokesley, 1826.[4]
 *p Tadcaster, 1710.
 *p Tinsley, 1711.
 *p Wentworth, 1711.

WALES AND MONMOUTHSHIRE

(*The spelling of some of the Welsh names in the earlier reports is so different from the modern forms as to be almost unrecognizable, especially as in the case of border parishes the county is often wrongly stated. The most notable variations are indicated below in square brackets.*)

Anglesey

  l Beaumaris, 1796, augm. 1840.
    Llanfailog, 1849.
  l Llangefni, 1823.

Caernarvonshire

  l Caernarvon, 1769, augm. 1840.
 *p *Llanrhos* (*Eglwys Rhos*), 1712.[5]

---

[1] For the library at Box, assisted by the Trustees though not founded by them, see App. II.
[2] This is Oldbury nr. Birmingham, formerly in Shropshire (and so listed in *Parochial Libraries*) but now in Worcestershire.
[3] Listed in early reports as *Burlington*.
[4] Listed initially as "Deanery of Cleveland".
[5] Listed as missing in 1849, but see *Parochial Libraries*, *s.v.*

pl Pwllheli, p. 1712, amalg. with l. 1770.

Cardiganshire

p Bangor, 1768.
l Cardigan, 1765, augm. 1823.
p Cellan [Kellan], 1765.
p Ciliau Aeron [Kilie-Ayron], 1765.
p Lampeter, 1765, augm. 1814.
p Llanarth, 1766.
pl Llanbadarnfawr, p. 1710, l. 1769. Cf. App. II.
p Llanbadarn Trefeglwys, 1765.
p Llanddewi Aberarth, 1765.
p Llandissiliogogo, 1766.
p Llandyfriog, 1768.
p Llandyssul, 1765.
l Llangynllo, 1811.
p Llanllwchaiarn, 1766.
p Llanwnen [Llanwannen], 1765.
p Trefilan, 1765.
l Ystrad Meuric, 1808, augm. 1809.

Carmarthenshire

p Abernant, 1765.
p Cyffic [Kiffig], 1766.
p Eglwys Cymmin, 1766.
p Egremont, 1768.
l Killymaenllwyd, 1764.
p Laugharne [Langharn], 1766.
Llanboldy, 1833.

p Llandawke, 1766.
p Llanddowror, 1766.
p Llandefeilog, 1765.
p Llandilo (Fawr), 1766.
p Llandygwydd [Lanewydd, Lancwydd], 1768.
p Llanegwad, 1766.
p Llanfihangel ar Arth [Llanvihangel Yeroth], 1765.
p Llangathen, 1768.
p Llanwinio, 1765.
p Newcastle Emlyn, *ante* 1730.[1]
p Penboyr, 1765.
p St. Clears, 1768.
p Trelech ar Bettws [Treleacht], 1765.

Denbighshire

l Denbigh, 1814, augm. 1840.
l Llanrwst, 1794, augm. 1840.
p Llantysilio, 1720.

Flintshire

l Mold, 1797.

Glamorgan

l Cowbridge (School), 1828. See also above under (c).
l Llandaff, 1760.
l Llandilo Talybont, 1802.[2]
l Swansea, 1793.

Merionethshire

l Bala, 1763.
l Dolgelly, 1796, augm. 1840.

[1] Recorded in Reports of the Associates as founded by Bray [i.e. by the Trustees], but though the Trustees considered the provision of a library there in 1718 (*Minutes*, 5th February, 1718), there is no record of the foundation.
[2] Listed as Llandeilo, Carm., but since Llandilo Fawr is separately entered (see above *s.v.* Carmarthenshire), the reference is probably to Llandilo Talybont, just over the border in Glamorganshire.

Monmouthshire

 l Abergavenny, 1784.¹
 l Caerleon, 1757.¹
*p *Chepstow*, 1712.¹
 p Llanover, 1829.
*p Monmouth, 1710.¹
*p Newport, 1711.¹
*p Trevethin, 1711.
 l Usk (School), 1828.¹

Montgomeryshire

*p Darowen, 1710.
 l *Deythur* [*Deuddwr*], 1766.
 l Llanfair (Careinion), 1768.
 p Llanwnog, 1764.

Pembrokeshire

 p *Clydey*, 1766.
     *Fishguard.*²
 l Haverfordwest, 1808.
 p *Little Newcastle*, 1766.
 p Llandysilio (West),   1766,
     1833.³
 p Llanwnda, 1768.
 p *Narberth*, 1768.
*p Prendergast, 1710.
 l St. David's, 1807.

Radnorshire

 l Rhayader, 1810.

SCOTLAND

 l Ballachulish, *Argyllsh.*, 1840.

---

¹ The remains of these six libraries were absorbed into the Llandaff Diocesan Library soon after its establishment in 1883 – M. Tallon, *Church in Wales Diocesan Libraries* (Athlone 1962), p. 53.
² Recorded from 1841 as a defunct library, date of foundation unknown.
³ The Reports record only the grant of a library to "Llandissilio, Carmarthenshire", in 1833. Actually the parish straddled the boundary of the two counties, but the parish church was in Pembrokeshire, in what is now Llandysilio West. The establishment of a library in 1766 is not recorded, but is known from other sources (see above, p. 112).

Report of the Manchester Statistical Society on Libraries in Hull, presented to the British Association 1839[1]

Circulating libraries, in the borough of Kingston-upon-Hull, may be ranged under the following heads: (1) Public subscription libraries. (2) Libraries attached to public institutions. (3) Congregational libraries. (4) Libraries attached to Sunday schools. (5) Private circulating libraries.

These public subscription libraries contain an extensive assortment of works in every department of literature. There are four, containing 25,671 volumes; of which, 2,537, or 9.88 per cent, are theology and ecclesiastical history; 2,674, or 10.41 per cent, are jurisprudence and political economy; 7,549, or 29.41 per cent, are history and biography; 9,566, or 37.27 per cent, are works on the arts, sciences, and general literature; and 3,345, or 13.03 per cent, are novels, romances, and works of imagination. The circulation is 102,180 volumes per annum, affording an average of 126 volumes annually to each member.[2]

There are four libraries connected with public institutions, and they contain 2,920 volumes, of which 467, or 15.99 per cent, are works in theology and ecclesiastical history; 26, or .89 per cent, are on jurisprudence and political economy; 1,016, or 34.80 per cent, are history and biography; 1,397, or 47.84 per cent, are arts, sciences, and general literature; and 14, or .48 per cent, are novels, romances, and works of imagination. This description of libraries appears to contain the whole amount of publications of a practical character, exclusive of religious works, which can be fairly regarded as coming within the reach of the working classes, and the whole of these, with the exception of 200 volumes, are in the library of the mechanics' institution, the number of volumes in which is 2,260, the average annual circulation being 17,992, exhibiting an average reading of 52 volumes per annum to each subscriber.

---

[1] This report is reproduced in full in the *Parliamentary Gazetteer of England and Wales* (1842–43), Vol. II, p. 579. It is summarized in the Transactions appended to the *Report of the Ninth Meeting of the British Association, 1839* (1840), p. 120.

[2] The most important of the four subscription libraries here mentioned was the Hull Subscription Library (founded in 1775), which by 1849 had a collection of some 21,000 volumes.

There are ten congregational libraries attached to churches or chapels, and designed to promote the religious instruction of the congregations. In these libraries are 2,994 volumes, which are, with scarcely an exception, of a religious character. The average circulation is 10,088 volumes per annum. The number of persons having access to these libraries, not being in all cases ascertainable, no estimate of the average number of volumes to each can be made.

There are twenty-eight libraries attached to Sunday schools, which have 5,655 volumes, exclusively of a religious tendency, with an annual circulation of 48,942 volumes, which takes place chiefly among the senior scholars and their teachers. Nearly the whole of the Sunday school libraries contain a variety of works of fiction, having, however, a religious object.

There are eleven private circulating libraries, having 17,474 volumes, 8 of which, or .04 per cent, are works in theology and ecclesiastical history; 9, or .05 per cent, jurisprudence and political economy; 220, or 1.26 per cent, history and biography; 26, or .14 per cent, arts, sciences, and general literature; and 17,211, or 98.51 per cent, novels, romances, and works of imagination. The average circulation could not be correctly ascertained, but the condition of the books, the number of libraries, and observations which fell from the proprietors, prove that it is very great, and is confined to the middle and operative classes. Laying out of view libraries originated by public-spirited individuals, for the benefit of these classes, and those promoted from religious motives, the taste of readers among the middle and working classes is strongly indicated by the description of works of which private circulating libraries are composed. The majority of works in these libraries may be characterized as mere trash, and not a few in some of them are of a more objectionable nature. When it is considered that the young form a large portion of the supporters of these establishments, and that early reading exercises no inconsiderable influence in the formation of character, it is much to be regretted, that no efforts commensurate with the wants of the public have yet been made to supply a desideratum which the progress of education is rapidly creating.

General Index

Index

Index

Fielding, Henry, 119
Fisher, John, Bp. of Rochester, 40
Fitzwilliam, Earl, 122
Foxe, John, *Book of Martyrs*, 81–2, 84, 197
Franciscans, 14, 17, 21–2, 24, 29, 87 n.
Frank, A. D., of Cranfield, 136
Franklin, Benjamin, 144
Fremantle, W. R., 191
Fuller, Thos., 42–3, 118

Galloway, Alex., 188
Gardenstone, Lord, 104
Garland, Augustus, M.P., 62
Garnett, Richd., 177 n. 1
Garrick, David, 157
Gaskell, Eliz., 236–7
Gatherer, Wm., of Elgin, 47
George II, 153, 160; — III, 157, 160; — IV, 160
Gery, Mr., Vicar of Islington, 61
Gibbon, Edw., 92, 158
Gilbert, Sir Humphrey, 167
Gladstone, W. E., 207–9
Glasgow, 18th-cent. development, 120; Mechanics' Inst., 211 n. 4, 230; Literary Soc., 224; Philosophical Soc., 224
Gloucester, Humphrey D. of, 17–18, 27
Graham, Arch., Bp. of the Isles, 101
Gray, Chas., M.P., 98
Gray, Rev. John, of Haddington, 101
Gray, Thos., 158
Greenwich, Soc. for Diffusion of Useful Knowledge, 229–30
Grenville, Thos., 163
Grieve, C. M., 211 n. 1
Griffith(s), Rev. John, of Llandyssilio, 112

Grinfield, Rev. E. W., of Bath, 200 n. 3
Grote, Geo., 209
Gutenberg, Johann, 38

Hacket, John, Bp. of Lichfield, 61–2
Hall, Rev. Thos., of King's Norton, 80
Hallam, Hy., 209
Hampden Clubs, 226
Hannibal, Thos., of Worcester, 35
Harper, Rev. Sam., 176
Harsnett, Sam., Abp. of York, 75
Henry VIII, 49, 154
Henry, Dr. Robt., of Linlithgow, 103
Hetherington, Hy., 227
Hildyard, John, bookseller, 65
Holcot, Robt., 26 n. 3
Holyoake, G. J., 188
Hook, Rev. W. F., of Leeds, 199
Horne, Rev. T. H., 176–7
Howell, Rev. Howell, of Llanboldy, 112
Hudson, J. W., 212, 214, 231
Hull, Literary and Philosophical Soc., 224
Hume, David, 158, 181
Hunter, Dr. Alex., of York, 65
Huntingdon, Henry 3rd E. of, 73
Huntingfield, Roger de, Rector of Balsham, 23
Hutton, John, M.P., 114
Hyde, Thos., librarian, 58

Imray, J., engineer, 190
Ipswich, early printing, 38

James I, 154
James, Dr. Thos., librarian, 54–8, 172, 174
Jewel, John, *Apology*, 81
Joanna, Q. of Scotland, 24
Johnson, Dr. Sam., 64, 104, 120, 158–9
Jones, Rev. Griffith, of Llanddowror, 110

Kiderminster, Sir John, 76
Kendal, Mechanics' Inst., 215
King, Dr. Wm., of Brighton, 227

Index of Individual Libraries

The following abbreviations are used: E. endowed library; S. private subscription library; B. book club; C. commercial circulating library; Br. Bray library.

For endowed libraries to 1800 see also Appendix II, and for a complete list of Bray libraries to 1850 Appendix III.

Man, Isle of, Bray libs., 106 n. 3, 107
Manchester, Chetham's Lib., 75, 77–80, 173, 185, 193; St. Mary's, 83–4; S. 126, 132, 143, 204–5; Mechanics' Inst., 191, 229–30, 232–5; factory lib. 235–6
Mansfield, S. 216 n. 1
Marlborough, E. 80
Marske (nr. Richmond, Yorks.), E. 80
Merthyr Tydfil, B. 141
Milton Abbas (Dorset), E. 69 n. 2
Monk Bretton (Yorks.), Priory, 44
Montrose, S. 126 n. 2
More (Shrops.), E. 94

Nantwich, Bray grant for lending lib., 106 n. 3
Neath (Glam.), itinerating lib., 217–18
Newark, E. 91, 94
Newcastle upon Tyne, St. Nicholas', (chained books) 25; E. 71, 73–4, 81–2, 96, 195; S. 126; C. 144; Nonconformist libs., 198–9; Lit. and Phil. Soc., 225; Mechanics' Inst. 230
Northampton, E. 91 n. 4; Bray grant for lending lib., 106 n. 3; Mechanics' Inst., 230
North Grimston (Yorks.), E. 80
Norwich, proposed lib. in 15th cent., 35; Cathedral, 24, 192 n. 2; St. Andrew's, 71–2; City Lib., 74–5, 97, 173–4, 195; St. Peter Mancroft, 75–6; S. 126, 173–4, 195, 204; Penny Lib., 217; Mechanics' Inst., 217
Nottingham, School, 91, 195; S. 94, 195; Operatives' and Artizans' Lib., 215–16; public house libs., 216

Oakham, E. 75
Ottery St. Mary, E. 80
Oxford, University, (mediæval) 15–18, 20, 26–7, 42, 45, (Bodleian) 48, 52–60, 167–8, 170, 172, 174; Magdalen Coll., 15, 18, 53; Merton Coll., 15; New

Coll., 18, 45; All Souls' Coll., 26; Durham Hall, 26; University Coll., 26; Corpus Christi Coll., 41–2; Radcliffe Camera, 53; Br. 109 n. 2; early book society, 121 n. 3

Peebles, Mechanics' Inst., 234–5
Pembrokeshire, Soc. of Clergymen, 136, 138 n. 2
Penrith, Mechanics' Lib., 215
Penzance, B. 139
Perth, S. 126
Peterborough, Abbey, 20; Cathedral, 192
Peterhead, B. 218–19
Plymouth, E. 106
Port Glasgow, S. 126 n. 2
Preston, Shepherd Lib., 91, 94, 193–4

Reading, B. 139
Reigate, E. 91 n. 4, 94, 96, 107, 195
Repton, E. 82–3, 95
Ripon, Cathedral, 63
Rochdale, S. 126 n. 1; Co-operative Soc., 227 n. 1; Weavers' Soc., 227 n. 1; factory lib., 235
Rochester, Cathedral, 63, 192 n. 2
Rotherham, School, 16; E. 94
Rothesay, E. 101; S. 126 n. 2
Rougham (Norf.), E. 93–4
Royal Library, 153–4, 160, 168–9

St. Albans, Abbey, 15, 17
St. Andrews, University, 26 n. 1; Priory, 42
St. Asaph, Cathedral, 15 n. 1, 63; diocesan lib., 107, 110–11
St. Cyrus (Kincs.), E. 198
St. David's, Cathedral, 15 n. 1, 62
St. Helens, B, 219
Salford, Public Lib., 237–8
Salisbury, Cathedral, 15 n. 1, 24, 44, 192 n. 2; St. Edmund's (chained book), 25; C. 144–5
Saltoun (E. Loth.), E. 87
Scarborough, C. 144
Scotland, National Library of, *see* Edinburgh, Advocates' Lib.
Selkirk, S. 126 n. 2
Settle, S. 126 n. 1